❧ Younger Women / Older Men ❧

Younger WOMEN

OLDER MEN

Beliza Ann Furman

BARRICADE BOOKS INC.

New York

Published by Barricade Books Inc.
150 Fifth Avenue
New York, NY 10011

Printed in the United States of America.
Design by LaBreacht Design.

Library of Congress Cataloging-in-Publication Data
Furman, Beliza Ann,
    Younger women/older men / Beliza Ann Furman.
        p.   cm.
    ISBN 1-56980-040-5
    1. Man-woman relationships. 2. Young women. 3. Aged men. I. Title.
    HQ801.F87 1995
    306.7—dc20   95-15360
                                                   CIP

First printing

To: *Laurie and Jill*

I love you from the bottom of my heart.
I'm sorry you had so much pain.

Sean and Ashley

The most precious moments in my life
have happened with you.

and especially Sam

My greatest supporter and best friend.
Our life together has been truly blessed.

A special thank you to:

DR. GEORGE BECKMAN
For sorting it all out and giving me the confidence
to feel comfortable with whom I am for the very
first time.

GENE BARNES, BARNES COMMUNICATIONS
AND PUBLIC RELATIONS
You always believed in me! I'll never forget
your caring.

TO JOYCE BORDEN VERNON, MARY WEIR,
AND BETSY FIFIELD
Thank you for your friendship, constant
reassurance, and understanding ear. You're what
friends are all about!

This book is dedicated to all my W.O.O.M.ies from around the world

Thank you for sharing your stories and for giving me the encouragement to write it all down.

Together, for the sake of love and happiness, we have motivated those who may be uncertain and intimidated to cope with controversy and prejudice. Our experiences have shown younger women in love with older men the way to face themselves, deal with and confront the concerns that surround their marriages and love affairs. We have reassured them how important it is not to worry about what others think and to follow their hearts.

I love you all!

In Appreciation

I am sincerely grateful to all the subscribers of Wives Of Older Men (W.O.O.M.) and my friends and acquaintances, the mental-health professionals, authors, sociologists, lawyers, and physicians who have graciously allowed themselves to be interviewed for this book. All the stories reflect true experiences of the people to whom I have spoken, but in several cases to protect their privacy, names may have been changed, the cities in which they live and some physical characteristics have been altered. To further protect confidentiality, I have occasionally created scenario composites. Because wives of older men experience similar concerns, any likeness to real people are a coincidence. I will indicate with an asterisk fictitious names the first time they appear.

I sincerely appreciate the confidence of my publishers, Carole and Lyle Stuart, and the patient encouragement of my editor, Sandy Stuart.

Contents

In the Beginning
There Were Beliza, Betsy, and Laurie / 9
Starting W.O.O.M. / 15
What This Book Will Do for You / 23

Beliza Ann Furman / 27

❧ Reflections of an Insecure Wallflower ❧ Annie
❧ Growing Up ❧ On My Own ❧ Dr. Furman
❧ The Affair ❧ The Price

So...You've Fallen in Love with an Older Man, Too / 49

❧ The Attraction
❧ Where Do Younger Women Meet Older Men?
❧ The Hurt and Pain of Being In Love with an
Older, Married Man ❧ You'll Hear It Often...
She's Just In It for the Money ❧ The Unwedded Wife
❧ The Palimony or Nonnuptial Agreement
❧ Negotiating Your Rights ❧ Dating an Older Playboy
❧ Dating an Older Widower
❧ Premarital Couple Therapy ❧ Breaking Up

What Kind of Woman Falls In Love with an Older Man / 95

❧ Barbie What! ❧ She's Definitely Not an Underdog
❧ The Proof's in the Pudding ❧ Androgynous Occupations
❧ Unsure Rebels ❧ A Jig Saw Puzzle...Nine Decades of
Not-Always-Interlocking Pieces ❧ Seeing It Her Way

❧ The Foretelling M.O.
❧ Watch Out! She Might Be After Your Job
❧ Vulnerability... The Impetus
❧ Packing It All In in His Lifetime ❧ Trophy Wives
❧ An Older Man's Springboard to Vivacity
❧ An Influential Counterpart ❧

What's He Like? / 115

❧ Image ❧ His and Her Demands ❧ Risking It All
❧ The Challenge ❧ The Pride Factor ❧ Midlife Crisis
❧ Erotic Savior Faire ❧ Chivalry ❧ Control ❧ Trading Up
❧ When At First You Don't Succeed...
❧ Sometimes It Can Backfire ❧ "The Johnny Syndrome"
❧ I Found Her! ❧

A Compendium of May/December Marriage Issues / 147

❧ Your Mom Won't Speak to Him, Your Dad
Won't Let Him in the House ❧ Friends' Reactions...
Prejudice and Isolation ❧ The Consequences of Living
with a Prenuptial Agreement ❧ The Generation Gap
❧ Dealing with Power and Control Issues
❧ Surviving Stepmotherhood
❧ The Issue of Wanting a Baby of Your Very Own
❧ Dad's Old Enough to Be My Grandpa
❧ Securing Your Future...The Emotional Side of Money,
Insurance, Legacies ❧ The Final Hours

Would You Do It Again? / 253

Acknowledgments / 256

In the Beginning There Were Beliza, Betsy and Laurie

In February, 1987 Robin Burns, the president of Calvin Klein Cosmetics, invited a few members of the organization, Cosmetic Executive Women, to lunch at her office. I was excited to have been included primarily because I hadn't been to see my friends in New York City since recuperating from delivering my daughter, Ashley, by caesarean section just before Christmas. But I also had an ulterior motive. My fifteen-year-old cosmetic company, Beliza, was facing financial ruin by way of the late 1980s' austerity and store bankruptcies, and it looked like I was going to be needing a job in the cosmetic field.

When I entered Robin's office, I noticed an attractive woman, a few years younger than me, seated at the table. She was very fashionable, but most noticeable was her fabulous mane of wildly long, curly black hair. I took the vacant seat next to her and introduced myself. Her name was Betsy Fifield. During lunch, she told me that she had quit her job as vice-president of McCann-Erickson to start her own marketing firm.

We hit it off right away and left the meeting together, filling each other in about ourselves. One of the first things Betsy mentioned was that she flew to Minneapolis every third weekend to visit her stepchildren, the daughters of her husband, Jim, the chief executive of EMI Music Worldwide. Remembering relinquishing weekends to visit with my husband's girls, Laurie and Jill, I said I had two stepdaughters also. When we realized we were both married to older men—my husband Sam is fifteen years older than me, Jim is thirteen years older than Betsy—we immediately bonded.

When Betsy wasn't shuttling back and forth from London to New York and L.A. with Jim, and on to Aspen to train for ski competitions, we would have lunch at Doubles, a private club at the Sherry-Netherland Hotel. Its dark, cocoonlike atmosphere made it a great place to talk, intimately, for hours about our travels, European trends, career aspirations, and marriages. Because I had been married longer, I was able to give Betsy insight into a lot of the difficult situations facing younger wives that I had overcome.

Even today, the intensity of our animated conversations, as we catch up on each other's lives, attracts attention wherever we go. Most amusing is that we both have the coquettish self-confidence younger wives develop from being married to an experienced and worldly older man. Combine that with the fact that we have both established successful careers of our own, married wisely and produced a beautiful family, we make quite an electrifying team.

Betsy and I are happy and proud to be dependent upon our older husbands. They like it that way, too. Because in turn, that gives them the confidence to be dependent upon us. As a whole, wives of older men are unique. They are mature for their age and prefer to indulge in sophisticated activities that are generally of little interest to their peers. These younger wives are very nurturing and sympathetic, but at the same time, extremely competitive—especially when their challenger is their older husband. Neither Betsy nor I (nor the majority of wives of older men) have any problem using our femininity to our advantage. Since we have fulfilled the current female obligation of "doing it all," we don't feel the need to embrace feminist organizations.

Having succeeded by having men on our side, Betsy and I graciously accept, but turn down, all flirtations as ego-boosting compliments that never get carried beyond just that. To stay in control, we find it's to our advantage and *always* great fun to make our husbands aware of the attention we receive. Being second wives, Betsy and I realize one way to secure our position is to keep our men on their toes. Many of my closest friends are married to older men, but Betsy has become my alter ego; she is also one reason I started my international network clearinghouse, Wives Of Older Men, more commonly and humorously referred to as W.O.O.M.— as in *womb*.

A few months after we met, Betsy introduced me to her friend, Laurie, wife of then RJR Chairman Ross Johnson, who was twenty years her senior. Although Laurie, who has two stepsons, was never a full-fledged member of our private "club," the stories she told of her marriage got me thinking even more seriously about starting a formal support system for younger wives.

Over the years, Laurie has had her share of backstabbing, as older women closer in age to their older husbands, ridiculed her inexperience and envied her firm thighs. Once, when Ross was CEO of Standard Brands and Laurie was twenty-six, they were invited to a dinner party. The hostess told her it was casual. When Laurie arrived in blue jeans, she found all the other women dressed in fancy cocktail dresses! It was an obvious ploy to make her feel like a real turkey.

I didn't get to know Laurie very well because she and Ross moved to Atlanta after he lost his job with RJR. But we did attend a couple of charity events together with Betsy. One of them was a benefit for the Martha Graham Dance Company.

Betsy was on the committee and saw to it we had front-row seats to watch Nureyev and Baryshnikov perform together for the first time. My husband, Sam, was so thrilled he promptly fell asleep.

Later, at the gala, Betsy, Laurie, and I looked fabulous on the arms of our charming, older husbands. Betsy and I, who wore very short pouf designer gowns, and Laurie in another spectacular frock, were interviewed by *The New York Times* about our dresses. As the writer was speaking with us, I proudly looked over at our three distinguished husbands, who were watching us with admiration, and thought, "How lucky we all are!" But the special moment was abruptly quashed when I noticed icy stares from some matronly women. Their disapproving expressions shouted, "Husband stealer, bimbo, gold digger." It was the final straw. The time had come for me to formalize my plans and establish a support group for age-disparate couples who could feel comfortable together—away from discrimination and disparagement.

Betsy was all for it, but she wanted to keep it just for *our* friends. I, who always do things on a more grandiose scale, suggested we advertise. That's when Betsy said, "That's absurd. Forget it!"

For months I tried to persuade Betsy to get involved with W.O.O.M., but she said Jim would be mighty unhappy having his personal life exposed. She still hadn't joined when Julie Connelly, senior editor at *Fortune* magazine, called me for names of some power moguls for a story she *said* she was doing about second wives of corporate CEOs. Betsy thought this was really great. I told Betsy she could be interviewed, but she had to join W.O.O.M. for at least one year. She groaned a lot, but she did write the check. Even though Laurie was in Atlanta, Betsy called her, and she and Ross were interviewed also.

Because I had helped Ms. Connelly so much with the story, she asked me to represent *Fortune's* fantasy of a trophy wife and appear on television talk shows to discuss the article. But when I read it, I was really upset. It was so sexist and portrayed the antithesis of my reasons for marrying an older man. Furthermore, I felt used. I had spent hours locating couples who fit Julie's profile, and she only gave W.O.O.M. one tiny paragraph. Angrily, I called and told her I had no intention of shilling for *Fortune*'s disgusting article, "Trophy Wives," and we ended up battling it out on CNN's *Sonya Friedman Live*. I was the advocate for love in marriage; Julie was sticking with her analysis that these marriages were based on bankbooks and good looks.

Within a few days, Betsy became the story's spokesperson. I was disappointed she was proud of the article and would help *Fortune* promote it. She now admits she made a mistake and refers to the whole episode as a weak moment.

Naturally, that was the end of Betsy's involvement with W.O.O.M. There was, however, a happy ending. Partially because of our friendship and my experience encouraging Sam that we should have a baby, she and Jim had a little BOOMie—a baby girl of an older man—Allison, who was born in January, 1994.

Starting W.O.O.M.

The first meeting of W.O.O.M. was held on September 19, 1988. I invited about ten of my friends who were married to older men to have lunch at my home. Their husbands were a little leery but most supported our idea. I knew it was a real ego-buster to be referred to as an older man because, after all, most of our older husbands married us to feel young. But what the heck, I thought, they *are* older husbands, and besides some of these men were younger than me!

The meeting was a great success. Everyone felt positive that W.O.O.M. would play an important role in their relationships, and it would offer them a safe haven to talk about dealing with stepchildren, family disapproval, friends' disgust, starting second families, aging husbands, and power and control issues. We decided to get together for an informal lunch or coffee klatch every month, either in New Jersey or New York City. However, I wasn't the least bit prepared for what happened after that!

A few days prior to the gathering, I thought I would test the concept with the media. I took the PR list that Gene Barnes, my publicist, used to promote my firm, Beliza Cosmetics, and sent a simple note announcing the formation of the self-help group, Wives Of Older Men. Within forty-eight hours, *The New York Times,* the *New York Daily News,* and the *Philadelphia Inquirer* were fighting over the story!

I couldn't believe it! Ron Alexander, from *The New York Times,* was *disappointed* he couldn't print the story for six months because the *Daily News* called me first and landed the feature. It was incredible. I had spent thousands of dollars on public relations for my cosmetic company and was lucky to receive two lines of free publicity. Now all of a sudden, I was the darling of the media with this little support group!

Sam was very supportive, a real sport. When the *Daily News* came to his office to photograph us, he bragged about it to all of his patients. But I almost died when the story ran! Sheila Ann Feeney, the reporter, depicted older men as if they were decrepit. She called them Daddy Warbucks! The paper came out the morning of a W.O.O.M. meeting, and my friends who saw it were squirming. How were they going to face their husbands? Nothing like jumping in with both feet. How would I ever get out of this one?

I bought the paper in a local deli, and everyone there couldn't help chuckling at my reaction. After I nervously ripped open the paper to the full-page feature, all I could manage was, "Oh my God!" By midafternoon, the story had been passed around so much, I was the talk of the town. Thrills! What a way to achieve fame, having my husband perceived as a reptile. Lord, I was scared to death Sam wouldn't let me in the house. He could sue me for defamation of character!

But Sam really surprised me. He loved it! He told me his travel agent, Marilyn Bell, had called. She just *had* to congratulate him. She did add that when she opened the paper and saw the story, she spewed her coffee all over the kitchen wall! Everyone was laughing except me.

About two weeks after that first meeting, Diane Superville from the Associated Press called requesting an interview. At the time, life was bedlam. Newspapers were contacting me from all over the country—people everywhere wanted to join W.O.O.M.! A social writer from the *Asbury Park Press* will remain forever angry with me because her story was usurped by the Associated Press story.

At first, it was very flattering, but the interviews were disrupting our lives. I knew it was too much when one day I arrived home from work, and a reporter was on the telephone interviewing Sean, our nine-year-old son! W.O.O.M. was appearing in print so much, patients were asking Sam if we had an interest in a newspaper syndicate. With all of the newspaper hype, the TV and radio talk shows came on the scene. W.O.O.M. meetings were turning into media circuses, and subscribers became famous overnight.

Hundreds of newspapers bought the Associated Press story and the one that appeared on the front page of *The New York Times* Lifestyle section after Ron Alexander's six months were up. Television producers were calling me at my office and at home— all hours of the day and night! Friends Sam hadn't seen since dental school called. They were flabbergasted that his sex life was being bragged about on *CBS This Morning*. People were contacting me from places like New Zealand and Saudi Arabia! But the funniest incident took place with *Geraldo* and *Sally Jessy Raphael*.

After the *Times'* story ran, I was deluged with calls again, one of which was from a producer of *Geraldo*. I was excited, but my mom was real unhappy. She said, "*Geraldo* is a *sleazy* show. All my friends will die if you appear with him. His shows are so trashy!" Soon after, I mentioned *Geraldo's* request to Amy Buxton*, a W.O.O.M. subscriber from Portland, Oregon. She said, "*Geraldo* is not our type. We're very high-class people. I'll be really disappointed in you if you appear on that show."

I called the producer back and politely begged off. Later that afternoon, Sally Jessy Raphael's producer called. She told me she was also involved with an older dentist, and would I please appear on her show? I thought my mom, her friends, and her charity committees would certainly approve of Sally. I said yes. I had just hung up the receiver when a second *Geraldo* producer called. I thought, can't these people take NO for an answer and said, "Thanks again, but no thanks."

The next day was a Saturday, and I wasn't at my cosmetics company office. The phone rang. It was my husband's dental receptionist telling me now a female producer from *Geraldo* wanted to speak to me. When I called her back, she said her name was C.C. something. I didn't pay attention. I was too furious with their bothering me continually. I said, "Look, Geraldo is a scum-bag! I can't go on a show with a host who gets beaten up by neo-Nazis and wallows in trash." There was silence on the other end of the line and then she blurted, "But I'm his wife...a younger wife, and I really want to do this show." Oh my God, I could have died!

After my tremendous faux pas, I explained that my mom and dad would be r-e-a-l unhappy if I appeared on *Geraldo*. I mentioned that even Sam, who will put up with most of my antics, was against it. But C.C., being the C.C. I came to know after spending hours with her on the telephone and at her home near ours, has the ability to get her way through gracious manipulation. Don't ask me why, but at great personal expense, I gave a reluctant okay. I got back to Sally's producer and told her I had promised C.C. an exclusive for *Geraldo's* fall season, and I couldn't do any other shows.

After the taping, we waited for weeks for the show to appear. I lost ten pounds worrying about how it would turn out. To my surprise and delight, it was the nicest show I have ever done. It was tasteful and compassionate and led to a lot of people, from all over the country, joining W.O.O.M. Geraldo opened with scenes from his own wedding which made it personally appealing. Ironically, this show has remained my mom and dad's favorite from the nearly twenty I have done.

While all this media hoopla was going on, I was conducting meetings in New Jersey and New York. But demand for membership was coming in from everywhere, and everyone wanted to start chapters. I didn't know what to do with these people! Meetings were being organized at hotels all over the country. I found myself involved in a national party-planning business.

Four years later, the media attention hadn't ceased. Once I did a thirty-six-hour turnaround stint from New Jersey to Seattle to appear on *Northwest Afternoon*. On another occasion, I raced from our vacation home in St. Thomas to appear on *Oprah* in Chicago. By then they were sending me first-class tickets. Soon after, I became totally overwhelmed and exhausted by the response and decided in September 1992 that I had to dissolve the organization. I just couldn't keep up with it anymore. I ignored reporters and the media. I'd had enough.

But the subscribers were upset. They needed W.O.O.M. Not because their marriages were rocky but because of the excess baggage that came along with them that interfered with their happiness. I told those who were disappointed that I would reconsider. Six months later, I came up with a way that I could continue with the work, although the load would still include fielding up to fifteen or twenty phone calls a week from women and men with problems—sometimes at three o'clock in the morning.

I lowered the membership fee to allow more people to join and dropped the national chapter meetings. Most women preferred a one-on-one friendship anyway. I set up a complicated and thorough computer program that lists everything about subscribers and their husbands, even including hobbies. Developing the software and entering the data was tedious because, at that time, there were close to fifteen hundred women who had contacted me. But once completed, it was a sophisticated international computerized networking system with which I can introduce subscribers to other age-disparate couples in their immediate area. At present we have about two thousand people catalogued. It is one of the largest collections of age-disparate couples in the world, and with my permission, sociologists, statisticians, and W.O.O.M. can use the data to conduct extremely valuable surveys.

The system allows me to introduce W.O.O.M. couples from all over the world to others with similar concerns. Some need information about such things as fertility programs, social security, and death benefits. Others may be contemplating marriage, experiencing trouble with stepchildren, or have husbands who don't want to have a baby.

On signing up, subscribers receive a packet of twenty-five or more informative newspaper and magazine articles featuring W.O.O.M. members who have told their own personal stories, along with a list of subscribers in their area, a newsletter that uses their letters to me as a jumping-off point for what is discussed, and unlimited phone calls for support.

The new format is gratifying and controllable. The letters pour in thanking me for being there. Many are quite moving. Using 1989 figures from the National Bureau of Statistics that 12 percent of the American population is involved in age-disparate marriages where the husband is ten or more years older and factoring in my own calculations over the past six years, I estimate that close to 17 percent of American couples will find a potential refuge from isolation and prejudice in W.O.O.M.

It has been seven years of turmoil and craziness, but this donation of my time and money as the Ann Landers of the older man/younger woman relationship has been the most rewarding of the many organizations I serve.

W.O.O.M. has been able to resurrect many failing marriages by encouraging couples to communicate. The dialogue in the newsletter suggests an agenda. For those who are single and concerned about marrying older men or younger women, I offer them the confidence to give it a try. When a mom and dad won't attend the wedding, our bride knows she can fall back on us. W.O.O.M. makes us feel that we are not alone. All of us have profited emotionally from the family we have created. We support one another in our endeavor to seek a happy and lasting marriage.

What This Book
Will Do For You

*I*f Princess Diana had been in a position to join W.O.O.M. or had the opportunity to read this book before her floundering marriage to Prince Charles dissolved, maybe there would have been a different outcome. *Or better yet*, maybe she wouldn't have married him in the first place.

A lot of women involved with or married to older men have a high profile. They are actresses or are socially or politically prominent. Many are successful in their own businesses or are married to famous and prosperous older men. They are somewhat uncomfortable joining W.O.O.M. Support groups don't fit into their self-image. Yet, the concerns of the very rich age-disparate couple mirror those from all socioeconomic levels.

Others who would like to join W.O.O.M. are afraid to tell their husbands about the organization for fear of insulting them or perhaps, letting on that life on the home front may not be altogether blissful. Women who are dating older men may not want their male friends aware that they have misgivings. Now, they can read this book and gain some insight into what may be in store for them.

Plenty of older husbands misjudge W.O.O.M.'s intentions. They regard it as a bitching post for younger wives and are offended that their younger wives would even think of joining. Some older husbands want to evade discussing concerns that could easily be allayed with one phone call to our network of members. Believe me, I have had my share of abuse from such older husbands! But, on the other hand, I have met many who are sensitive and concerned about their marriages and the welfare of their younger wives or girl friends.

This book will offer any man or woman, whether enthusiastic or reluctant—or just curious about age-disparate relationships—the opportunity to benefit from W.O.O.M.'s experience and information. I deal with younger wives from the ages of nineteen to seventy. Even if the concerns of someone just entering adulthood are very different than those who are senior citizens, this book can be useful as a handbook on how to achieve a successful May/December marriage.

Younger Women/Older Men will address future issues and problems that many don't realize face them. No one is ever prepared to be a widow, but when you are a widow at thirty-two, you have to carry on and be certain you are covered financially. Asking an older husband to increase his insurance or prepare a will can be touchy, but it has to be done. I can help you with that. I will also talk about how, to please her older husband, a twenty-year-old bride may swear she doesn't want children but later be resentful when she nears the end of her childbearing years and realizes she can't live with her pledge. I will address the age-gap issue and discuss the burden a younger wife can be for an older man.

There is a great deal that therapists can learn from younger women/older men relationships. Many subscribers tell me they can't find a therapist who fully comprehends the many problems that face a couple with an age difference. Or worse, they have found one who disapproves of their marriage.

And finally, at the risk of offending first wives who have been left for a younger woman or those who suspect their husbands may be having an affair with one, this book will reveal a secret strategy for you to consider in your next relationship or to use to hang on to your present man...a winning combination of hyphenates: seductress-challenger, mother-wife, housekeeper-businesswoman, time for him-time for you. The lesson we, as next wives, have learned from your mistakes (because our husbands have told us) is that there is no room for complacency in marriage.

In a recent telephone survey conducted for the cosmetic company, Clinique, 1001 American women, sixteen years and older, were asked about their attitudes on their looks, cosmetics, and aging. What particularly startled me was the response to the question, "Thinking ahead ten years, what do you fear?" Forty percent of the women said they fear being more like their mothers; 25 percent said they fear losing their mate to someone younger. Don't think for a minute there weren't some younger wives included in that statistic.

Younger Women / Older Men will help couples bridge generational differences. Enjoy it privately or share it with your older husband or male friend. But keep it close by. It will be useful throughout your relationship.

Beliza Ann Furman

❧ Reflections of an Insecure Wallflower ❦

It's difficult to write about myself. I'm not so sure I want to know who I *was*. I've spent years marketing and packaging myself to be anything other than that! I've glossed over my vulnerability and inadequacies, preferring to be in complete control of who knows what about me. Actually, I've trained myself to be an enigma. It's a matter of what I haven't told, often leaving out just enough to create an illusion. Now, compared to who I was, I may be a figment of my *own* imagination.

In writing this book, I learned that in some respects, I have lost a part of my identity—the very thing that made me...*me*. But it was a small price to pay for what I have become. I attribute the bulk of my successes to my marriage to an older man. With my husband Sam's guidance, I have achieved more than I ever thought I could. He saw the potential and helped me regain my confidence that was shattered by childhood rejection and heartbreaking defeats in figure skating. I met Sam when I was nineteen—uncertain and scared. I'm forty-seven now; confident and capable. Without his encouragement, I never would have made the effort to strive to be the very best I can. His unconditional love for me has allowed me to trust loving someone once again. He's my best friend; sometimes my worst enemy! Sam challenges me to be my personal best. Our quarter-century love affair has been bonded by the great respect we have for each other.

In retrospect, I hadn't given much thought to the "old me" until one October day in 1993. I had just signed a contract with my New York City publishers, Barricade Books. The owners, Carole and Lyle Stuart, offered me a ride uptown. Maybe, because I was sitting in the back of Lyle's Mercedes and couldn't see his face, I just rattled off my life story as he shot out questions. Being a former newspaper reporter, he was very good at rooting out the past. He called it dialogue; I call it invasion. When I got out of the car, I was stunned at what I had revealed. I felt stripped and unsheltered.

Minutes later, I met my husband, Sam, at La Caravelle and downed two glasses of Moët before I could speak. Confused, I was angry at him, and it took me a few moments to define my emotions. After all, it was he who first received Carole's Fax about writing a book when it came into his office. It also took him ten days of constant encouragement to get me to call her back! Barely touching my food, I thought *"this will never work...I never write about me...Sam and I are very private people."* I was ready to return the book advance and thought about doing just that for weeks.

Each time I sat down to begin writing, I was stopped short of pulling up the shade to reveal our innermost private moments. It was disconcerting, but I knew without talking honestly about the intimate aspects of Sam's and my love affair and marriage, the book wouldn't be honest. But if I told the whole story, I might hurt people I care about and that would prevent me from going on. I was also horribly afraid that after opening myself up, the project would fail.

It is not easy for me to admit I have been through a lot. Like most people unhappy about their beginnings, I've developed a veneer. It often makes me appear hard, but the truth is when you peel that away, I am terribly insecure. I'm frightened by rejection, paralyzed by failure, and I've never really felt good enough. Since I have worked hard at trying to conceal my insecurities for years, I hadn't planned on dredging up the stuff that's been tucked away in a far corner of my memory bank. But, I feel it's important because some psychologists and mental-health specialists believe early childhood experiences influence women to marry certain individuals.

Agreeing with them, I am aware that much about me is pertinent to why I married an older man. I think it's important to tell you who I am and who I was so that you may understand why I was attracted to someone so self-assured, in control, honest, and trustworthy.

But first, I want it to be known to those who still think I am a ruthless home breaker that I am just like all other mortals. I've heard the unkind whispers behind my back and those that are sometimes said rudely to my face. Contrary to some opinion, I am not an insensitive, brainless gold digger. I am merely someone who fell in love.

In essence, my life has two chapters, *BS*...Before Sam and *AS*...After Sam.

✽ *Annie* ✽

World War II had ended, and my dad had just resigned from active duty. A full colonel in the army, he took a job in the executive department of IT&T and remained in Europe. I was born in Basel, Switzerland, on October 7, 1947. My parents named me

Margaret Ann Gilardi. Dad was thirty-three, an Italian Catholic. My mom was a twenty-seven-year-old Scotch-Irish Protestant.

The circumstances of my parent's marriage and my birth were never made very clear to me. I undoubtedly blew out of proportion what wasn't said, but it created a strain on my mother-daughter relationship. I silently blamed myself for any problems they had early on. Somehow, I felt responsible. In looking back, I realize I was pretty grouchy. I played the middle-child syndrome to the hilt. Childhood was a drag that I would have preferred bypassing altogether. In fact, to this day, I hate being called Annie since it reminds me of when I was a kid.

Sometime after I was born, an older brother materialized. Literally, he appeared one day out of thin air. His name was Bingham McMaster Coe. I guess my dad adopted him at some point because I've only known him with the last name of Gilardi. Even though he wouldn't tolerate any little sister nonsense, I adored my big brother, Bing. He helped me with my homework and looked out for me as I was growing up. To me, he was powerful because he was older and could protect me. He always acted tough, but sometimes, Bing could be really sad. He wouldn't admit what the problem was, but I used to find him rummaging through old trunks up in the attic. I think he was desperate to find a shred of information about his natural father. I found it so appealing that Bing's vulnerability softened his superiority—combined traits I have found so inviting in all my older men.

As I grew up, I favored my Italian side, especially my Grandma Gilardi. I'm proud of my Scotch-Irish half, but it's so terribly Protestant. Grandma was stubborn, feisty, and very independent. She was an orphan who never went past the fifth grade, but she was smart, and she saw to it that my dad got a college education. At seventeen, she decided to join her older sister in California. I always admired her for traveling alone from Turin, Italy, to California without speaking a word of English. And that was in 1909! After she arrived, she met and married my Grandpa Joseph. When he "nipped" a little too much wine, my grandma would take over running the ranch they owned in Santa Rosa. She was an original. A real woman's libber who instilled in me the importance of marrying a responsible man.

Grandma was very religious. Once, when we were at St. Patrick's Cathedral in New York City, I let her convince me we had a saint in the family. By then I was her only soulmate. Dad had converted and become a Presbyterian, and all my grandma's Hail Marys made my mom really nervous. The mixed cultures and religions made the Gilardi children more responsive to other people's differences. I married a Jew, and Bing and my younger brother, Richard, both married Catholics. Poor mom needed a diagram to figure us all out.

It is interesting to note—and it should have been so obvious to me since I started W.O.O.M., yet escaped me altogether until I wrote this book—that all the older men in my life were very special to me. My happiest experiences were with them.

My dad was the first older man in my life, and I just adore him. He taught me to appreciate opera, travel, speaking different languages, and the finer things in life. I've always loved his soft voice and his genteel manner. As a little girl, he was really proud of me and treated me as if I were a contemporary. Once when I was about nine, he took me to Toots Shor's, a very fancy restaurant, during a business trip to New York. Dad had me taste scallops, and I've loved them ever since. Unfortunately, dad just wasn't around enough when I needed him. He traveled all over the world on very long trips.

My Grandad McMaster briefly filled the void. Now there was a man who knew how to make a little girl feel great! When I was very young, we would both wake up before anyone else, and just the two of us would have breakfast in a restaurant. He made an absolute ceremony out of removing my first tooth. He tied pretty strings around my tooth and attached them to Coke bottles.

Then he invited all the neighbors in his trailer park to attend the "coming-out party." Grandad taught me calligraphy and how to fish. We would talk for hours and became real pals. Many of my fondest childhood memories are of our times together. He died when I was eleven.

Growing up, I always knew I wasn't mom's favorite. In retrospect, it's easy to understand. I argued too much and demanded too much attention. I did everything to get my mom to love me more; but I knew I wasn't in her heart. Until I was twelve, I really tried, but knowing she favored my brothers' less complicated personalities, I became a defiant brat. I was easy to hate. If mom said the sky was blue, I said it was pink. She liked everything pasteurized. I preferred things a little bit moldy. I drove her crazy.

As a young woman, mom had hidden agendas and suffered from severe mood swings. I couldn't help feeling responsible. She was very beautiful, but her beauty was often obliterated by unhappiness. I would have walked to the end of the earth to have filled her well with love. But she didn't want it. Physically she took very good care of me, but I needed her emotional support. She always bragged about me to others but never praised me directly. I was desperate for her love, but in those days, I don't think she could give it. Deep down inside because I love her, I believe she did her best.

Happily, my mother and I have worked out our differences. I've grown up and she's mellowed. We have developed an affectionate understanding and respect for each other as individuals. And the friendship we enjoy now is not taken for granted. However, the effects of my mother's earlier discontent created a turbulent childhood that influenced me to marry Sam.

Many schools of psychology contend that younger women are attracted to older men because they are searching for a father figure. To some degree, I concur. However, after talking with many W.O.O.M. subscribers, I have come to believe that a strong and domineering mother who clashes with her insecure daughter is the greater governing force behind younger women gravitating to older men.

❧ *Growing Up* ❦

When I was three, we moved from Europe to Fort Wayne, Indiana. We lived on Beaver Avenue in the only house I've ever lived in with my whole family together. I met most of my friends at Miss Jane's nursery school. We went through grade school and high school together until the third month of my senior year. My dad was then promoted to vice-president of IT&T. He had to work out of the New York office, so we moved to New Jersey.

I was really athletic when I was little. We belonged to Orchard Ridge Country Club where I played golf to please my mom, and I joined the swim team. I won a lot of trophies. When I was six, I discovered ice skating. It was the most wonderful thing that ever happened to me. I couldn't get enough of it. As I twirled and leaped, I noticed a lot of people watching me. I enjoyed the attention it brought me.

As I improved, a woman named Bette Bramel told my mom I should have lessons. At first, my mom wasn't too excited by the idea. The rink was very far away, but Mrs. Bramel promised she would drive me there as often as possible. With her encouragement, I had something of my very own. Until tenth grade when I started dating a senior boy, I was an unpopular loner, a not-very-pretty, insecure wallflower—I suffered from a significant inferiority complex. Ice skating became a passion and filled the void. I was good at it and felt beautiful when I did it.

One of my coaches was a Swiss named Nino Minelli. He was very nice to me and thought I had a lot of talent. When I was about eight, I developed an enormous crush on him. Mr. Minelli encouraged me and shaped my future. I always felt special and important when I was with him.

Over the years, I became a graceful and talented skater. It took a lot for me to practice. When my mom couldn't drive me, I would take two buses to get to the rink which was about twenty miles from my house. Often, I could only practice on a small patch of ice reserved for me when the ice was covered by boards for the Pistons, a professional basketball team. That was such a happy time. During the week I would skate before school and return in the afternoon. On weekends, I skated all day.

Unfortunately, one disaster after another kept setting me back. The first year I was qualified to compete, I developed food poisoning the morning of the event; but I skated anyway. The year after that, I was really on top. This was going to be my year. A few days before the competition, my coach and I collided, and I tore my Achilles tendon. I was devastated. I began to believe that I must be a bad person and nothing good could happen to me.

When I recovered, I really practiced to make up for lost time. It was too late. I was getting older, and my competition days were numbered. I skated summers, sometimes six or seven hours a day. But when you stay out of competition for two consecutive years, nothing short of a miracle will help you secure a title. It was November, 1964, when my dad was transferred to New York. My parents took an apartment across the street from an ice rink in West Orange, New Jersey, and I practiced every day from about 4:00 A.M. to 8:00 A.M. I'm glad I did, because shortly after we moved, my father lost his job to a younger, less expensive executive, and little did I know, skating was going to be my livelihood. My mother was understandably depressed. Jealous that I had a happy future before me, she saw only bleakness ahead for herself. I had no one to turn to. It was a very unhappy time for all of us, and I wanted out.

I desperately needed a friend, and I found one in my older British ice-dancing teacher, David Owen. I was seventeen and he was about thirty, single and a real lady's man. I was crazy about him. David gave me the attention I needed. He taught me how to dress, how to be a proper English lady, and I really enjoyed being with him. But he was too fast for me, and I had no intention of going to bed with anyone, so I cooled it.

By this time, my dad was emotionally at his lowest ebb. It broke my heart to see him come home, job interview after job interview. My mom had a terrible time leaving her club and friends in Indiana. And I was graduating from West Orange High School where I knew no one. Our security and future were uncertain. I took a job at Korvettes department store changing toilet paper in the ladies' rooms and was shortly "promoted" to the hair salon where I swept the floor. After work, I baby-sat or did ironing for neighbors in our apartment complex. For a girl who had taken college preparatory courses in high school and was only proficient in geometry because she repeated it twice, very little was open to me.

I wanted desperately to go to Ohio State University where my skating would be a valuable asset. But that was out of state and not financially feasible. Bing was at Purdue and Richard needed to be educated. I feebly sent a couple of applications to nearby junior colleges but was rejected.

❧ On My Own ❦

After graduating from West Orange High School in June, 1965, I was offered a job teaching skating at the Beacon Hill Country Club in Summit, New Jersey. It was an offer I couldn't resist. For seven months, I lived in the beautiful country-club mansion and ate delicious meals with the chef in the kitchen. It was a relief from all the melancholy at home. At seventeen, I was completely on my own. My parents weren't able to offer any financial help. God, was I scared.

Soon, an opportunity to skate for Holiday on Ice International came my way. Because I had gained so much weight, I was relegated to the chorus line even though I was by far the best skater in the show. I didn't care. I had a hotel roof over my head and money in my pocket. I hadn't skated with them long when a boss, a very old and unpleasant man, took me to a fancy restaurant for lunch. He alluded to letting me understudy the show's star if I spent some time with him.

A trainer and his wife who worked for the show were helping me on the sly to prepare for that very position. Jack was a chubby teddy bear of a man who pummeled off my weight. He taught me how to eat properly and genuinely cared for me. Early in the morning and after shows, he would open the rink for me and teach me how to sell to an audience. We spent hours working out routines that were far superior to anything they had in the show, but after my lunch with the show's lascivious boss, I realized the price was too high.

In January of 1967, I went with the show to South America. We performed in Argentina where I spent a lot of time with the Bertas, my grandmother's family. We later played Brazil where I met an orthodontist, Dr. Carlos Vogel. His family was German, but had moved to Brazil after World War II. I fell head over heels in love with Carlos who was twelve years older than I was. I couldn't get enough of the most incredibly handsome man I had ever seen.

Carlos was a rich playboy who took me to his private sporting clubs, to the jockey club, and to meet his family and friends. He taught me how to shoot for sport and introduced me to all the most elegant nightclubs and restaurants in São Paulo. I thought I had died and gone to heaven, but I knew he would never be faithful to me. So I came home. It was August, 1967.

Dad had taken a job at Fort Monmouth, and I was staying at their house in Tinton Falls, New Jersey. I knew I only had a few weeks to decide my fate. The opportunities were limited. I could return to the ice show which paid well, but the life-style didn't promise much in the way of a future. I could get a job, but doing what? Finally, but not a real option, I could marry the man of my mother's dreams and be miserable the rest of my life.

One day, as I started to pull out of my parent's driveway, I got a flat tire. A young neighbor, David Cohen, came across the street and asked if I needed help. As he was fixing the tire, I mentioned I was looking for a job. He said his friend worked at Dr. Furman's office, just down the street, but she was leaving. "Maybe you could be a dental assistant," he yelled from underneath the car. I laughed. About all I knew about teeth were a few things I learned in Carlos's office and that you should brush twice a day.

But it gave me an idea. I'd go to dental assistant's school. It was cheap and the training took less than a year. So I signed up. At the same time, I called Dr. Furman's office for an interview and asked if they could use someone part time who was attending dental assistant's school. An older-sounding woman named Mrs. Strachan gave me an appointment for an interview in the early afternoon.

❧ Dr. Furman ❦

I waited in Dr. Furman's private office for what seemed like hours. It was freezing in there! I had worn a corduroy pumpkin-colored mini dress that was totally wrong for the occasion. Among all the white starch, it stuck out like a sore thumb. Desperate for the job, I mulled over how I could embellish the oral resume I would soon be giving. I'm laughing now as I think about it. Toilet-paper changer, floor sweeper, ice skater—oh yes, baby-sitter. Really experienced. I wondered whether I should mention the job I had for two days at Don's, a drive-in restaurant in Livingston. The owner fired me after I spilled a large vat of multicolored sprinkles.

As I was daydreaming about my lack of qualifications, Dr. Furman walked briskly into the office. At first, I was startled by his brusque demeanor. He wasn't old, but he wasn't young. When you're nineteen, everyone looks older than you. Actually, he was kind of cute. He had long black eyelashes that looked fake and really slender hands. Within a couple of minutes, he was ushering me out the door. I just knew I didn't get the job.

Later that afternoon, I was astonished when Mrs. Strachan called and told me I could start the next day. She was pretty firm about the white uniform. The hem should be two inches below the knee, and my arms were to be covered by three-quarter length sleeves. This was quite a switch from all those skimpy show costumes.

The job turned out to be better than I expected, and I really enjoyed the work. Over the next couple of months, I continued the schooling, worked afternoons for Dr. Furman, and also started teaching ice skating at night and weekends at nearby Navesink Country Club. I made enough money to move out of my parents' home into a lovely apartment. It meant eating a bagel every night for dinner, but being on my own again was worth it. Dr. Furman taught me how to take X-rays, and when I became proficient at that, he suggested I quit the school and work full time for him. When I told one of the other assistants about his offer, she warned me, "Don't accept sixty dollars per week. He's paying the other assistant sixty-five."

I was sitting on a yellow Cosco stool when Dr. Furman came into the lab and asked me if I had made a decision. Even though I knew he was having financial problems, I still asked for the sixty-five dollars per week. Amused by my boldness, his grouchiness, often caused by the financial difficulties, disappeared. He softened, flashed me his brilliant smile, and said, "Okay." That was the first time I noticed his charm.

I met some really nice people at dental assistant meetings. One of them introduced me to her boss, Dr. Steinberg, who was older than Dr. Furman, but he was single and asked me out. We dated for several months, but I could tell he was really in love with another assistant who was attending dental hygiene school.

I decided it was time I made it to college where I belonged. I would apply to dental hygiene school, as well.

I told Dr. Furman about my ambition to become a hygienist, and he set up an interview for me at the University of Pennsylvania, his alma mater. His friend, Dr. Ray Johnson, a professor at Penn, drove me. It went very well, and it was decided that I would start the following fall. I worked on my weak chemistry background with one of Dr. Furman's patients and was really excited about the future.

But soon, I noticed a change in Dr. Furman. He joined the ice-skating club where I taught and asked me to give lessons to him and his five-year-old daughter, Laurie. He kept falling all over the place and quit after the first lesson. He said it was too humiliating to be picked up by a ninety-pound waif. But Sam continued to bring Laurie. Soon after, I mentioned I was going to visit some friends who were performing in an ice show in Scranton, Pennsylvania. He told me it was very dangerous to drive there alone and asked if I knew what I was doing.

This man was really naive. I had just completed a stint in South America where the bathroom was usually a hole in the ground, and my hotel in Buenos Aires was bombed, and he's worried about Pennsylvania! I went anyway.

Then I really rocked him in November and asked if I could take a two-week vacation. I wanted to go to Brazil. He said, "Brazil! Why would you want to go there? Who are you going with?" I told him I was going by myself and staying with a friend. He was beside himself and said, "By yourself! You're only twenty." Stupefied, I thought this guy was really sheltered. After all, I went there when I was nineteen and nothing happened. Besides, why did he care?

Actually, I wanted to go to Brazil because I couldn't get over Carlos who had recently married. I knew if I went back, I could get him out of my system; but I had to bury the dream on Brazilian soil.

Dr. Furman said I could have the time off, but I would have to wait until February when he and his wife were taking a Caribbean vacation and the office would be closed. That was fine with me because I needed more time to save money for the trip.

Over the next few weeks, Dr. Furman started spending a lot of time with the assistants in the lab. Mrs. Strachan said she had never seen him happier. He really enjoyed letting down his guard. Sheepishly, he was discovering a different side of himself and liked it. But behind it all, I noticed a sadness I didn't understand. I joked with him that he needed to have fun more often and shouldn't take life so seriously.

Soon after, he asked Mrs. Strachan and me to visit the expensive, new home he had just purchased. That was when I met his wife, Joan. I had seen her in the office, but she seldom spoke to the assistants. Joan didn't fraternize with the help.

❧ The Affair ❦

If I had been older and more mature, I would have realized Dr. Furman was falling in love with me. But I wasn't and mistook his attentiveness for fatherly concern. In reality, I had an abundance of boyfriends and probably needed the paternal attention more.

One day when Mrs. Strachan and the other assistant left early, I was helping in the business office. Dr. Furman and I were finishing up some paper work. I was sitting at a desk that was tucked away in a corner. He came over and asked me a question about a patient, and while I was answering, he bent down and kissed me. It was terribly exciting, a beautiful moment filled with admiration and love. But it was wrong. He was married.

Thoroughly bewildered, I left the office wondering what it was supposed to mean. Over the next couple of weeks our emotions escalated. We were a mixed bag of lust and confusion, but we held back and tried to collect our thoughts. Mrs. Strachan was dying from resentment as she noticed Dr. Furman's change toward me. It was obvious we were in love. It was amusing to watch Sam—he is so ethical and totally straight. He was slapping himself on the wrist, while at the same time patting himself on the back. It was a struggle to control our feelings. I was counting the minutes until I left for Brazil. I needed time alone to work this all out.

About a month into the attraction, we were a tandem of passion. I was infatuated with Sam's gentleness, his genuine concern, and deep devotion. With emotions running wild, it was time to make a decision. Realizing there was no turning back, we confirmed our deep affection and made love in his private office. Actually, Sam made love and I found out what it was all about. I was a virgin.

I was still confused and uncertain and continued to date other men. I wanted to be sure I knew what I was doing. I knew that lots of men say they will leave their wives but don't. I was also unconvinced about the stolen moments in obscure hotel rooms. Could the excitement of love-on-the-sly have been the real attraction for both of us?

About two months after our affair began, I told Sam we needed to spend some time together—more than the hour or two of after-work passion. Sam found a legitimate two-day dental meeting in New York where we could stay overnight.

In retrospect, it was all rather hilarious, especially since we thought we were being so clever. I packed an old Samsonite cosmetic bag with absolutely everything I would need, including a skimpy slip dress I borrowed from a friend. I parked on a side street near Sam's office while he waited for the staff to leave. Within minutes, he drove up and I jumped in and sat on the floor until we got on the highway. We arrived at an out-of-the-way, cut-rate, hotel on the West Side, where Sam was sure he wouldn't bump into anyone he knew. We walked into the lobby and the first person he saw was a dentist who practiced near his office, a classmate of his at Penn. Great!

Figuring we had nothing to lose after that, Sam boldly made a reservation for dinner at La Côte Basque, a fancy Manhattan restaurant. What a laugh! I walked in with my twenty-nine-dollar dress. Quite a sight in comparison to the Chanels and Adolfos aligning the banquettes.

Intimidated by the French menu, I was relieved when the captain suggested I order the restaurant's famous artichoke. When it came, I began to eat it...spines and all! Practically choking on all of the needles sticking in my throat, I'm sure I gave the staff and anyone watching a real snicker. A courtly British gentleman, sitting adjacent to me, came to my rescue. With a twinkle in his eye, fully aware this was a seduction scene, he leaned over and discreetly suggested I watch him demonstrate how to eat an artichoke. As he meticulously scooped off the meat with his upper teeth and placed the finished leaf in the side dish provided, I realized again just how comfortable an older man can make a young woman feel.

Weeks later, I was still not convinced that Sam and I were a fait accompli. It was a relief to go to Brazil. I had to think. But Sam was miserable during his vacation in St. Thomas. He came to the realization that his marriage was a failure. The mix of hysterical mood swings, constant fighting over money, and infrequent sex was pushing Sam further and further away from his wife. He learned that with me along or not, he couldn't stay with Joan any longer. It was a sad time for him.

Sam returned to the States and called me in São Paulo. He asked me to come home early. We needed to talk. My sensors picked up that we might have a problem. Barely into our relationship and already he was telling me what to do. I became consumed with guilt that I might not want to commit to the relationship. I loved him, but I was a proud renegade who'd made it on her own. Mainly, I was concerned that my free-spirited nature would collide with his possessive overprotectiveness.

However, common sense told me he was good for me, and I would never find someone again who cared so much. I struggled and fought with my misgivings all the way home from Brazil.

The permanence of marriage was encumbering my decision. While mulling it over, I realized the problem was me; I wasn't accustomed to so much attention and almost resented it. I distrusted love. In the past it had been based upon performance, but Sam's came without conditions. By the time I landed, I opted to give it a try because in my heart, I knew Sam would always be faithful to me and that his affair with me was an aberration. I also knew that Joan had handed him to me on a silver platter.

❧ *The Price* ❦

Sam told me Joan was suspicious of the hushed late-night calls. Certain she knew he wasn't in love with her anymore, it annoyed Sam that Joan was trying so fervently to win him back. He felt her rediscovered love and concern came too late and that any effort on her part to revive the ill-fated relationship was in vain.

Friends who were around years before their separation and divorce tell me Sam and Joan were seldom able to hide their discontent. It was obvious from their frequent public outbursts that they were a very unhappy couple. By the time I came on the scene, Sam and Joan's marriage had been reduced to them both begging. For Sam, it was debasing and emasculating.

Aggravating their marital strife was Sam's financial condition. He was strapped. Sam wouldn't have been able to afford Joan's expensive taste under the best of circumstances. In trying to do so, he was headed for a meltdown.

In 1967, at the age of thirty-five, Sam found himself saddled with three mortgages. One was on the costly new house he had bought for Joan, the second on the professional complex he built because his dental practice had been in his bachelor house. Having trouble selling the latter, meant there was mortgage number three.

If that wasn't bad enough, he also owed his father a pile of money and was carrying sizable balances on nearly thirty department and specialty store charge accounts. He knew a divorce would wipe him out, and Joan would get any remaining cash. The uncertainty over his financial survival brought on severe stomachaches. Under a doctor's care, he was living on medication.

Tragically though, the tougher and more heartbreaking impasse facing Sam was leaving Laurie and Jill; emotionally, it was tearing him up. Knowing for years that his marriage was an unfortunate mistake for both Joan and him, his concern for his young daughters' welfare kept him from walking out. While he knew he was very much in love with me, Sam did not know how he could face his little girls and say, "Daddy's not going to live here anymore." Maybe they could take it, but he wasn't sure he could.

It was obvious, when I watched them together, how much he adored his six-year-old daughter, Laurie. She was the apple of his eye who made the botched marriage bearable. Jill was three. She was witty and smart, and Sam was crazy about her as well. Yet during our private moments—alone together—Sam also recognized how much he needed me. However, the guilt of abandoning his daughters was constantly on his mind. I hated seeing him so torn—vacillating back and forth.

Bogged down by my own uncertainty, I was relieved Sam might be having second thoughts and was taking his time. At this point, neither one of us had promised each other anything except devotion. We were in love, but we knew the traumatic expense could easily have dissolved the affair.

Early one Sunday morning, Sam went to his office to work out treatment plans for patients he would see on Monday. He was barely in the door when his private telephone line rang. It was his friend, Ron*. He wanted to come over to the office—they had to talk. Not knowing what Ron had on his mind, Sam agreed to see him.

Visibly concerned, Ron told Sam he was upsetting the apple cart for their circle of "upright" Jewish friends who didn't believe in divorce. Their wives were threatened and afraid Sam was opening up Pandora's box. Ron said, "If you leave Joan, none of us will talk to you again." He tried to persuade Sam to stay with Joan, set me up in an apartment (he didn't know I was able to afford my own), and keep me as a mistress. "Lots of guys do it."

On the surface, it seemed the easy way out. Have your cake and eat it, too. But Sam couldn't live with the hypocrisy—he wouldn't humiliate Joan by playing around behind her back. And he loved me too much to even think about it as an alternative solution.

About a month after Ron's talk with Sam, I was in absolute agony with a toothache. I was in the process of orthodontic treatment, and one tooth was acting up. Earlier that morning, an endodontist removed the nerve, but I had no relief. At midnight, I called Sam at home. I needed him to remove the tooth. Concerned, he rushed over to the office. He picked up an instrument and poked around. As he examined the tooth, he discovered an orthodontic elastic had popped off and wrapped itself around the molar. He removed the elastic, and the pain disappeared.

Because he had never seen this happen before and we were able to save the tooth, Sam was ecstatic. In this mood, he returned home where Joan made it clear that she thought he had met me for anything but a dental reason. That was the end. He knew the marriage was over. Thanksgiving weekend, 1969, an opportunity arose when Joan took the children to visit her family in St. Louis. Sam packed his belongings and a few household items and left.

It broke my heart to watch a man who had worked all his life move from a four-thousand-square-foot luxury home into a tiny, dumpy place and live on a budget. In my confusion, I felt I was to blame. Sam was ruined financially. Knowing it would be a struggle and a strain to rebuild his life, I urged Sam to return, but he said he couldn't.

Meanwhile, Joan fought to retain her position until the bitter end. In fact, when their divorce case came to trial more than a year later, she withdrew her complaint. To this day, Sam has never understood why. He says, "I was never good enough, successful enough, for her. Why the sudden change of heart?"

Sam was forced to proceed on the basis of mental cruelty. The judge insisted he state from memory the overwhelming number of charge accounts and outstanding balances Joan had incurred that he was having difficulty paying. At that point, Joan came to the realization it would be detrimental for her to fight the divorce. She reopened her case and eventually won.

Ironically, Joan, who was thirty-two and beautiful, came out of all of this smelling like a rose. Freed from an horrendous marriage, she met and fell in love with a physician whom she flaunted as a rich "real" doctor and was flashing a huge engagement ring, a few weeks after the divorce. Three months later, she remarried. She sold the house (taking Sam's premarital equity with her) and built an even bigger one with her new husband in an exclusive area in central New Jersey—in some people's eyes, this was a real trade up!

With Joan happily remarried, you would think things could only get better. On the contrary, Joan and her husband, Earle, carried on a vendetta against Sam that consumed them. And vice-versa. There must have been twenty visits back and forth to court. The legal files filled a trunk! Sam's lawyer, the Honorable William Himelman, had never seen anything like it.

The divorce and custody trials, where Laurie was allowed to live with Sam and me, were among the nastiest and most horrific in the history of Monmouth County, New Jersey. Even Sam's rabbi, Jack Rosoff, testified against him (I am Christian)! Sam, Joan, and Earle were a troika of hate—all at the expense of two very precious children who were the innocent victims of insane animosity.

Sadly, Laurie and Jill became the pawns of their parents' squabbling. Each, worrying they would be shunned by one parent if they expressed their love of the other, closed up. Their innocence and trust of parental love was destroyed by us. For years, Laurie, in particular, was emotionally wounded, insecure, and uncommunicative.

Jill regarded Sam as an outsider. Understandably so. Although her father never missed a visitation day, supported her financially, paid for her private school and college education, and loved her very much, she had lived with her stepfather since she was in preschool. When Jill became engaged, there was no discussion— her stepfather would walk her down the aisle. As much as it hurt Sam, he had to accept that he would be merely an invited guest.

Daring to reflect back, I realize I have no regrets. I merely consider myself the catalyst that finally broke up an already failing marriage. If it hadn't been me, it would have been someone else. But I will never get over what it did to Laurie and Jill.

So... You've Fallen in Love with an Older Man, Too

✻ The Attraction ✻

Falling in love with an older man is a delicious experience. It's a love affair you will savor. The one you will never forget. It's the liaison you should search out to catapult you into womanhood... the benchmark on which to base every passion. Especially because, many of us have never been cared for so much.

Yes, we've been in love before with high-school and college sweethearts, and even first husbands, but that was puppy love compared to the incomparable high a younger woman feels when she has attracted the attention of someone so worldly. I know because, since I was four years old, I have fallen in love with older men lots of times!

I do not stand alone in exalting the attributes of older lovers. University of Michigan psychologist, David Buss, author of *The Evolution of Desire*, found in his study of human-mating strategies that women in thirty-seven cultures preferred older men. When we examine the reasons, it makes perfect sense.

The juxtaposition of female reckless youth and male vintage savvy is magical. A sublime potion of power and beauty. *Dynasty's* Blake and Krystal Carrington revisited. For those of us who don't mind being considered a priceless ornament, with all the perks, the encounter is very much like being a kid in a candy store. Life is full of surprises, as we are spoiled with the goodies and safeguarding love lavished upon us. But it's a complicated relationship, chock full of antitheses, that requires respect and compassion for each other's age-related, differences.

When we articulate our variances and blend our generations, we become an unstoppable power couple. Add to that our undying love, and we're infallible. There's conceit in knowing we've beaten the odds. For younger women, it's the certainty that selecting the historian over history-to-be-made elevates us from our peers. But at times, we both miss the adventure of fitting in with those our own age.

To be the protégée of an older man is rewarding. You are privy to years of experience without paying the price. Under his tutelage, we can develop a competitive edge that's inaccessible to women involved with men their own age. Our guy's seen the world and knows the ropes. He's not competing with us and is seldom jealous of our accomplishments. Many of us get to where we are going because we let him help chart the course. However, the price you pay is, at times, you'll resent not being able to reinvent your very *own* wheel.

It's very easy to be infatuated with the strength of an older man. He's been around, coped, and survived many of the things we are experiencing or may soon be facing. It's reassuring to be with a big brother who is there to break the fall and encourage us to continue on. Because he has been through it, he knows this crisis is only a momentary setback. Whether we are young or middle-aged, an older man will continuously come to our rescue as a supportive Band-Aid. He never tires of watching out for us, even as he occasionally smothers us.

Just as most older men are patient and more affectionate lovers, second marriages often make for more understanding husbands. The next wife gains from their trials and tribulations, failures and successes. Being with an older man is a fail-safe method in bringing out the best in yourself. The security of being with someone who's seen the world gives a younger woman certain powers of her very own. An older man is our Ouija board. Through his experiences, we gain knowledge and foresight others our age can only obtain by living longer.

For those of us who are in love with older men, the relationship is heady and intoxicating. The effervescence of tasting, touching, and burrowing oneself between its layers of nourishment and demand...flexibility and brittleness...lust and sin is compelling. There is no equal.

❧ *Where Do Younger Women Meet Older Men?* ❦

The older man you have fallen in love with is no ordinary guy. And undoubtedly his position of power adds to his prowess. He may be your college professor, hold a very senior position at your firm, or be the firefighter who rescued your cat. Wherever you met, your youth and outlook have caught his eye, and he's chosen you to remake and energize his life. Some men look to glamorous younger women to heighten their image; others are bored with their wives and desperately seek debs to recapture their youth. For an older guy who has money in his pocket and no one to spend it on, a younger woman can make all the difference in changing the quality of his life.

According to a survey I conducted in August, 1990, polling 183 W.O.O.M. subscribers, where the majority of women who completed the questionnaire were between the ages of twenty-six and thirty-four, 51 percent of the respondents met their older men—single, married, divorced or widowed—in the workplace or a work-related setting.

The other 49 percent met their husbands or male friends at self-help groups, volunteer organizations, on blind dates, or at bars and social clubs. One woman's soon-to-be husband was a friend of her first husband and another met her future husband at the train station. The most ironic was the lady who met her intended at a "How to Become a Successful Single" class! Since so many women meet their mates as a result of working for them, I want to examine this group up close.

For those who said, "He was my boss," or "I was his secretary," it's important to determine the sincerity and honorableness of *his* intentions and explore just where the relationship is going.

If you are involved with a man at the office *sans sex*, in a proverbial "water-cooler romance," you're probably more serious than he is because lots of older guys like to flirt with younger women. If kept at that, it's fun and flattering and can sometimes lead to a career-enhancing friendship. But be careful that you don't become ensnared in a once-a-week tryst that leads nowhere. Often these guys have a wife at home they have no intention of leaving.

Many people advise against getting involved with a man you work with—especially your boss. Many women end up losing their job and man when the affair's over. But the reality is: Who do you get to know, but the people you know? A boss and his secretary or associate have a very close bond. If there's even the slightest spark, it only takes an "off-guard" moment between the two to kindle a romance.

However, if you're incontrovertibly in love and are convinced of his undeniable ardor, the two of you can set the world on fire! You'll develop a sense of history from him, and he'll explore new and contemporary worlds with you. The relationship is heady and intoxicating as you delve into each other's very separate but fascinating spheres. An older man is cuddly and warm, protective and supportive. He is unabashedly proud of his young lover's endeavors and is pleased as punch that you adore him. There is no stopping you. But sometimes, even if there is genuine love between you, these older charmers are married.

❧ *The Hurt and Pain of Being In Love with an Older, Married Man* ❦

*T*rusting the intentions of an older married man may be an arduous and degrading exercise. If you are a younger woman involved in an affair with a married man, you will pay a heavy emotional price to determine if and how badly you're being used and if his love is sincere. The uncertainty creates havoc with your sensibility and half the time you won't be able to think straight. Even the most sophisticated women find it unnerving to remain in a risky affair. It makes no difference whether you are young or middle-aged, all women vacillate between love and hate for their married lovers as they spend lonely hours waiting by the phone. The affair will disrupt your life as you suffer through weekends and holidays by yourself, obsessing over what your lover is doing with his wife and kids. I know I couldn't eat or sleep.

The good part, though, is that you'll find out quickly how committed he is. A "let's meet Tuesday night when *she* takes her course in ancient history" is passion not love. And a quick test of his availability and devotion is to make a date to see him on the weekend. If it's never convenient, you can assume he's very much married and considers you a plaything. The bad part will be freeing yourself from a spellbinding, dead-end relationship that is dangerous to both your self-esteem and health. For those who enjoy the attention and are afraid of being alone under any circumstance, being able to let go will be painful.

On the other hand, if you get roses every day, hourly love-Faxes signed "your secret admirer," and take daily two-hour lunches in dark, intimate restaurants to discuss pressing business, it's safe to say he's smitten, and you should go with your heart. But prepare your defensive armor for a lot of prejudicial backlash because it is generally assumed younger wives of previously married men *seek out* and steal other women's husbands.

The ramifications of wanting to be the next wife of a married man can be cruel and consuming. Whereas, coupling on the sneak is passionate and exciting, it is nothing like divorce which is sheer hell! The chance of your love affair surviving is better than Ivana and Donald Trump reconciling, but be advised that you may be in for an arduous uphill battle. Going through his divorce will be a real litmus test of your devotion. And you may have to do without the luxurious gifts he has been lavishing on you, because unless he has a concealed Swiss bank account—*this* is going to cost! The expense is not only monetary. The consequences of defying the religious precept, *Thou shalt not commit adultery*, looms ominously over those involved.

I was consumed with guilt. My love affair with a married man frightened me. It contradicted my innermost personal values. Spiritually religious, breaking up Sam's marriage was destroying me emotionally. Yet I couldn't help myself. My conscience screamed, "This affair is immoral, sinful, so *not* me."

But it wasn't Sam, either. He was, still is, conservative, unbending, traditional—an introvert. I'm effusive, abstract, unreserved. At the time I thought, "What do I see in him?" I constantly chastised myself. But I was hopelessly in love. Many people in similar situations develop phobias. Mine was the fear of flying. I was sure God would blow me up to get even.

For most, it is the emotional, gut-wrenching guilt that's the relationship killer —particularly if he has kids. If he does, the decision to leave his unhappy marriage is monumental. I emphasize "unhappy marriage." *You* shouldn't shoulder the blame for the failure of the marriage. If he was contented and blissful with his present wife, he wouldn't be fooling around with someone else!

As innocent as your relationship started out to be, it's a lonely road for a woman who "breaks up a home." Society has very little compassion for the *other* woman. Many feel home wreckers deserve emotional and maybe even physical punishment. You will become the object of the scorned wife's wrath and her threatened friends will make mincemeat out of you. Even though in your eyes, his unhappiness justified the affair, the sweetest of you will be labeled sluts. You will always be blamed, while his dalliance will be passed off as a weak moment. Although everyone knows the guy and his wife are a miserable mismatch, the sanctity of marriage is a *tough nut to crack,* and you will become a gossipmonger's dream come true. I can testify to that from personal experience!

Sam was one of the first among his young, professional Jewish friends to get divorced. Perturbed that Sam was upsetting the applecart for those played around but didn't leave their wives, as Ron* had suggested he should, most of these "friends" wouldn't speak to him after he left Joan and still don't to this day. His side of the story wasn't important, and the inattentive wife he couldn't afford was absolved of any responsibility.

I was the one who received all the attention. From a competition-level professional figure skater, I was transformed into a show girl. Even though my father resigned from active duty before I was born, suddenly I was an Army brat with no roots. I was lewd with a disreputable past, when in fact I was a virgin until I met Sam. And of course, I wasn't Jewish. Oh yes, in 1970, the phones were ringing! "Dolores! Can you *b-e-l-i-e-v-e* it? Sam's shacking up with a shiksa harlot! A dancer who's sure been around. Her dad's in the *army!*"

While I knew Sam was undeniably in love with me and that it was only a matter of time before I would be his wife, others aren't so lucky. And for many I talk with, the heartbreak of walking away from a love affair with a married man leaves deep scars.

My friend, Simone Fortier*, literally fled Gordes, a small city in southern France to get away from her married, older lover. She said, "I knew if I stayed, I wouldn't be able to resist continuing the relationship." But she paid a heavy price. Simone left a comfortable home, loving parents, and her brothers and sisters. "It broke my heart to quit college," she laments. "In France you have to pass a stringent test to be accepted."

Simone, who barely spoke English, accepted a position in Connecticut as an au pair. It has taken her years to get over the relationship that disrupted her life; he was constantly on her mind. Eventually, she put herself through New York University, supplementing her income teaching French at the Alliance Français. Now she is a happily married mother of two. But the regrettable experience cost her her country and the proximity of a loving family. The loss stays ever fresh in her mind.

I hear from so many desperate women looking for support. They are in need of a friend and confidante, someone who won't pass judgment. Younger women, hopelessly in love with older married men fighting with their conscience as they consider divorce, are frustrated as time often stands still. Sarah Morgan*, an account representative in Ontario, Canada, is having an affair with her boss. "I know John* loves me more," she said, "but he has left me three times to go back to his wife and children. I am tortured by this love affair." Women like Sarah are at the mercy of the man's convictions. I can't give them a definitive answer about what to do because there isn't one. However, I can guarantee, until you have the ring on your finger, you'll never be certain of his intentions.

Over the past several years, Janet Martelli*, a young and talented, national television producer has called me often for advice. She was agonizing over her affair with a much older, married actor. He was conscience-stricken about leaving his second wife for her. Holidays spent alone, knowing he was with his wife and family, were painful but no worse than his inability to come to grips with a decision.

She often lamented, "He is trying to have the best of both worlds. He talks incessantly about me when he is with his wife,

but worries about 'trashing her' to me when we are alone together—as if he wants us to be friends!" On one occasion, he invited
them both to accompany him to a movie!

Ms. Martelli was frustrated but often sympathetic in expressing her lover's concern that, "Failing at a second marriage scared
him because it confirmed his pattern of not being able to be
faithful to any wife." And she also worried that if she became his
third wife, would *she* be the last? Eventually, he left his wife but
not for her. Three years later, Janet's confused, "He's still crazy in
love with me, gets jealous when I see other men, but can't bring
himself to commit."

Some older men stay in miserable marriages because they don't
want to lose the respect of their family and community and perhaps their boss. Others may be in high-powered political positions
where divorce is just barely accepted. Rich older men, who have
been around long enough to be ensnared in investments or tax
shelters that have been put in their wives' names, may keep you
dangling. Divorce proceedings could ruin them financially and
may even bring to light illegal acts that could land them in jail.

Twenty-nine-year-old Allison Schmidt*, a department manager at Henri Bendel in New York City, said that her male
friend's fraud case, of which his wife knows all the details, hasn't
stopped him from setting her up in an apartment nor from buying her fine art and expensive jewelry over the past five years.
But she doesn't see him leaving his wife while the case is being
litigated.

Some see divorce and breaking up a family as immoral. To
solve the problem, many older men keep mistresses who wait
hopelessly for a change in attitude or a wife's death. Others who
don't want emotional ties, resort to escort services (we've all heard
about Heidi Fleiss and the Mayflower Madam) to provide young
and beautiful out-of-town dates; but often, even *they* fall in love.

Extramarital love affairs are wrong, but many wives just aren't
tuned in to their husbands' emotional needs. Often for good rea-

son their husbands seek out a surrogate. Sidney Biddle Barrows filled this void, and it's a real eye-opener. She and many other madams admit that a lot of married men they deal with are really not interested in rough-and-tumble sex. It's a compassionate, attentive listener they're seeking. Harvey Hendrix, Ph.D., author of *Getting the Love You Want,* concurs. He often asks couples in his relationship-therapy sessions to be each other's live-in, lifelong therapists.

The despair of loving a man torn between his happiness and the happiness of his family is universally wrenching, whether you live in California or New Zealand. Recently, twenty-seven-year-old Jillian Moore* called me, frantic, from Manchester, England. "I'm just desperate," she wept. "I just don't know what to say to my boyfriend to make it better. Andrew's* children won't speak to him, and he's lost all contact with them. He is just sick over the matter. His world is crashing in on him." Hopelessly down-hearted, she told me about her anguish and her forty-four-year-old, married lover's plight.

It all started when they met ten years ago. Jillian was a receptionist for Andrew's firm. In the beginning, the relationship was strictly business. She left the company two years later when she set up home with Robert*, a gentleman eight years her senior. Their love affair was fairly rocky, but they had a child together.

Over the years, Jillian would pop in to visit old friends at Andrew's company and returned there to work several years later. "In February of 1993," says Jillian, "Andrew began to show more interest in me. He invited me out for dinner. I thought that it wouldn't do any harm, so I agreed. He took me out for a very nice meal, and we made arrangements to meet up again."

However, the secret meetings were very difficult for Jillian because she had to hide her feelings about Andrew at work as their love affair became more intense. "I know it sounds a bit corny," says Jillian, "but our relationship just seemed to develop more rapidly than expected, and we found ourselves falling in

love. It filled a cold void, and we were both finding it very difficult to go back to our partners."

Knowing that her relationship with Robert was over, Jillian
moved into a one-bedroom apartment. "At this time," says Jillian,
"Andrew was still at home with his wife and children and had
never once promised that he would leave them and set up home
with me." But Andrew's wife became extremely suspicious and
took steps to confirm the affair.

In an attempt to make amends, Robert took his family on a
vacation. "But on the second week of his holiday," Jillian says,
"Andrew called me and said things were going very badly and
that it was likely that upon their return, he would be leaving her.
The next phone call came on the day he got back to England.
[He] asked if I'd collect him from the airport. He has not lived at
home since that time; he stays in a hotel or sometimes with me."
Ruefully, Jillian adds, "I can understand that both [Robert and
Andrew's wife] feel very hurt and betrayed by us—but our rela-
tionship was not planned—it just happened. We cannot help our
feelings for one another. I love him very much indeed."

Andrew's children have turned on him. They refuse to see or
even speak to him. His wife swings from one mood to another—
from wanting him back to wanting a divorce and never seeing
him again. "I've asked Andrew if he wants to go back with his
family if it would make it easier," says Jillian. "He says that he is
not so sure that it would work out. What he wants is to be able
to see and get on with his children and to also have me, but it's
not that simple, as we both realize. What his children have basically said is that he should choose between me and them. He is
very distressed. I don't want to lose him and feel very guilty about
this—I also feel selfish—as his children really look up to him and
have always gotten on very well with him. I feel he should go
back with them, but I don't want him to."

This is a heavy burden for a young woman and a rude awak-
ening to the struggle that lies ahead when one's involved with an

older man who is thinking about leaving his wife or is separated and contemplating divorce. In essence, he's at the controls.

For older men who are not the typical cheaters, and may be in the only affair of their lives, the emotional hassle can propel them back to a thankful and forgiving wife who doesn't mind his extra thirty pounds and to the kids who take him for granted. Grateful that it's over, wives with blinders can chalk it up to a midlife crisis. The husband and wife kiss and make up, and the relief of the reconciliation obliterates the memory of the mistress.

Love affairs with married older men may be regarded as déclassé, but the affair bug has no class boundaries. It bites the upper crust as hard as it does floozies, and those who fall between.

At the beginning of World War II, Pamela Churchill, who is presently President Bill Clinton's ambassador to France, was the new bride of Randolph Churchill, the playboy son of England's prime minister, Winston Churchill. Within months after her marriage, she fell madly in love with Averell Harriman. At that time, the millionaire Union Pacific heir was Franklin Delano Roosevelt's special liaison to Britain. Pamela was twenty-one; Averell was forty-nine. Two years after the torrid affair began, Harriman's wife, Marie threatened to divorce him, and they left London immediately for "another assignment" in Moscow. Pamela, fed up with her husband's gambling debts and excessive drinking, separated from the debauched Randolph about the same time.

It didn't take the irresistible Pamela long to become the paramour of a number of internationally renowned gentlemen including Élie de Rothschild, Frank Sinatra, and Prince Aly Kahn. She was manipulative and charming in her endeavors to make a man believe she was captivated by him—whether the man was married or not. In 1960, Broadway producer Leland Hayward divorced his third wife, "Slim" Keith, to marry Pamela. He was sixty; she was only forty. After a series of strokes, he died eleven years later.

It wasn't until 1971 that Pamela finally captured her first love. Shortly after Hayward's death, she was reunited with her old beau, Averell Harriman, at a dinner party at the home of *Washington Post* publisher, Katherine Graham. Marie had died and the bittersweet romance was rekindled. Harriman was seventy-nine, free at last, to marry Pamela—thirty years later!

Even when the two of you are so in love a crowbar couldn't pry you apart, there are going to be times when you'll have to adapt to being an outsider. It will be difficult for you to not resent the people and emotions that have to be considered. A few years ago, I appeared on a nationally televised show with Michigan resident Betty Lou Stanlonis. I was struck by her honesty in expressing what many of us are afraid to: That her first concern was that she wouldn't be able to help her boyfriend, nine years older, get through his divorce. "It was an emotionally traumatized divorce, and I was troubled by what effect it would have on our [pending] marriage...I worried things would come between us because there still was a physical attachment to his former wife—child support, alimony, and visitation."

The illicit relationship between a younger woman and an older, married man garners ill will and contempt within every social stratum. Many men are reminded, not always subtly, that their dalliance will result in split loyalties. Even the famous, jet-set friends of Donald and Ivana Trump overtly took to different slopes in the winter of 1990 when the forty-three-year-old, millionaire financier starting schussing on the sly with Marla Maples, a voluptuous model, seventeen years his junior. Barely off the ski lift, "the girls" rallied around "poor" Ivana.

Was Marla really the home breaker of one of America's "royal" families? Or was she merely the catalyst that opened up the Trumps' already failing marriage? Many who knew them told of the complete disregard bordering on contempt "The Donald" displayed toward Ivana and felt that it was only a matter of time before he would divorce her. He also, like many men, didn't leave his marriage explicitly for Marla and after the divorce sowed his wild oats dating celebrities and models. But Marla comes from a new generation of aggressive and assertive women. She held her ground, confronted him publicly, and did it her way. Shortly after giving birth to Donald's baby, she married him in a lavish ceremony at the Plaza Hotel in front of six hundred guests.

Lynn Gold-Bikin, a divorce attorney from Norristown, Pennsylvania, came to the rescue of younger women involved with married men when she appeared on a television talk-show panel with me for Lifetime Television's now-defunct *Jane Wallace Show*. She opined, "The bulk of men don't leave their wives unless they have a replacement lined up. This doesn't necessarily mean these women break up the marriage, but it's what I refer to as the *Springer Concept*. This guy finds someone else who makes him happy. She holds up a mirror to his marriage that shows him things could be better somewhere else—she literally *springs* him into another life."

❧ You'll Hear It Often... She's Just In It for the Money ❧

Insulting lots of W.O.O.M.ies, many people misconstrue our intentions and needs. They look at security as "$ecurity" and completely miss the real point of the appeal. Unfortunately, it can put a younger woman on the defensive, and often her intentions are misunderstood.

What I find so interesting is the hypocrisy in all of this. If a younger woman falls in love with a rich man who is close to her age, everyone celebrates her good fortune. If the man happens to be ten or more years older, the respect for their love affair diminishes, and the younger woman's motives become questionable. She must be out for his money. Go figure out the difference.

For those who are cruel and relish the sensational, our relationship gives them the opportunity to resurrect the insulting "sugar daddy/gold-digging bimbo" image that creates a black cloud over our relationship. We are often misjudged and can feel isolated. However, lonely as it is, this isolation brings us closer to our older partners. If we are in love with someone who is successful—it is often assumed we are in it for the money. Many think our careers catapulted when we fell in love with the boss and our talents are insignificant. Just look at twenty-four-year-old, Mariah Carey. In 1990 her album, *Mariah Carey,* sold six million copies and she won two Grammys. Now that she's married to Sony's head, Tony Mattola, who's forty-three, certain critics attribute her success to being the former lover and now wife of the chairman of the board. Sure!

Many women who write or call me worry bitterly about being accused of dating an older man for his money. Talk show producers relish how unsavory it all is. And deep down, most people think it. In January, 1993, I called the United States Department for Health and Human Services for some information for *The New York Times.* After several attempts to find out the percentage of marriages where the man is ten or more years older, I was finally referred to a statistician who offered an unsolicited comment describing the relationship as a "pretty package" for a young woman. She went on to tell me that one can forgive the paunch and lack of hair for the money. She then bragged that she was going to write a book about it because she had the numbers to prove it. In response, I said, "You're the exact reason I appear on so many TV talk shows...to dispel this kind of stereotypical prejudicial attitude."

Many years ago, Sam and I were sitting with several guests at the dining-room table of our good friends Clare and Gil Cornick when the conversation turned to the popular and profitable cosmetic store I had recently opened. One of the older female guests commented, right in front of me, that Sam's money and brains were the reasons for the store's runaway success! It has been seventeen years since I heard the unfortunate remark, but I can still see her face and remember her name. Most noteworthy, though, was her stupidity: how Sam could have sold lipstick and prepared teeth for crowns at the same time never crossed her mind.

Yes, I agree, there are a select few who have contributed to the "she just married him for his money" myth, and because the relationships are sensational, the press has a field day. But Jacqueline Kennedy Onassis, who was twenty-nine years younger than her second husband, Aristotle Onassis, the ultrarich shipping magnate and Patricia Kluge, the former nightclub dancer who married John W. Kluge, one of America's richest men—thirty-five years her senior—are the exceptions, not the rule. Only a handful of us will ever see a million dollars, but the media love a good story and promote a myth as reality. Everyday, younger women in love with just ordinary older men want to be exonerated from the bad rap and respected for simply being in love.

Ad agencies can be just as bad. A few years ago, I boycotted Smart Food popcorn. The company launched an ad campaign that featured a young bride and a very obviously older groom. He reminded me of Uncle Fester in the *Addams Family*. Above his head was a bubble that indicated he was dreaming about popcorn. Over her head was a bubble that featured a bulging sack of money!

About a year before I fell in love with Sam, I was dating Robert Ireland, a very wealthy, handsome army officer who was only a few years older than me. His parents' home, outside of Los Angeles, was filled with servants and was right out of *Architectural Digest*. What impressed me most was the four-car garage. I had never seen one before. Bob was very much in love with me and almost as if she had handpicked him, my mother was ecstatic. His social prominence, portfolio, and impeccable lineage meant nothing to me. I didn't love him.

"Carolyn Morton is young and beautiful," wrote Maureen Downey of the *Atlanta Journal and Constitution*. "Her husband is twice her age and has a receding hairline. According to marital mythology, that adds up to a match made in mink.

"Meeting the Mortons dispels all the stereotypes of the gorgeous young woman and her wealthy older man," Downey continued. "The couple live in a modest two bedroom, Atlanta apartment. Their sofa is early Salvation Army and the only access they have to the good life is MARTA [public transportation]."

Carolyn was one of my first W.O.O.M. members, and I was excited that C.C. Rivera wanted her to appear on the *Geraldo* show with me in August 1989. When we met, I found her to be a breath of fresh air. It was obvious she would have given up anything to be with George. She told the audience it was a real hardship but well worth it for the love they shared.

George was a divorced father of three and nearing retirement when he went to the grocery store in Charlotte, North Carolina, and came home dreaming about Carolyn! As he was leaving the grocery, he noticed her tangling with a broken shopping bag and came to her rescue. Soon after, they developed a friendship and when Carolyn, who is twenty-seven years younger, went to Atlanta to attend fashion school, George wasn't far behind. But it was a tough struggle. Whatever cash he had was wiped out in alimony and child-support payments, and George, who had been a director of a manufacturing plant, started over in Atlanta with a five-dollar-an-hour position.

Not all older men are rich financially. They are wealthy with experience. And 99 percent of the time, for younger women, that's the appeal.

❧ The Unwedded Wife ❦

Older men who come off horrific and expensive divorces, obligating them to pay huge settlements, tend to have cold feet when it comes to tying the knot the second or third time around. As much as they don't want to admit it, marriage is a thorny issue that prickles the silvery hairs on the backs of their necks which is why they opt for helping with the rent and perhaps, after a while, the living-together arrangement. Even monogamous and devoted older men, who have been burned by the first divorce settlement, balk at the mention of a licensed partnership.

One spring day, I was surveying the needs of my garden with landscape architect Linnie Chandler*. It was the first time we had met, and we hit it off right away. Soon I was telling her about myself and the W.O.O.M. newsletter, and it was as if a plug had been removed from a dike holding back a flood of repressed feelings. Normally vivacious, Linnie, at forty-six, was forlorn about her love life; she had no one to turn to. Few of her friends could understand her predicament of being in love with a man unable to commit. And fewer were patient with her staying in a dead-end relationship.

On and off for the past ten years, Linnie has been dating the twice-married Peter Brice*, eighteen years her senior. Peter's last divorce wiped him out financially and destroyed his trust in women. His second wife was a very meek woman who didn't have any particular career skills. He took her by the hand and brought her into his manufacturing firm—teaching her every-thing he knew. She was a sharp student, possessing great poten-tial, and soon became a valuable asset to Peter's company. That's when she dumped him and took most of the company with her! He has never forgiven her, and unfortunately, this lack of trust in women has put great pressure on his relationship with Linnie, who remains sympathetic but is losing patience.

Peter is very generous with Linnie. He takes her on vacations, helps her with her rent, buys her nice clothes, leases a Jaguar for her, is like a father to her three children, and is practically a mem-ber of her family. Still, he finds all kinds of excuses for why they can't live together.

Very possessive of Linnie's time, Peter simmers when he calls and she's not at home. He interrogates her on her whereabouts.

When she threatens to leave him, it's as if he doesn't hear her as he sends over the plumber to fix a leaky faucet in her apartment. Trying to remain sensitive to Peter's distrust, Linnie is finding the conditional love affair has taken a toll on their relationship, and she often feels defensive and used. But she's very much in love, and she knows he loves her, too.

In analyzing the relationships of my unmarried dating or living-together W.O.O.M. subscribers, I have found most of the previously married men are perceived to be charming, understanding of women's needs, sensitive to feminist issues (except when they pertain to him), and very much in love with their younger girl friends. Many have a commendable level of commitment. They are monogamous, comfortable in domestic situations, and are proud to include the younger girl friend in every aspect of their lives: family parties, business dinners, and other social occasions. In many cases, these younger women are put on a pedestal and often treated with more deference than the former wife. But for these guys, the mere word marriage sticks in their throats.

Dr. Marlin Potash, a psychotherapist specializing in couple and family therapy in New York City, co-authored *Cold Feet: Why Men Don't Commit* with Dr. Sonya Rhodes. They write, "The dreaded 'M' word is a very big deal. [Some men] shy away from the 'symbols' of marriage, particularly if they have been through a horrible marriage and divorce." Afraid marriage will stifle them, some nonetheless feel a deep commitment is just fine.

It's easy for a young woman to get caught up in this nurturing web where they are supported and coddled, but boundaries can easily be confused. The relationship that so resembles marriage makes it is easy for the woman to forget her male friend's distrust and dislike for the institution. After a while, the relationship for the woman becomes clouded by her efforts to change his mind. Many, thinking there is something wrong with them, don't understand that their free-at-last partners want to remain just that.

"Marriage is not a necessity if a couple can make a deep commitment to each other," write Potash and Rhodes. "In general before you move in or he moves in with you, you should have an understanding about marriage—that it's on the way (and only one short step away). It is not an experiment to see how it will work out, and if you decide to move in together simply for convenience, that's fine, but be clear that that is *all* it is."

Eager for my readers to learn if commitment characteristics in men changed in any way when a man was involved with a much younger woman, I asked Dr. Potash, "Does an age gap create a different set of circumstances than what is described as 'The Five Levels of Commitment' in your book, where most couples interviewed are similar in age?" She felt that it very definitely did and said, "I think one of the reasons older men pick younger women is so they *don't* have to commit, if they've been through a lousy marriage. They figure, if she's not forty-one, needing a baby tomorrow, and she doesn't have children, they're not going to be pressured to make decisions right away. And *right away* turns into maybe it will never happen, if I'm lucky."

My opinion, reached after talking with W.O.O.M. subscribers and those who call anonymously, is that there comes a point when the living-together arrangement just isn't enough for women. As they turn thirty, they want more out of the relationship. Once the party's over—when good sex and the *good* life just aren't fulfilling anymore—these women become angry with the status quo and threaten to walk. They don't really want to leave. They've been out of the dating scene a long time, and this relationship is going to be a hard act to follow. Many find themselves in an untenable situation, yet the compromise of living by his rules, being completely dependent upon his whims, weighs heavily on them. While considering the alternative, many live-in ladies become silently hostile, lashing out when it's too much to take.

"You can threaten to leave," says Dr. Potash, "but you have to be prepared to follow through. If someone is complaining for six years, all the while putting up with it, you're not going to be taken seriously when you finally do say enough is enough. There's a difference between a threat and a promise and (if not carried out), it's not worth a heck of a lot when you finally do get to the end of your rope."

Despite their thirty-three-year age difference and her Italian-Catholic upbringing, Lucille Colantonio moved into the lavish, New Jersey home of millionaire restaurateur Ralph Rosenblum in 1985 with her young son, Michael. Lucille is a very classy redhead, a witty, street-smart rebel who knows what's best for her. At twenty-three, alone with a young child, she felt solid and secure with a stalwart Holocaust survivor, who worked himself up from the bowels of lower Manhattan. Together they redecorated his home, traveled, and enjoyed a traditional family life together, which included Ralph's three (some older than Lucille) children from his first marriage.

Four years later, Regis Philbin asked Ralph during a W.O.O.M. segment of the *Regis and Kathie Lee Show*, "I know it's *absolutely* none of our business. You've been together for four years now. Is there some obstacle about why you haven't thought about getting married?"

Lucille jumped right in as if prompted by previous, nosy queries and responded assuredly, "We've both discussed this from the very start, both being married before, having our own children. We're happy and we're afraid we're going to rock the boat. We don't know what the future holds."

For those who have lived with divorced older men for years and have given up or put on hold their careers, or weddings to others to be the *unwedded* wife, the uncertainty is frightening and can become an ugly, controlling issue. In the final analysis, most younger women cohabiting with older men don't *have* any rights, except for a weekly allowance, a leased vehicle in his name, some designer clothes if the guy has money, and his roof over her head. "The older man holds the cards," attorney, Lynne Gold-Bikin pointed out to me in a subsequent interview. "It's what I call the Golden Rule: Him who has the gold, rules.... *They* are powerless."

I met Marlie Hamilton*, a cosmopolitan advertising executive from Philadelphia, when she became a member of W.O.O.M. in 1991. Sharing a passion for gardening, we became very close friends. I often felt she was hoping that somehow my secure and happy marriage to Sam would rub off on her. Two years before we met, Marlie, like most younger single women who can't get their older male friends down the aisle, crated and stored her old life, and moved with her two children into the home of her former boss, Marshall Ross*.

Marshall, who was thrice married, had just turned a very energetic sixty when Marlie introduced us. A few weeks later, she invited Sam and me to a lavish birthday party for him at New York's Pierre Hotel where one of the things I noticed about the guests was that many were older men /younger women couples. I remember thinking how easily Sam and I fit in among *our crowd*. Having found too often that older women never gave me a chance, I was relieved at how comfortable it was to be there. Nobody stared.

Marshall has an aloof attitude that can drive a woman crazy. Once he took a month-long jaunt to the orient *sans* Marlie. In many respects, he was torn about his relationship with her. He liked his freedom, yet he enjoyed having a young, attractive woman waiting for him when he returned home. Unfortunately, the two mix about as well as water and oil, and soon Marlie was beginning to fear for her future, having given up her job to spend most of her time with Marshall who was offering no solid financial nor marital security.

One troubling time, after she and Marshall had returned from a grueling rough-it trip to the Amazon, Marlie called as she often did and said, "I am so upset I haven't been able to sleep for weeks." She loved Marshall more than anything, but the uncertainty of the relationship was coming between them.

At the beginning, she was attracted by Marshall's thirty-one year age difference and felt comfortable that he was solid and unbending. She loved the stability of knowing that what she saw was what she got. But what was she getting? A two-year reprieve on having to support herself and children? Or, was this investment in wishful thinking actually going to pay off with an "until death do them part" contract?

Feminists would howl at the relationships of their male-reliant sisters. But the truth is, many women are dependent totally on men whether they are wives or girl friends. There is no real financial security for younger women, living for years with non-pledging older men who control their fate. They depend upon the generosity of the man. In all fairness to many of these freedom-loving Daddy Warbucks, they usually don't promise any long-term future, but many do take very good care of their younger girl friends.

If the men are well off, the younger women are often bestowed with *special gifts* far more extravagant than they likely would have received from a lover closer to them in age. However, after several years the *live-in* gets caught up in the wife thing (easy to do when you're scrubbing the floor). If she proves invaluable, she is often rewarded with a palimony agreement if marriage is not in the cards or a prenuptial agreement if it is. Often, women who challenge the arrangement as it was verbally contracted are replaced.

Supermodel Jerry Hall is, by any estimate, successful, beautiful, and smart; someone who could land the cream of the crop. She waited out a thirteen-year live-in arrangement with Mick Jagger, thirteen years her senior. Even though Jagger fathered their two children, Elizabeth and James, he would brush aside all questions of marriage with giggling. He said early on, "Doing it more than once is a waste of time." Personally, when I saw the two of them together in 1985, on the island of St. Martin, I thought *he* was the lucky one! In my eyes, Jagger's appeal was overrated; he was no match for Hall's languorous sensuality and style. Obviously though, she found him irresistible.

By 1988, after years of waiting, Hall groaned, "The 'M' word—golly I'm tryin'! Would y'all quit rubbin' it in?" When Jerry finally got an engagement ring, she would facetiously joke to the press, "He kept on begging and begging me to marry him until I finally gave in." But it hasn't been bliss for Jerry. Her marriage has been rocky due to another "other" woman. They're together again now, but who knows for how long? Maybe marriage turned Jerry into that most feared person, a wife; and what Mick really wants is a full-time lover.

For many it may be worth the risk of waiting out a long-term live-in arrangement. But many W.O.O.M. subscribers feel the brunt of the compromises that get them down the aisle are absorbed by the younger woman. Lucille Colantonio eventually did marry Ralph about a year after he suffered a heart attack and underwent bypass surgery. She told me they were married without pomp on an autumnal November morning in 1992. On their wedding day, she was eight months pregnant with their son, Harry Michael. Shortly before, she had converted to Judaism.

❧ *The Palimony or Nonnuptial Agreement* ❦

Several years ago, I had a phone call from an hysterical younger woman who had been living with a well-to-do, older man in Coconut Grove, Florida. I could tell from the clinking coins, she was calling me from a pay phone. Breathlessly, she chronicled her plight. "My boyfriend just threw me out! I have nothing! He's taken my clothes, my car—everything! I had to leave the house on a dilapidated bicycle I found in his garage! Can you believe he sold my Toyota and pocketed the money when he leased the Mercedes for me! God, don't I have any rights?"

I told her probably not. She was living proof of just how bad it can get. Without a living-together contract, younger women who don't financially secure a future with noncommitting older lovers are really dumb to stick around.

In a recent W.O.O.M. survey, I asked my subscribers to help their sisters, who may be in this debasing "pickle," root out what would be equitable for both parties in the relationship. We must consider though, that most of these women have married their older lovers, and their remarks convey that confidence. However, their hindsight and advice is an objective eye-opener for those who may have misplaced their personal value.

"[This is] a tough question for both sides," writes Caryn Hackett, a thirty-two-year-old, private-club reservations clerk from Singer Island, Florida. "Should the woman actually be assuming the role of the wife—without the legalities of marriage—then I feel she should be treated as a spouse under the eyes of the law."

Grace Martin*, a forty-something realtor from southern New Jersey who chose an older man for her second husband wrote, "If there are no children involved, sometimes, it is financially beneficial to remain single (tax wise). On an emotional level, the man has made a physical commitment to the woman, and she deserves the security of a marriage commitment for her own peace of mind. If that is not acceptable, a written document similar to a prenuptial agreement could be drawn up outlining her entitlements." She added if they can't come to an accord, "Perhaps she should start looking somewhere else."

Katie Scott, a twenty-four-year-old homemaker and mother from Pittsburgh, wrote, "If they act like husband and wife, then to me they are. A woman, or a man for that matter, should be compensated accordingly. I do feel the women should push for the legal commitment to protect them[selves]."

Linna McAuliffe, from Nine Mile Falls, Washington, who has been married to two older men (her first marriage ended in divorce after eight years) had this advice to offer. "If women don't get their financial act together before they are married, then they are damn fools!"

Marvin Mitchelson, the controversial Hollywood divorce lawyer, drew up the first successful palimony agreement in 1976 while representing Michelle Marvin, the former common-law wife of actor Lee Marvin. Mitchelson stated in a *Vanity Fair* interview that "Women are fools to sign these things!" But in reality, they are not stupid. Many who have doctorates, medical degrees, or are successful in business are willing, for the sake of this "very special" relationship, to put up with much more than they would if the man was closer in age. There's another underlying factor. Younger women are more easily intimidated by their older partners and stand on less solid ground when they are unsure their priority under any circumstance is not to risk losing the relationship.

Wanting to have firsthand information from the man who pioneered the palimony concept, I called Mitchelson, who was acting as a consultant while he awaited the appeal of an income-tax fraud charge. I found him to be equally fair to both parties and particularly sympathetic toward females involved with older men who want to make sure they're being loved for just being themselves. He prefaced the conversation with, "People are very reluctant to sign palimony agreements. Usually, somebody resents it because you're giving them a lot less than what they would be entitled to under the law."

"But what if a party insists upon it?" I asked.

"I was always against palimony agreements," he said, "but it does provide a blueprint or recipe in case the parties break up. In a way, there is something good about delineating the reality of what can happen if people don't get along. There's a 50 to 60 percent divorce rate, and people break up about that often, too. It's sort of like estate planning, and there's nothing wrong with it. The only trouble is that it's usually done in a way that is unfair to one party. It's overbearing, and someone is usually trying to take advantage of someone else by getting the better of the deal if it doesn't work out."

Palimony agreements are documents that are explicitly supposed to protect both parties. They are contracts that are almost always beneficial to men—usually older—and to a lesser extent women, with assets. When I talk with W.O.O.M. subscribers who have been presented with palimony agreements, I worry about these younger women signing without being represented by their own counsel. Many say they can't afford an attorney. I asked Mitchelson how he felt about that. He said, "Some women don't [insist upon representation] because they are so anxious to sign it and kind of get it over with. They don't want to put up a roadblock." More often than not, people are represented on both sides, as they should be. I asked him, who pays the legal fees? "If the guy wants it, he usually pays."

Compensation is a rotten issue and an intimidating subject to address. Putting a price tag on a love affair is degrading enough, but while younger women await the verdict about marriage, they lose sight of the years that are slipping by. College educations and careers are thrown to the wind for an old shoe that doesn't even belong to them. Often, the aggressive independence that attracted the older man to the younger woman in the first place is replaced by dependency as he insists she be more and more available to him.

According to Dr. Potash, "A big part of the appeal of the younger woman is these guys can kind of escape and be young. They sort of forget, though, that if they want to retire some time soon and go sailing, they pretty much have to insure her future or else let her work. You can't have it both ways. You can't have her doting on you, running off to the Caribbean and playing golf, and expect that magically, she's not going to need you anymore and be independent."

Mr. Mitchelson was helpful in defining how a woman can utilize a palimony (an expression coined by the media) or non-nuptial agreement (coined by Mitchelson) to secure her future if she does decide to devote all of her time to her older lover. He chuckled as he said, "You can write anything you want into the agreement if it isn't against public policy. People get very pedantic, who's going to take out the garbage...who keeps the pets, etc. They write in all kinds of things." Mitchelson has seen many younger women set forth their career goals, making certain they and the hours they take are recognized by their lovers. Women can also bargain for income-producing property, stock, or an insurance policy, but it's harder to make that kind of a deal when you are beginning a relationship. I asked him if you could write in that a woman can't have a baby? He said, "Yes, but you should outline what will happen if she does."

The prenuptial, if the parties intend to marry, and the nonnuptial, if they don't, are cold and calculating as lawyers work over conditions. In essence, they are a divorce before the marriage and emphasize it may not work out which is very upsetting every time an argument occurs.

However, Mitchelson's comments, assured me of one thing. If a woman is strong and not afraid of walking away from the relationship if she's treated unfairly, she can make demands, too, and in certain ways, it lets everyone know where they stand and gets issues out in the open. Some W.O.O.M. subscribers have mentioned that they have signed documents that award them absolutely nothing. Mr. Mitchelson said, "I wouldn't write a contract like that, unless she has money of her own and doesn't want anything." And added, "She better be certain to keep something for herself"—protecting her own assets.

What are her options? If she refuses to sign and chooses to stay in the relationship for a considerable length of time, she is protected by common-law case laws, but they are not as airtight as the nonnup, and as Mitchelson said, "Suing on oral agreements are hard to prove." However he added, "Whether it's an oral, written, or implied-conduct agreement, they have terms to them. And usually the predicate is that someone breached a contract and [the offended party] is entitled to a jury trial when a party files a breach of contract lawsuit." Mitchelson went on to say that the palimony law in forty-four states recognizes the Marvin case and that more and more of these contracts are considered valid in every court of law.

Commenting on what it would cost a woman to hire a lawyer and fight a guy who renounces his "Don't worry, I'll always take care of you" oral agreement, Mitchelson said, "It would usually be a ten to fifteen thousand dollar retainer fee which would be applied to the percentage counsel would receive from the award going to the attorney."

"But what if a woman can't afford that," I asked, "can she use a public defender?"

"No. They are only available for criminal cases. There may be some states, not many, that have some legal aid available for these purposes. Usually, I try to get her fees covered though; but it's a good idea to have a little nest egg for your own peace of mind."

In the Trump/Marla Maples relationship and marriage, The Donald had a point in trying to protect himself against any ambitions Marla may have had to get at more of his estate than he was willing to share. He said, "I hate the concept of a prenuptial contract, but that doesn't mean it's not necessary. It's for my own peace of mind." Ours, too, Donald.

When the older man is well off, a hassle-free, dignified real-estate deal put in the younger companion's name might be preferable to a nonnup or prenup, something in the way of an all-expenses-paid duplex or condominium building that would give her a place to live and an income if the relationship broke up. She would still need a lawyer to assure her that the deal was on the up and up. But in lieu of signing an ugly contract, the woman and her male friend get on with their love affair out from under a contractual black cloud. Some women have mentioned to me that they have a stock deal, and others work it out with airtight (meaning he gives you the check to pay the premium) whole-life insurance policies that they can cash in if the relationship ends or their lover dies. It's all cold, hard, and unromantic when you are in love; but so is a park bench when you're not.

❧ *Negotiating Your Rights* ❦

*I*t is disheartening to bargain a love affair. It's an issue of control. But if you are the one with fewer assets, you assume a subservient position that makes it difficult to grasp power and negotiate a deal. Yet, if you have given up income-producing prospects, you have to be compensated. Because this is a touchy topic, being assertive and insisting upon fair compensation is an altogether different matter.

Love is based on mutual respect for each other's life-style and self-worth. Older men can be very set in their ways and self-centered. And those who are insecure prefer their younger women to be in a position of asking for money and worldly goods. Many older men are very possessive and proud of their women but tend not to want to give them a lot of rope. It's all very endearing to be worshipped, but remember—you are not a possession. You can't let a man take away your freedom and having pocket money has a lot to do with freedom.

Remember, though, it's not just money. Time, dreams, goals, babies, careers, a wedding date, and your future happiness are all priceless considerations to be respected. In order to love somebody 100 percent, that person has to let you move around confidently within the relationship, or resentment will eat you up. You can't give away the very thing that makes you one of a kind—your individuality.

Many younger women respond and react to confrontation with older men emotionally, rather than calmly stating facts. I know it is especially difficult to verbally spar when you've been

reared to respect your elders. On the one hand, you must continually remind yourself that you are not this man's child nor his
chattel. But on the other hand, as disconcerting as it may be, you
will have to develop the mind set that the relationship's success
will rely heavily on your complying to *his* demands. In some
cases, that can give you an advantage. If you are strong and
assertive, he will have to compromise.

In some respects, I feel as if I have lost a part of my identity.
It's because I gave up a portion of my youth when I tried to grow
up too fast to cope with Sam's maturity. I turned the pages too
quickly on what was synonymous with my age, and I can never
recapture that chapter of my life. If I had been more in control,
I would have told Sam from the very beginning that I needed a
night out once a week with my younger girl friends or that a
Rod Stewart concert wouldn't kill him. But I didn't and that was
a mistake for both Sam and me because we spent many unhappy
moments during the early years of our marriage skirting around
what was really bothering me.

Younger women, take note! The only way a couple can reach
a compromise is if one of them balks—so balk! An "oh nothing"
response to "what's the matter?" does no good. You have to talk
about it. Take the bull by the horns and say: "This is what I need.
Can you deal with it? If not, I can't stay in this relationship."

Standing firm also applies to middle-aged younger women
considering marrying an older man. If you are forty and want to
work and maintain your career, spell out the conditions *before* you
tie the knot. No matter how lonely you may be without him, it's
worth jeopardizing the relationship to hang on to *you*. If your silver fox wants to winter in Florida with the old folks, and you
can't stand the thought of conversation at every social event
revolving around pill popping or blood pressure, compromise
with the Caribbean or Arizona where you can take up scuba div-
ing or hot-air ballooning. Relocate to an area that has a broad
mix of ages yet is conducive to the needs of retirees.

Some younger women have successful positions they don't want to give up to accompany their older men for months at a time. It's a tough decision to walk away from a job you have worked hard for and earned. If this applies to you, you could suggest that you will fly down on weekends or take the bulk of your vacation concurrently. Married couples with businesses in separate parts of the country do it all of the time.

Georgette Mosbacher, wife of Robert Mosbacher, twenty years her senior and former secretary of commerce during the Bush administration, runs her Manhattan-based cosmetic company, Exclusives, five days a week. On weekends, she flies to Houston where Bob's business is based. "As cornball as it sounds," says Bob, "the time we spend together is real quality time." With private time at a premium, the two rarely attend galas or make dates with friends and opt to spend time alone on Bob's boat. "We get really excited about seeing each other," confides Georgette who carries a folder marked *RM* that holds tidbits of gossip and information she wants to share with him when they are together.

If you find you can't be away from work for extended periods, you can rework things at the office. Faxes, computers, telephones, and modems make it all very easy to conduct business from afar. And sometimes, you just have to trade off having a lot of time together and make the most of the precious moments you do have. Football commentator, Frank Gifford, twenty-three years older than his entertainer wife Kathie Lee, told *Pinnacle* magazine, "I have to work on weekends; Kathie works during the week, but we spend every minute together we can."

If you are dating a virile older man in his sixties, discuss what will happen when he is in his eighties and perhaps not able to get out. Find out if you have his blessing to go out alone and be with friends your age, go to the movies by yourself, or take a course. If you get stuck in the house day and night without a life of your own, you can feel trapped by the ravages of his old age.

During one of my appearances on CNN's *Sonya Friedman Live*, a gentleman in his late seventies called the show and said he was encouraging his wife, who was twenty years younger, to divorce him. Although he loved his wife very much and she loved him, it was time to let go. He felt guilty that his advancing age was infringing upon her happiness and expectations.

This is a drastic way of handling the situation, but nonetheless an eye-opener on what goes through a man's head when he is aging. Wouldn't it have been nice if they had been able to communicate all of that before he was totally demoralized? And worked out a way in which both of them could have stayed happily in the marriage for the rest of his life?

❧ *Dating an Older Playboy* ❦

Women who fall in love with older men who have never been married before or had a quick "starter" first marriage long ago have it easier socially, but often these guys are very set in their ways. They have been single so long, they are not accustomed to the duality of a partnership. Compared to men who have been divorced or widowed, they aren't as sensitive to women's needs or the feminine mystique. They're less willing to accept faults and imperfections. These guys are going to need a quick lesson in dealing with women on a long-term basis.

Younger women will require a great deal of perseverance to fit into his life-style of coming and going as he pleases. Also, don't expect him to give up the black-leather couches so fast. Many are playboys who have dated numerous, glamorous younger women who find these men *and* their interior design irresistible. Don't dwell on scrapbooks or old photos, either. You'll find yourself being unnecessarily jealous and resentful of past competition and comparison to other women.

Supermodel Cindy Crawford, told Richard Gere, leading man in *American Gigolo* and *Pretty Woman* and confirmed bachelor, seventeen years her senior, "I can't wait. I gotta move on if it ain't happening." So on December 12, 1991, they flew to Las Vegas and exchanged vows in the Little Chapel of the West. But even though she landed Gere, Crawford made concessions and gave up a lot to be with him by slowing down her career and following him all over the world from one movie set to another. Some might wonder who got the better deal in this relationship. Why would Cindy, who was valedictorian of her high-school class, entered Northwestern to study chemical engineering and dropped out to become a top fashion model, even need Gere, an erstwhile drug abuser who turned to Buddhism to clean up his life?

It all goes back to the smart younger woman/handsome successful older man appeal. Yet according to those who have been there, the younger woman is going to have to give in more—especially if he comes with a past of steamy bedroom scenes followed by dates with a stable of gorgeous models, artists, and fashion moguls. Cindy captured an idol. And way down in the depths of her female psyche, she was where she wanted to be. "More than anything, I want a family," she said. "I feel being a mother is the thing in my life I'm going to be best at." But she would have a tough time convincing Gere who is open-minded—but resistant—to the idea of having children. "I am a child," he has said.

It didn't take long for the Crawford/Gere union to hit the rocks. Gere was linked with British model, Laura Bailey, a twenty-two-year-old university honors graduate (seems Gere is attracted to intellectuals) and fellow Buddhist. Reading about Crawford and Gere's ad proclaiming fidelity and sexual preferences, followed quickly by a separation, we have to wonder, "Can these guys really deal with younger wives—or any wife, for that matter—when they have been single and focused solely on themselves for so long?" As Cindy catapults herself into an eighteen-million-dollar career, Gere has said, "I'm over the hysteria of the career thing." Who is he kidding?

Hugh Hefner ended his ten-year marriage to Millie Williams in 1959 and spent the next thirty years making it publicly clear he did not plan to get married again. Over the years, Hef—bachelor of bachelors—filled his mansion with live-ins, as many as five at one time. He cohabited with Barbie Benton for nine years and even got hit with a thirty-five-million-dollar palimony suit (which was later dropped) brought by model Carrie Leigh, thirty-seven years his junior. It has been said that Carrie wanted her rightful due after living with him for five years and nursing him through a debilitating stroke. Hefner's response to the litigation was, "I'm a very romantic person, but marriage is not for me."

However, in 1989, Hefner, sixty-three, had a change in philosophy. He fell in love with and married Playmate of the Month and aspiring model, Kimberly Conrad, twenty-six, ending his three-decade bachelor party.

Presently, the Hefners have two sons: Marston, four, and Cooper, two. Hefner told *Maclean's* magazine, "This relationship has made my September years the best time of my life....It couldn't be sweeter. With Kimberly, I realized I found something better than what had come before, and very clearly something better than what would be lying over the hill."

But perhaps Hefner is still living in his old fantasy world, unable to face the reality of change in his women, just as he was blind to the changing taste in erotica that hit his magazine empire financially between the eyes. When he says, "I've managed to romanticize marriage and children. To see children's toys in the Playboy mansion is romantic," you sense he's still trying to live in Candyland.

His wife Kimberly wasn't as enthusiastic. She said in a separate interview with the same magazine that life with Hefner has taken some adjustment. "Hef has had a lot of control over me," she said, "but I'm breaking away from that." She admitted Hefner is really a good father, a really good husband, and her best friend, but you get the impression there is an underlying disappointment in either him or herself. "I'm thirty-one, I don't do anything."

Later she mentioned, "When Hef and I were going through our downswing—like all marriages go through ups and downs, and we have been going through a down for the past year—people treat me differently. It's everyone from staff to people who I thought were good friends." Kimberly feels Hef has his spies and added, "I go everywhere with a security guard, so they can keep an eye on me."

It may be time for Kimberly and Hefner to take a hard look at her needs and assets. The disparity between Kimberly's pragmatic assessment of their marriage and Hefner's euphoric romanticizing may be an indication that Kimberly must reclaim and define her identity, recapture her self-esteem. Hefner will need to be progressive and secure enough to deal with that.

For a younger woman who finally lands a confirmed bachelor, the insecurity of knowing that pre-her there were many romances that didn't work can interfere with her trust in the relationship. It can be difficult to appreciate that her man was single so long because he simply wasn't ready to settle down. Or maybe it had to do with money. He just didn't want to give up half of what he's got. Sometimes older, aging bachelors finally marry because they don't want to face the ravages of old age alone. They might not realize this at the time, but it can leave a new wife questioning her older lover's motives—especially if he insists she spending an inordinate amount of time with him.

Radio talk jock Don Imus was married in the early sixties. He sired four daughters then left the marriage after a little more than ten years. Over the past twenty years, he has had his ups and downs with alcohol and drug abuse and volatile firings and rehirings—leaving very little room in his life for a significant other until December, 1994, when he married track-star-turned-actress

Deirdre Coleman, twenty-five years his junior. Talk about the juxtaposition of personalities! He's a wan chain smoker with very little regard for taking care of his body; she's fit and healthy, a personal trainer even. Yet, she dotes on him and is very protective.

Last winter Dr. Georgia Witkin, NBC's resident psychologist, appeared on *Imus in the Morning*. Months later, when I interviewed her for this book, she told me that Imus was concerned that people were teasing him for marrying someone so young. He asked her, "Am I normal?"

To which Dr. Witkin inquired, "At what age did you start to do drugs?"

"I was twenty-nine."

Dr. Witkin then asked, "When did you quit?"

Imus answered, "About six years ago."

Dr. Witkin went on to assure Imus that not only was he normal, but technically, he was only about thirty-five emotionally. She said Imus blurted, "Yeah! Yeah! I should be perfect for someone who is twenty-nine."

On the other hand, another older bachelor may have played the field for years to find out just what he was really looking for.

When Patricia Richmand, a social worker, started dating Herb Gutentag, a forty-something dentist, who had been married only once for about a year, she felt she had to seriously ask him, "Are you *sure* you are ready to commit?" She knew Herb, twelve years her senior, had dated various women and was concerned that maybe he didn't even know if he could answer that question. But he fell deeply in love with her and was she ever the lucky one! Herb asked her to marry him, in spite of the fact that she came to the relationship with a toddler, a dog, an ex-husband, and housekeeper! Quite a load for a man who had lived alone for the previous ten years! The fact that Herb didn't have any of this baggage was to her advantage. Herb has focused solely on them.

❧ *Dating an Older Widower* ❦

It is more complex dealing with an older man who is a widower than a divorced man who hated his former wife. Usually, it's the mourning for the deceased wife that makes a younger woman feel inferior. As she listens to the accolades of the glorified wife who has passed away, a young woman's self-esteem can be easily deflated. She's being compared to a level of perfection that's impossible to achieve.

Lisa Johnstone*, a friend I exercise with, is dating a man who divorced his second wife and then remarried her shortly before she died. Lisa's boyfriend suffers from the compounded guilt of the lost years he and his deceased wife could have been together when they divorced and ultimately losing her altogether. Exasperated Lisa confides, "What's it going to take for me to replace her?" To her, the relationship is a triad in which she respectfully relives the good and bad points of his marriage and wonders if she can accept forever being in the deceased wife's shadow.

The struggle is worse if the widower has children. Younger women will question his motives. They worry, "Does he really love me for me, or does he want a mother for his kids and a housekeeper to clean up?" Many feel as if they will never be as good as or loved as much as the wife who died.

Seventy-year-old Lee Iacocca recently set about divorcing his third wife, Darrien Earle, a fifty-five-year-old former beauty queen and model. They were married for three years. In 1986, Iacocca had married Wife Number Two, thirty-five-year-old flight attendant Peggy Johnson. That union lasted eight and a half months. Both his second and third wives claim he wasn't a pleasant husband at times. Ms. Johnson said Lee wouldn't let her have a credit card or bank account in her own name. If she wanted to buy something major, she had to submit—in writing—the reasons she wanted the item before he would pay for it.

In divorce papers filed in Los Angeles in October, 1994, Darrien charged that Iacocca used assistants to spy on her—making her feel like a prisoner in her own home. She also claimed that while he was encouraging a reconciliation in Los Angeles, unbeknownst to her, he had filed for divorce in Michigan.

Iacocca was married to his first wife, Mary, for twenty-seven years. She died from diabetic disorders in 1983. His second wife, Peggy, contends he was still deeply attached to Mary. She asserts that his Bloomfield, Michigan, home was a "mausoleum" dedicated to preserving Mary Iacocca's presence. "Everything remained," Peggy has said, "pictures, photographs all over the house." Mentioning that she was relegated to the maid's room, Peggy feels she "probably would have been crucified" if she had ever walked into the master suite Mary and Lee had shared.

Some of this may be sour grapes. Some, undoubtedly, comes close to the truth. It would be tough to make up if you hadn't lived at least some part of it. I have heard many similar stories from younger wives married to widowers. Older husbands, unable to get over the death of a spouse, is not news to W.O.O.M. nor is the revenge some husbands exact on their younger next wife for not being *her*. But then again, wives shouldn't be unreasonable and ask that a husband completely cast off his former existence.

When dating a widower, you have to take things slower. You have to quietly make changes that won't belittle his grief even if it has created a shrine to the dead wife. "It's all very complicated," remarks Toby Lane*, a younger woman living with a widower. "I just can't act too excited about buying a new mattress to replace the one *she* slept on or even rewallpapering. It takes away a lot of the fun in being a couple. I always have this ghost looking over my shoulder."

My neighbor, Bobbie Van Anda, met her future husband, Allen, a widower, through his daughter, Lynn. Once a year, Bobbie, a teacher in Lynn's school, participated in a program for orphans. Wanting to give special attention to Lynn because she had lost her mother, Bobbie asked her to help. Bobbie had never met Allen, but he offered to make dinner for her in appreciation for all the time she had spent with Lynn. Well, it was a match made over beef! "He made the meanest prime rib dinner I ever had," remembered Bobbie. "And I thought, *are you kidding*, I'm not going to miss out on this guy!"

Recently, I called Bobbie, who is fifteen years younger than Allen, and asked her if, when she was dating her husband, she ever worried that he would love her as much as his first wife? She said, "Boy that's a good question! I think probably in the beginning I did. I was living in a small apartment with my mom, and I walked into this beautiful home, and here was her picture with these little Hummel angels around it. There's a lot to keep up with when your predecessor is dead."

Bobbie went on to say that if she hadn't loved Allen so much, she could have been easily defeated. "The deceased become sainted in memory....They never did anything wrong. [The family] just forgets any shortcomings they had. They are venerated; and in the back of your mind, you know he didn't turn away from her. It was real hard to face that."

She continued, "Until I reached the same number of years married to Allen that he had with his first wife, I never felt as secure. When I finally surpassed them, I knew he was more mine than hers. It was a real milestone to reach that time."

Carla Manchester* from Birmingham, Alabama, says her five-year-old marriage may not make it. Her husband's first wife died very quickly from cancer, and John*, who is eighteen years older than Carla, has never really gotten over it. When he married Carla, he made her sign a prenuptial agreement which gives her absolutely nothing. Even after five years of marriage, she still shares many expenses for the upkeep of the house he owned with his deceased wife. "If the marriage breaks up," says Carla, "it will look as if I never existed." She's also responsible for purchasing her own clothes and personal items. John wants to invest very little in her and even less in the marriage.

When he couldn't clone Carla, who owns her own manufacturing firm, into his dead wife, who stayed at home and doted on him, the marriage started to splinter. "It's as if he wants his old wife back and is taking it out on me because he knows it's not going to happen."

Living in the deceased wife's home is a real trial for any next wife. It will never be your house and in most cases, you will feel like the "odd man out." If you've signed a prenuptial, leaving the house in his name, you'll be cleaning and maintaining a home that doesn't even belong to you. When a wife dies, the decorating and the decor in her house is hallowed and often any changes you make will be resented. One W.O.O.M. subscriber from the Southwest told me she had to pass her husband's dead wife's picture on the hall table every night on the way to bed. Needless to say, it didn't do much for her sex life. Finally after six years of living together and marriage, Nancy* mentioned to her husband, Lyle*, who was married to his deceased wife for twenty-six years, that the photo really upset her. He was insulted and hurt that she didn't understand how much the picture meant to him.

Another W.O.O.M. subscriber from Maine said her forty-four-year-old stepdaughter bawled her out for cutting down a lilac bush her mother had planted thirty years before. All the subscriber wanted to do was see out of her living-room window. She hadn't realized the significance the bush carried for her stepdaughter. To her, the lilac bush was sacred.

Particularly if there are children living in the home, it may seem insensitive to uproot a family after a mother's death. But if at all possible, try to persuade your future husband to sell his house before you get married or at least, let you redecorate. When a man is comfortable in his home, among the possessions he's lived with for years, he'll be slow to realize just how important it is to a woman to be surrounded by her own things. You may have to put your foot down. He'll be taken aback at first, and you may even risk losing the relationship. But you'll find out quickly just how much he really loves you and what he will sacrifice to be with you. I can almost guarantee most will comply with your wishes to the best of their ability. If they don't, move on—you'll never live up to the first wife's sainthood.

❧ *Premarital Couple Therapy* ❧

*I*n this section of *Younger Women/Older Men*, I hope to make you aware of all the circumstances that evolve when you fall in love with an older man—I'm also hoping *he* sneaks a peek! Even though it wasn't my intention, some of my comments may scare you out of your love affair. But bear in mind, they are reflections of the frustrations women, and sometimes men, have expressed to me over the last seven years since I founded W.O.O.M. And because of these tales of woe, I have discovered the importance of working things out *before* you get too far along. Actually, I cannot stress it enough. Hidden agendas can be fatal to any relationship! How you set yourself up now and deal with the power and control issue (who's the *real* boss) will affect every discussion you have during your relationship and marriage, if it reaches that point.

Don't ever think that "After we're married, all of the pieces will fall into place." That's precisely when problems will intensify and become more difficult to deal with. It's also important to be aware that how your lover perceives you *now* will influence all issues that come up for the rest of your relationship. Older men are not as malleable as younger men, and they will hold you to your word and drive you crazy if you deviate from it. Lay your cards on the table from the very start, and be sure to stress that you are young and your attitudes could change as life's circumstances change. Find out in the beginning if he can live with that!

I've been married for twenty-four years and would be lying if I said Sam and I didn't have some things to work out to sustain our love through all the years. We have locked horns over things

I wish I had *known* were coming up. Fortunately, we both wanted our marriage to work so badly that we were able to compromise on many issues to stay together. Many of our points of contention still remain, but at least we have an understanding of how to approach them. I want you to have that same comfort zone.

It took me a long time to have the confidence to talk to Sam as an equal. Because I was so much younger, I dealt with problems thinking I might be punished—like a child—for expressing something that did not comply with his wishes. I am not ashamed to admit that the age difference did make me feel less in control. Because all of you understand that! Once I established, in my head, that our partnership was on equal terms, meaning equal happiness and equal power, I was successful in getting on with a healthier marriage. Sam got a wife in exchange for a little girl, and we became a team.

The relationship works best when you emphasize the positive aspects of the generation gap and personality differences and take advantage of them. When your older partner is set in his ways and has a hard time changing, you should be strong and farsighted. If you are impulsive and want to jump in without holding your nose, let him come to the rescue with experience and brawn. You can grab the upper hand if you understand and manipulate the fact that the woman he was brought up to perceive as a wife is *not* you!

But it won't always be easy. Everyone has to work hard to make a marriage work. However, we may need professional help because of the excess baggage that comes with one partner having a longer prior history. As Sam pointed out recently when asked why, if we were so happy, we needed W.O.O.M. and counseling books, "Annie inherited a lot of problems that needed to be talked about."

Many of the happy couples, married or living together, who subscribe to W.O.O.M. suggest precommitment couple therapy. They feel it helped them define their needs and outline what can or cannot be expected from each other. Through therapy, you will see a problem that you may not even know exists.

If you are unable to afford counseling, contact your community mental health clinic and find out if it is available at a reduced rate. Often, churches and synagogues, and religious orders offer this service. You are both responsible for making the relationship work. Just because he's older doesn't mean you can't speak up. Earnest communication, before you commit, will be invaluable to the success of the relationship.

❧ *Breaking Up* ❧

*B*reaking up a relationship, especially if it has been a long-term love affair, is wrenching. It's like throwing away a portion of your life that still touches you deeply many years later when something reminds you of it. Even though I knew Carlos, the Brazilian dentist I was very much in love with, didn't love me enough to marry me, it was hard to walk away from the relationship. I was leaving behind a man and country that were integral parts of my growing up. Because I was happy in Brazil, it further ignited my passion. I wanted to stay there the rest of my life.

Carlos taught me how to love a man, approach his emotional needs, and make him feel like he was the only man on earth that existed. He developed my sensuality; and all the men I have had relationships with since have reaped the rewards of my learning how to please a man.

Although our relationship had no future, Carlos gave me insight into what *I* was looking for: an older, charismatic, dynamic, chivalrous, and successful man. My infatuation with Carlos set a standard against which I would measure other relationships. I would try to find something comparable—and I did. There is no replacement for a young woman's first love with an older man. It's tough to get over; but you will.

Susan, a tennis friend, spent eight years in a marvelous relationship with a father of two, eighteen years older than she. They had everything in common and enjoyed being with one another immensely. "And even though we had many struggles in the beginning," she remembers, "we were so perfect together.…We never fought."

Susan was twenty-six when the relationship began. She just loved his kids and was certain she didn't want children of her own. But three years later, a maternal urge changed her mind. "I knew I had to have a baby to fulfill my life." Unfortunately, he didn't.

After seven years invested in the relationship, Susan and her boyfriend mutually broke it off. They were still friends and dated occasionally, but she knew it would never be the same. Several months later, her boyfriend realized he couldn't live without her. Susan remembers, "He offered me a marriage proposal, and said, 'I'll even throw in a baby! Let's fly to Paris for a springtime wedding. It will be so romantic.'" Susan was tempted to accept, but she knew it was over. "He would never be as excited as I was about the baby. He would hate me for the burden. I didn't want it to be an issue of forcing."

Even though it is years after the ill-fated relationship, Susan hasn't forgotten. "It was sad to have to start again. I thought I would never find someone who would have all the qualities I had admired in my older boyfriend." Eventually, she did. She said, "He is an absolutely gorgeous hunk—seven years *younger* than me!" Excitedly, Susan added, "He came equipped with all the values I was looking for." Soon after, they started a family, and she is incredibly happy.

Many women's first loves are with older men. For a multitude of complex reasons, they don't work out. The man is married and hasn't any intention of getting a divorce. He prefers a more sophisticated woman. Her family disapproves, or they can't agree on the parameters.

Jeannette*, an early subscriber of W.O.O.M., was in her late forties when she was dating sixty-eight-year-old Seymour Goldman*, who had been divorced for many years. The relationship was really special, and everyone thought they were perfect together, *except* his kids, who were grown, married, and independent of their father. They made family holidays miserable by barely speaking to Jeannette. No matter how she tried to win them over, they collectively did everything to break up the affair and eventually did. Rather than see their father happy, they needled him about "what it would do to mom!" Seymour relented and left Jeannette. And now, they are both painfully alone. But in one way it worked out for the best. Their relationship would have been consumed by his worrying about offending his kids.

There is no equal to a love affair with an older man. Because you can't repeat first feelings with the same spirit the next time around, it will leave you reminiscing for many years. It is heartbreaking when it doesn't work; but all of us are better off, with or without professional help, to be out of a love affair that will eventually have an unhappy ending.

What Kind of Woman Falls In Love with an Older Man?

❧ Barbie What! ❧

As charming and effervescent as he is, Phil Donahue knew just which button to push to rankle me and provoke my anger during one of my appearances on his show. He referred to women who marry older men as "Barbies" and guys who get involved with younger women as having "Barbie" mentalities. Of course, he based his attitude on neither theory nor study but on what he *assumed* to be the personality of the woman who marries an older man—something he undoubtedly picked up from Hollywood-type marriages, where on celluloid, the "half the age, half the brains factor" is sensationalized.

I knew differently, but Phil was on a roll and any attempt at changing his mind was futile. Today, older men find stimulating, intelligent younger women who are successful in their careers to be very attractive. More often than not, these women are the opposite of their husband's first wives (if they were married

95

before) who chose a traditional path in marriage and more resemble the stereotypical woman society thinks marries an older man.

Of course, I can't blame Phil completely for his attitude since it is so widely held, and going on the attack sells shows. Yet in fairness to all those younger wives with brains, I do have to make an effort whenever given the opportunity to persuade people to give these women a chance.

On one occasion, I thought I found a significant platform. I was invited by a New York radio marketing firm to talk to a panel of metropolitan radio stations about W.O.O.M. and its purpose. I looked forward to these people helping me change the public's perception of age-disparate marriage through the radio shows they represented.

I had barely begun my presentation when I was interrupted by one of the guests, who belittled my concern that wives of older men feel their intellect undervalued and often ridiculed by the media. He wanted me to name a younger wife who got where she was without the help of her older husband.

Stunned, off the top of my head I blurted: Linda Wachner, president, chairwoman, and CEO of Warnaco (her husband, Seymour Applebaum, who was thirty-four years her senior, is hardly in the position of helping and influencing her business decisions since he's been dead since 1983). And there is Betsy Gotbaum, former New York City parks commissioner in the David Dinkins administration. In charge of 1,765 parks, I doubt her sixteen years older, former labor leader husband, Victor, was able to advise her much about preserving Indian paths and setting up solar-powered communications systems. And what about Susan Lucci, the soap-opera and movie-of-the-week star? I can't imagine how her chef/restaurateur husband landed her the role of Erica Kane on *All My Children*. These women *earned* their positions without anyone's help.

Having no comeback, my interrogator sat down; but he made me realize how ingrained this stereotype is and how difficult a road I faced in changing public perception.

❧ She's Definitely Not an Underdog ❧

To corroborate my thinking, I'll discuss a noteworthy study of my group, conducted in 1989.

A few months after I founded W.O.O.M., I received a phone call from Nancy Nelson, a Seton Hall University graduate student in her midthirties. Nelson was planning to present a dissertation, "The Marital Satisfaction of Women Married to Older Men," to complete a Ph.D. in psychology. What piqued Nancy's interest in this topic was the disparity in what the theorists thought versus the dynamism and go-getting traits that she saw in her sister, sister-in-law, and several friends married to older men. None of them viewed themselves as underdogs because they were female, and most were working in fields usually reserved for men.

As Nelson began her research, she noted that a few other researchers agreed with her philosophy: that profeminist younger women who were involved in androgynous (united male/female characteristics) fields or male-dominated occupations were probably more happily married because they selected older men to be their husbands. But she needed to prove it. Nancy asked me if she could use the W.O.O.M. membership in a study that would require three separate mailings to the members. Thinking that our association would also benefit from the study, I told her I would be happy to help her with her research as long as the anonymity of my subscribers was protected.

Prior to her study, Nelson found research on marital satisfaction had been limited to establishing if such satisfaction is achievable. (The consensus: It is.) However, no one had investigated which factors account for this despite evidence to suggest that societal attitudes toward such marriages remain pessimistic. This negative attitude reflects speculations by Freud and other psychoanalytic theorists that marital satisfaction for such women is rarely achievable—predicated on the existence of traditional gender-based characteristics. More specifically, these theorists propose that women who marry older men seek to marry a "daddy" figure so they can remain childlike and dependent. In other words, traditionally feminine.

❧ The Proof's in the Pudding ❦

The results of Mrs. Nelson's research proved my ire with Donahue and his producers was justified. After surveying 70 percent of the membership in a defined category, she found the majority confirmed her suspicions. The women proved to relate to an androgynous sex-role identity, a profeminist sex-role attitude, and participated in male-dominated occupations. And because of that, uniquely or in combination with these characteristics, our group achieved marital satisfaction when married to older men.

Until recently, I wasn't sure her research data was credible if compared with all women married to older men, particularly because she indicated in her dissertation that the W.O.O.M. subscriber was unique. Additionally, she confined the study, in order to control certain demographic criteria, to the majority of W.O.O.M.'s membership which in 1989, was basically white, middle- and upper-middle-class women ranging in age from twenty-six to forty-four. Most of them joined W.O.O.M. after reading Ron Alexander's front-page, *Living Section* feature, "A Support System for Younger Wives," in *The New York Times*, a newspaper usually read by more educated and affluent people. Criteria guidelines included that the women being surveyed have a minimum of twelve years of education and were in a first marriage of at least three years in duration with the husbands being ten or more years older.

Concurring with me, Mrs. Nelson was quick to point out that to be totally conclusive, her study needed to be duplicated with other women married to older men. However, it was not possible in 1989 because lists of these women in significant numbers were not available and searches using national marketing firms were prohibitively expensive. However, now that W.O.O.M. has been in existence for seven years, I was surprised when I found her results were remarkably similar when I performed an unscientific survey of my own where I included many of the same factors, except race.

I was especially amazed to find exactly 70 percent of today's members met the same standard as they did in 1989. Because our subscribers' socioeconomic backgrounds at this time are so vast, I was certain the results would be different. I attribute what I thought should have been a change in subscriber profile to the lowering of the organization's fee schedule and increased size. In 1989, the membership fee was fifty dollars and was open to only a select 125 members. In 1993, when I conducted my own survey, the subscriber fee was fifteen dollars which attracted 400 subscribers (the maximum I can handle). I haven't even begun to survey the two thousand profiles in my computer bank, but I can almost guarantee the results would be similar.

❦ Androgynous Occupations ❦

While conducting my personal survey, I did not have access to the sophisticated testing procedures Mrs. Nelson used that would indicate marital happiness, sex-role participation, nor those that would assess profeminist sex-role attitudes. But I do have access to the occupation of both spouses and was able to determine the level of education (pretty much all I was interested in) and class criteria based upon job descriptions.

Interestingly, I found that the selected candidate belonging to this more diverse group of W.O.O.M. members, born between 1946 and 1964, was well educated, also. There were a number of women who were physicians and lawyers, one is a rabbi, another a minister. Mari Bottom, of Miami, Florida, performs security surveys that check the efficacy of safety devices and systems in hotels and corporate buildings. Connie Rahner-Platt*, Buffalo, New York, is an hydrogeologist. Johanna Taliaferro, Phoenix, Arizona, lays telephone cables. Michele Hahn, New York City, is a family private investigator. Others were college professors or administrators, and many had obtained executive positions in finance or business—all generally male-dominated fields. I found it amusing, though, that most of the women's hobbies are feminine with gardening and maintaining more beautiful bodies topping the list! I have also discovered that W.O.O.M.ies reserve their profeminist attitudes to work-related issues and graciously welcome any chivalrous offer of help outside that arena.

❧ Unsure Rebels ☙

Wives of older men, as a group, confess to being renegades who defiantly march to a different tune! Ironically, they often contradict even themselves. Many operate with an "I don't care what you think attitude," while inwardly worrying very much about what others think.

A few years ago, I had a W.O.O.M. pool party at my home. It was the first time we had an event where husbands and wives got together. Mattie Stern*, thirty years younger than her husband, Mel*, turned to me and said, "Does it bother you, Beliza, that we look funny even to me?" I laughed at her newfound consternation and realized Mattie, who was always the advocate for the group, protesting any article that was unfavorable to the age-disparate marriage, was a bit unsettled.

Against her parents' wishes, Maria Delmonte*, a white, upper-class former resident of the United Kingdom, followed her black, physician male friend, nineteen years her senior, to Wyoming. Even though she knew her parents would be very upset and society would not be kind, they eventually married. She told me, "I know I loved him very much, but the fact that he was forbidden fruit intensified my affection for him. With many odds against us, we've made a very nice life for ourselves and have adjusted to each other's different backgrounds. But along with the hurt and pain of being snubbed by both our races, I do miss having my parents' blessing and sometimes wonder, 'How would my life be different if I had listened?'"

Ellin Mackay was a beautiful heiress—a postdebutante— when she met Irving Berlin at a dinner party on May 23, 1924. Berlin, fifteen years her senior, was a world-famous composer— and he was Jewish, a cantor's son from the Lower East Side. Ellin was Catholic, the daughter of millionaire Clarence Mackay. It was a chance meeting. Berlin was a last-minute fill-in for a guest who couldn't make it. Ellin, who also came solo, was engaged but not really in love. He was a Democrat, she a Republican. They came from two different worlds, worlds that would shun them because of their religious differences. Despite this, they fell deeply in love. But Irving was cautious.

In her book, *Irving Berlin*, author Mary Ellin Barrett, Berlin's daughter, mentions her father attempted to keep things light. He described Ellin and himself as "a couple of idiots suffering from a bad, but fortunately, temporary attack of spring fever." "But one night," she writes, "it being leap year, my mother proposed. Joking, of course. Not joking at all."

Unable to resist one another, the courtship created a scandal. They were a threat to New York's rigid society. In those days, in Southampton where the very rich summered, "Old-guard Protestants and new-guard Irish Catholics belonged to the same clubs," Ms. Barrett writes. "Jews were something else, alien people who didn't figure into the equation and were not welcome." And certainly not at Harbor Hill, the Mackay's fifty-room Long Island mansion, where a party for the Prince of Wales was being planned. Yet, Ellin was determined to have her man—at all costs.

Her father threatened to disown her. Berlin was totally unsuitable, he argued. According to Ms. Barrett, Mackay said, "The *impossibility* of this man, fifteen years older, a Broadway songwriter, someone from a completely different background, of no education, no position, leading God knows what sort of life." Mackay insisted Ellin leave the country for six months. If she still felt the same way about Mr. Berlin when the trip was over, they would again discuss the issue.

Meanwhile, Irving Berlin was having second thoughts. Ms. Barrett writes, "My father, though also in love, way beyond spring fever—it's nearly autumn now—has not made up his mind. He worries about the difference in age, in backgrounds, about religion. Ellin wanted to be married by a priest (it would help soften up her father); Irving, the cantor's son, didn't see himself being married by a priest. His world and hers may meet at New York dinner parties, yet they still retreat into sternly different backgrounds. And then there is his simple reluctance of a longtime single man to give up his freedom." His song "What'll I Do?" never seemed more appropriate.

Ellin stuck out the six-month agreement with her father. She wanted so much for him to accept her happiness. She pleaded with him to reconsider his rejection. Yet, she was determined ultimately to have her way.

Months went by. Many father-daughter arguments ensued. Mackay added other points to the cauldron—the impact on children of mixed race; the extent of Irving's devotion; Ellin's youth; and more.

To make matters worse, newspapers and periodicals were eagerly reporting the principals every move. It was all too much to take. Ellin and Irving were hopelessly in love. "On Monday,

January 4, 1926," writes Ms. Barrett, "my father telephoned Ellin. He could stand it no longer. He had a ring. Would she get married that morning? Could she come to his apartment right now and from there they would go to city hall?"

Ellin was wearing a wrinkled gray dress. Not bothering to change, she ran! Irving was panicky. He forgot his wallet and had to borrow two dollars to pay for the marriage license. They eloped. Clarence Mackay disinherited his daughter as promised. "Ten million dollars down the drain," Ms. Barrett writes. (Years later, Berlin and Mackay became friends.) The newlyweds sailed for a month-long honeymoon in Europe. On board ship, Irving Berlin presented his young wife with her wedding present, a song he wrote especially for her, the moving and best-selling hit, "Always."

And yes, even today, those of us who defied our parents and found dating someone out of our religion a novelty before we married are confronted with circumstances that tend to isolate us from our older partners. We keep our religious feelings to ourselves. Neither partner is ever very comfortable broaching the subject; and even when everything else is perfect, it remains for many couples a silent disparity. Too touchy to talk about. Nevertheless, because they were brought up at a time when intermarrying was less acceptable, many older husbands are less tolerant of religious differences than their younger wives.

When age-disparate couples argue, clashes usually occur over the very divisions they both found so beguiling at the outset. Unfortunately, these conflicts escalate into war when the older husband realizes his younger wife is not going to move very far from her position. Because women of his generation didn't take such stands, the husband may have a hard time coping with his wife's attitude. What complicates things further and results in a difficult-to-compromise predicament is that neither one of them is wrong when considering the other generation's point of view.

❧ A Jig Saw Puzzle...
Nine Decades of Not-Always-Interlocking Pieces ❦

I'm continually amazed that I deal with younger wives from the ages of twenty to seventy. They pose a half century of female age-related ideologies I have to piece together when dealing with their concerns.

Intermix them with another sixty or so years to include the men's variables, and that adds up to about nine decades of age-disparate combinations I need to master.

For example, the issues of a twenty-five-year-old female newly married to a man who is sixty compared with a forty-five-year-old woman newly married to a sexagenarian have to be handled in a profoundly different manner. Even though their husbands' outlook may be similar, the younger young wife's perception of what to expect in her marriage will undoubtedly vary from that of a middle-aged younger wife's. When a man considers remarriage, it would be wise if he made himself aware of the commitment differences and demands upon his time fifteen to twenty years can make when selecting a younger next mate.

A twenty- or thirty-something wife will have to rely more upon her husband's cooperation in fulfilling her goals. She will need his agreement to start a family, perhaps buy a bigger house, or to pitch in and help juggle her career and family. Often she will appear more demanding in her need for him to accept change. Yet more distressing, because of the vast age difference, he may not be able to comprehend what she has in mind.

Think about it. Sixty-year-old men generally don't have a clue about Lamaze, breast-feeding, and natural childbirth. And forget about changing a diaper, separating the wash, giving up a Sunday game of golf to watch the kids while his wife works—

shared responsibilities! Most older husbands have never had to participate in any of that when they were married to a woman closer to their age.

In comparison, a middle-aged younger new wife has probably finished having babies, comes to the relationship involved in an established career, and is often more financially independent than a younger younger wife. If she has been a single parent for any length of time, she is accustomed to juggling job and family by herself. In general, the middle-aged younger wife will accept indirect domestic participation from her sixty-year-old husband and will appear less self-centered and more willing to compromise about little things—including his physical appearance. This couple's domestic affairs will center on less disruptive decisions such as: in whose home shall they live, can she change his former wife's carpet selection, and/or can he stand her kids?

Depending on which part of the country the couple reside, I find a greater imbalance with the middle-aged younger wife's assertiveness when she has been married to an older man for many years in comparison to those who have married older men when they are already middle-aged. These women deal with male/female equality from a more contemporary point of view. And it appears easier for them to work out problems.

On the other hand, the middle-aged younger wife who married her husband in her twenties will simmer internally as she views her marriage from a more subservient position. At times, she is more timid in stating her personal needs and demands. As a result, problems blow up out of proportion because they haven't been faced head-on at the outset.

It is mind boggling trying to counsel couples with age-discrepancy conflicts. Further complicating matters is, more often than not, both parties are right when their ages and positions in life are considered.

❧ *Seeing It Her Way* ❦

A common favorable trait of older husbands is their inability to stay mad at their younger, medium younger, and older younger wives for very long. This female rebel who wants to be dared gets under an older man's skin. She's an amusingly outrageous handful—persuasively irresistible, innovative, and crafty. Utilizing this killer combination, she'll manipulate you into thinking your argument is dumb and unfounded. Before you know it, you'll be seeing things her way. Let's face it, she's cute enough to her husband to get away with it. But she doesn't just save these skills for her older partner! Younger wives are apt to succeed in business and other ventures by trying out new or zany ideas others are afraid to attempt—such as marrying an older man.

Yet the glitch for the marriage is that she doesn't resemble any woman an older man has ever lived with. His mother and former, similar-in-age wife (if he had one), more often than not, centered their activities around him. While he discovers the younger woman's independence and accomplishments are enticing, the older husband may find it difficult to cope with the fact there are going to be nights when he's popping a TV dinner into the microwave while she's doling out food to the homeless at a local soup kitchen, is at a business meeting, or taking a course. Betsy Fifield told *Fortune* magazine, "I give Jim one wife day a week," when she'll run errands for him.

Lyn Lear, forty-six years old, the younger wife of television producer Norman Lear, seventy-two, is just the type of younger woman with whom older men want to spend the rest of their lives. But the trade-off is, she and those like her are going to be off doing their own thing just when their older husbands want them around.

Lyn is fresh, stimulating, and diverse in her talents. In addition to a Ph.D. in psychology, she has spent most of her adult life in school—either as a student or as a teacher of psychology, philosophy, and world religions. Add to that her participation with an all-female team that formed the Environmental Media Association, an organization that attempts to get environmental messages included in television shows and films, the time she spends helping her husband with shows he is producing, and mothering their young son, Benjamin, and you can see why she attracted a megamogul like Lear. Lyn is a bolder new breed of younger wife who insists, "I can be involved in [Norman's] life as I wish to be, creatively and in other ways." Being the exception, not the rule, she adds, "I don't feel threatened, and I don't feel competitive."

❧ *The Foretelling M.O.* ❧

Fortune-telling is not my specialty, nor do I run a dating service—even though I am occasionally asked to matchmake. However, I am pretty good at spotting single women who would be better off if they chose older men to be their husbands. These are usually dynamic women who discover men they date in college are too immature and those their age at work, not sophisticated enough. These women are light-years ahead of their peers and are often frustrated and bored with men their age.

Twenty-four-year-old Lisa Miele, the oldest daughter of our friends, Joe and Ceile Miele, has recently completed her master's degree in business administration. Far more mature than many women her own age, Lisa doesn't shun her parents' circle of friends. She fits in at dinner parties and enjoys the gracious lifestyle the Mieles have given her. She is well-spoken, a real powerhouse, and possesses the confidence of a much older woman. When Lisa was in high school and college bound, she took a course at a local manicure school and worked at a nail salon to earn pocket money. Most of her schoolmates, who came from similar well-to-do families, didn't have her enterprising nature. They wouldn't have been caught dead working in a trade profession. But the right older man would appreciate Lisa's ambition immensely.

❧ Watch Out! She Might Be After Your Job ❦

Many women married to older men are multitalented—like Lili Zanuck who left her job at the World Bank in Washington, D.C., married producer Richard Zanuck, who was twenty years older, and started puttering around his office—without pay. Her fresh attitude and youth paid off for both of them, and now, she is a salaried producer with movies *Cocoon, Rush,* and Oscar-winning, *Driving Miss Daisy* under her belt. Even though she had to push her way past her husband's misgivings, Lili has become an integral link in his business—without any prior experience!

Certainly, a younger wife's talents are realized sooner by having husbands who have a couple of decades on her in experience and knowledge. But it is this penchant, as twenty- to seventy-somethings (yes, they're younger wives, too) to outdo their older husbands and prove to them they're just as smart by keeping up with their successes that makes marriage to a younger woman—or any woman for that matter—exciting. Being competitive is a noteworthy characteristic of most younger women involved with older men. Sometimes it takes a few years for it to manifest, but much to their chagrin (they created a monster), older husbands will become dogged by it.

In the biography, *Writing Dangerously: Mary McCarthy and her World*, Carol Brightman chronicled McCarthy's turbulent marriage to Edmund Wilson, a book editor nearly twice her age. She said of the late author of *The Group, A Charmed Life,* and other powerful novels, it was in her view a woman's prerogative, certainly her pleasure, to take on any man and beat him at his own game.

Although McCarthy was provoked by her older husband's radical, undue control, all wives take heed. Could this drive to succeed be the real intrigue? Is it our self-worth and value to others—the constant confirmation that *he* made the right choice—the adhesive that makes a man stick around? Remain interested? Or as in Hanko Rosenblad's case, the net that lures an older man?

Several years ago, Hanko was determined to teach herself how to sail. She started on a sixteen-foot sailboat and graduated quickly to a twenty-one footer. After a high-seas romance, she married her Swedish older husband, Axel, an experienced seafarer, in 1987. Hanko told the *Two River* (New Jersey) *Times* that in their first competition, they came in first place in their division, in the Marion, Massachusetts, to Bermuda Race, and ended up fourth in the entire field of one hundred and sixty-four entries! But Hanko's competitive spirit didn't stop there! She joined her yacht club as the first female full member in the eighties when most yacht clubs only accepted women as auxiliary members. She reasoned, she deserved to be a full member.

Charging ahead, she encouraged the club to consider her idea that they be the first yacht club in New Jersey to offer sailing lessons for mentally challenged people (Hanko's niece was born with Down's syndrome). This resulted in her starting a Special Olympics sailing program. Hanko is confident she and her crew will set sail to Hartford for the 1995 Special Olympics!

❧ *Vulnerability... The Impetus* ❦

*A*bly handling a multitude of things at once seems to be the younger wife's forte. This perpetual motion sets them apart from women who don't have the need to prove themselves to a discriminating older partner or anyone else for that matter. It's actually the younger wife's vulnerability that produces this enormous expenditure of energy. Many of their husbands left a former wife who they say "just didn't keep up."

Several years ago while sitting on the Riveras' dock, I was casually chatting with C.C. Rivera and the wife of Geraldo's agent at the William Morris agency. At some point, the conversation veered toward marrying divorced men. I said, "It is very insecure to be the second wife." C.C. briskly interjected, "Try being the third or fourth wife!"

At that moment, I realized that my thoughts echoed those of so many next wives. Yet, our zeal to impress irritates those who don't feel like competing. Especially some of the so-called age-appropriate wives of our older husband's friends who find being around us a threat.

❧ *Packing It All In in His Lifetime* ❦

*R*ecently, I was playing tennis with a woman who mockingly teased, "Just what *can't* you do?" When I mentioned that 1994 was going to be my year of coping by jumping in and just doing it, she was aggravated that my ambitions belittled her less-aspiring life-style. I must admit even *I* bit off almost more than I could chew! That year, I wrote this book, was chairwoman of the Monmouth College Scholarship Ball, produced three newsletters for individual businesses, served on the executive committee for the Central Jersey March of Dimes, ran W.O.O.M., and kept an eye on my two kids ages seven and fourteen!

I don't feel I am any smarter or more special than anyone else. I look at it as making the most of myself. Living with an older man, I know my married life can be significantly shorter than those whose husbands are closer to them in age. Taking advantage of an enormous energy that matches my love and admiration for him, I want to pack it all in while Sam is around to share my accomplishments. But I know just what Yvonne Tovar Galanoudes, who is building her career as a real-estate agent, meant when she told the Torrance, California, *Daily Breeze*,

"I am very ambitious and goal oriented, and my husband, George [a real estate agent, also] wants me to make something of myself, too. But sometimes I feel pushed, like I'm in a rush. I feel like he's saying 'come on Yvonne, try harder. I don't have all the time in the world.'"

Yes, in some cases, we have an edge over women married to men their age—a coach. But it can be exhausting trying to live our life and have him relive his through us—all at the same time!

❦ *Trophy Wives* ❦

*O*ccasionally, an older husband's watchful eye can be a nuisance. But it develops a vast self-confidence in younger wives and lovers and accelerates them to a particular level of perfection that fulfills her goals and his expectations. Viewed as icons and treated as handle-with-care packages by their husbands, these women have been coined *Trophy Wives.*

Even when these women attempt to downplay their personal merits—which to some could include his assets—many still have trouble maintaining and making friends. They unintentionally border on cocky or uppity to peers and associates who don't realize the impetus for all of this is the younger wife's concern to continually impress an older husband who may have traded in a less-interesting model for her. Not wanting to repeat the mistakes of a former wife, younger women are driven to overdo and prove themselves accordingly.

Having the advantage of learning from his mistakes, these women can exude an assured maturity (sometimes bordering on being old ladies in young bodies) and successfulness far beyond the years of women who are married to men similar in age. There are some people who don't want to give these women credit where it's due. They maintain the younger wives' successes were achieved only because of the husband's financial backing and pull. And if she falls on her face, he's going to be there to help pick up the pieces. In some cases that may be true, but on the whole, these ladies are a pretty talented lot.

Cecilia Silver is a forty-three-year-old younger wife, twenty-six years her husband Seymour's junior. Now she could be easy to hate! Cecilia is a piano teacher, a certified advanced scuba diver, a gourmet cook, a sailor, and somehow finds the ambition to attend classes at night to obtain a master's degree in business administration while she practices law by day—quite a repertoire of accomplishments! She walks the extra mile to make the most out of her life and represents the younger-wife prototype so appealing to older men.

❧ *An Older Man's Springboard to Vivacity* ❦

*Y*ounger women who get involved with older men come in all sizes and shapes. They can be model-like and glamorous or average, maybe even "plain Janes." And whether they are obtaining degrees, working their way up the company ladder, the head of a company, or are outstanding volunteers serving their communities, you'll find them continually striving to better themselves. To older men, their looks are a secondary consideration. It's their fresh and perky attitude that's so appealing. Norman Brinker, the founder of the Steak and Ale and Bennigan's chains and CEO of Chili's, a fast-food outfit from Dallas, Texas, said of his third wife Nancy, sixteen years his junior, "I was attracted to her brains, wit, and vitality." Many younger wives are quick to please and have nurturing temperaments. You'll find a lot of them enter healing or helping fields.

But those aren't the only characteristics that older men find captivating. In my computer bank, I have a myriad of races and nationalities. There are all types of interracial and intercultural marriages. Actually, *interanything* seems to be the rage. I know of men who leave a politically or socially correct marriage to marry someone who completely opposes their friends' and families' milieu.

Many of us read about the family chill that erupted when Barbara "Basia" Piasecka, a Polish chambermaid, married billionaire Band-Aid heir, J. Seward Johnson, Sr., who was forty-two years her senior. We also remember the horrific and spectacular legal fight his children precipitated, when he died twelve years later and *tried* to leave Basia $400 million. For many May/December love affairs, polarity seems to enhance the appeal. And if it's a care-less, to hell with the others *liaison dangereuse*, it's even more titillating.

❧ *An Influential Counterpart* ❦

*T*ina Brown, the editor of the *New Yorker* who propelled *Vanity Fair* to the front of the magazine sales rack with her risqué covers and intriguing articles, knew what she was doing when she married Harold Evans, the current head of Random House's trade book division. She linked herself up with a man who appreciated her talent and wouldn't compete with nor impede her enterprising nature.

When Tina met Evans, she was an Oxford graduate and aspiring writer in her early twenties. He was an editor of the London *Sunday Times* in his midforties. They became a power couple among literary circles, and together, their influence among writers is exceptional. However, behind her back there are those who might think, "Where would she be today without him?" But why not ask, Where would he be today without her? It is the dynamics of the team that makes the younger woman/older man couple so impressive.

Anyone who knows Jim Robinson, former CEO of American Express, and his wife Linda, seventeen years his junior, a chief executive with Robinson, Lake, Lerer, and Montgomery, a highly successful New York public-relations firm, is aware that their personal successes relied heavily on each other's input. Whether a man is CEO of a major corporation or CEO of a local bakery, he is going to find it a real ego-booster and business builder to have an articulate wife by his side in whom he can confide and discuss business. In a way, it's all very flattering. She will become his legacy and carry on where he's left off.

What's He Like?

❧ Image ❧

What does a man who survived Viet Nam—or for that matter, fought in World War II—see in a woman who was in diapers when President Nixon resigned from office? That's the question that haunts former wives who have been left for younger women. In 99 percent of the cases, oldsters are seeking a new lease on life—a fresh attitude. Many have the need to maintain or recapture their youth, and there's nothing like firm flesh to get the juices flowing. But there's more to it than just feeling young and exciting sex. There's the importance of image.

When Michael S. Broder, a psychologist from Philadelphia, asks his older male clients why they are attracted to younger women, he discovers their answers are so blunt, they'll propel *any* wife who wants to save her marriage off to aerobics classes and a *year* at Elizabeth Arden! One of Broder's clients was graphically succinct when he told him, "Would you rather have somebody like so-and-so who is thirty or forty years old and is young and attractive or someone who looks like Barbara Bush?" Broder commented, "It makes perfect sense."

In her book, *Secrets About Men Every Woman Should Know About*, author/therapist Barbara DeAngelis writes, "Men are turned on by visual stimulation. Men are more visually oriented; women more verbally oriented. This means your husband's primary source of sexual arousal is your appearance." Ms. DeAngelis explains this is why men fixate on a woman's body or what she is wearing.

Image and success go hand in hand as the American dream for the majority of older men. Achieving it is all part of the game. Holding onto it may be the break point. When I asked the men I interviewed how they view image and success, their replies were candid and near unanimous. A good job, a beautiful, attentive wife, and family was the formula that kept them going. They believed this trio enhanced their ability and increased their chances of making it big—whatever *big* might be. Additionally, I learned that managers and others who have made it to the top, find the security of hanging onto power jobs is not as simple as professional shrewdness and an application of Grecian Formula. However, all agreed an active libido, strength, keeping trim, and vitality added up to staying power.

One solution for threatened middle-aged men, keeping ahead of youthful counterparts who are chasing them up the corporate ladder, might be to secure their positions with accoutrements that they believe signify youth—like Harleys, living in the fast lane, and changing wives. Although they may find this route expensive and exhausting, these men brashly discover ignoring the personal consequences could prove to be too critical to not make the effort. Divorcing an old wife for a perky, beautiful wife, who resurrects a man's youthful outlook and bonhomie, is the quick fix some corporate lions losing a foothold will try. The new spouse often gets labeled a power wife—an attractive younger woman, successful in her own right, who abets and endorses her older husband's accomplishments.

In *Fortune* magazine's cover story, "The CEO's Second Wife," psychiatrist Helen Singer Kaplan said, "In some cases, the man with the old wife is looked down on. He's seen as not keeping up appearances. Why can't he do better for himself?" Historically, if an executive divorced his wife, his partners and coworkers frowned upon it, and it could have cost him his job. Sadly today, it could save his job! As sexist as it is, marriage has become big business for CEOs and other corporate powerhouses, and wives have become a quintessential asset just as important as stock options and golden parachutes.

But what's good for the gander is good for the goose. Visible, successful American women are quickly surveying the field for exciting—usually older—accomplished mates who can keep up with their achievements and not shrink from humiliation when referred to as Jane Doe's husband.

In an article for *Working Woman* magazine, Nikki Finke wrote that successful women who have put off marriage for the sake of making it big in their careers often choose men with three or more of five attributes: fame, prestige, position, brains, and money. Sound familiar? "He's an ego prop," she said, "like a Trophy Wife. Marry this guy and she becomes one half of that phenomena known as the Power Couple."

How does this all relate to John Doe, a construction worker from Little Town, U.S.A.? In very much the same way. Hermosa Beach, California, psychotherapist, Myrna Miller said, "An older husband makes a younger woman feel protected and sophisticated; she makes him feel young and accomplished. By her standards, he's really successful." When a younger woman considers an older mate, prestige, power, and wealth are all relative to the world from which they come. Miller agreed. "If he makes fifty thousand dollars a year, that's a lot of money to a twenty year old, but for a woman of forty, that's not that much."

"It truly boils down to not how much you feel about the other person," says psychologist Broder when describing his older male clients, "but how you feel about yourself when you are *with* the other person."

❧ His and Her Demands ❦

The whole concept of trading up, or keeping a present wife on guard, is self-centered and belittles the holiness of marriage by replacing vows with a type of ultimatum, but it's a moral gamble many are willing to take to simply feel good about who they are for as long as *she* produces the fodder: respect and adulation. It sounds humiliating, but in reality, it's a fact of life, and any woman involved with a man who expects this type of treatment is going to find herself out in the cold if she doesn't follow along.

But it's equally true that if wives would have the presence to demand the same consideration in return, there would be a turn-around in the divorce rate. That would require assertiveness (not bitchiness) and regard to cause and effect; characteristics considered to be traditionally unfeminine because women wear their emotions on their cuff and don't always follow through with demands.

Fifty-year-old Sheldon Linz, photographer of Presidents Nixon, Reagan, and Bush and now married to a much younger woman, told me, "If my first wife had demanded more and hadn't given into my whims, I would have had more respect for her. When she started to put on weight and not caring about her appearance, I didn't want to be married to her anymore. Now that we're divorced, she's lost the weight...takes care of herself. She looks great!"

You may be asking yourself just what kind of cad would put a wife under such pressure by requiring such trivialities as good looks, social prowess, and successful careers? Many men, but not all may be so direct in his demands, nor carry out a drastic change in his marital life-style. But understand, women are no different. Their guidelines for marital bliss are mighty blunt, also. Show me a woman who doesn't consider power, success, and having the rent paid on time important elements in a good marriage. I didn't make this up. In David Buss' book, *The Evolution of Desire*, he notes that universally, women across the board, "Prefer men with resources and status—usually the province of the older man." He also said, "On average, American *college* women say their prospective mate's earning power must be in at least the seventieth percentile—or better!" Hardly something they are going to find in a recent male graduate.

❧ *Risking It All* ❦

Fifty-eight percent of the husbands of W.O.O.M. subscribers list gambling as an extracurricular activity. This implies that these men are risk takers. Because many of them have risked it all to be with their younger wives, understand the power these younger women wield by constantly making their man or someone else's man feel good about himself.

You're probably wondering, "Who is this sugar daddy who robs the cradle, may have left a wife, splits his family, and works day and night to pay off his investment?" He can be as simple as the guy next door or as high powered as seventy-four-year-old multimillionaire, John Gutfreund, former head of the investment banking firm Salomon Brothers.

He married former flight attendant/rich divorcee Susan Penn in 1981. She was thirty-five. Overnight, Susan transformed Gutfreund. As he began to smell the roses, he switched from being frugal and unsociable to an international jet-setter who lavished Parisian homes and rooms full of eighteenth-century furnishings on her. Obviously happier than he has ever been, John says, "My wife has spent all my money, but it is worth it."

Everyone is entitled to marital happiness, even those who are expected to be above moral reproach, such as the clergy. A friend of mine told me about her uncle's friend who was a minister from Oklahoma. He was miserable in his marriage and eventually left his wife and married a friend of his daughter's, twenty-four years his junior. It was a real scandal! Driven out of town, he left the state, left the church, and is now happy building yachts and running charters on the island of Anguilla. At great emotional and professional expense, he traded in his old life as he sought personal happiness. Starting over, he has three young children who get along famously with the children from his first marriage, an intellectually stimulating wife with two degrees, and a new lease on life. Seldom looking back, he changed his world in search of inner peace. If you look at it from a man's point of view where acquisitions, tangible and emotional, are his most sacred assets, it's easy to comprehend the trend. Some would refer to it as pride in ownership.

Wives close in age to their husbands have to pay attention to what a man will give up to feel good. If these women can keep their relationship stimulating, there's every reason to believe they will grow old together with their husbands. But too often couples grow apart, get lazy, and take each other for granted. That's when the husband starts to look outside the marriage for someone who will give him that shot in the ego that keeps his juices flowing.

Women who have been left by their husbands for younger women are intrigued by my organization. On one hand, they loathe the concept and want to hate me; but on the other hand, they feel compelled to ask me where they went wrong. My answer to them is similar to what I used to say to women buying my cosmetics.

When my would-be customers resisted change or told me they didn't have time to wear makeup, I would suggest they "stand by the check-out counter at the local supermarket some morning and tell me which woman catches your eye?" Many responded, "Very few; but usually the one who is made up, trim, and well dressed."

Continuing, I would recommend they note the juxtaposition of the nearby glamour magazine covers and the unmade-up women in baggy sweatsuits collecting their groceries at the check-out counter. The comparison is a shock to anyone's senses. Men work day in and day out with women who are aggressive, challenging, and smartly dressed. If they don't come home to someone comparable, trouble will soon be in the air.

Never discount that the chase is often more exciting than the catch. Once a couple marries, it is up to the wife to maintain the charm that initiated the pursuit. To keep my marriage stimulating for both Sam and me, I like the idea of challenging surprises.

Something elementary like "Oh by the way, I met John Doe today at a fund-raiser. He was so interesting! We talked for hours. Did you know that he _ _ _ *(make something up if you have to)?*" is very effective.

It is likely your husband will say, "I didn't know you were going out."

You say, "Oh I just decided at the last minute."

You needn't let your husband know, beforehand, your every move. You're not connected at the hip. That's one pathway that leads to marital ennui!

All wives need to keep their lives interesting—not get so wrapped up in housework and the kids that they don't see something in their marriage might be amiss. Take courses, read the newspaper—surprise your husband with your intellect. Threaten his brainwaves. Give him a reason to be proud of you.

A lot of wives who have been left tell me they were treated like doormats. But I have learned that no one can treat you badly, unless you let them. If the woman is used as a doormat, some of the responsibility is hers. If a wife keeps taking it, she's giving a guy permission to walk all over her. If you fit this category, watch how fast your husband's attitude will change when you walk out the door. And if it doesn't, it's his loss. Command respect. And continually remind your husband how lucky he is to have *you*—just be sure to live up to the hype.

❦ *The Challenge* ❦

Sam has been asked, "Doesn't your wife being involved with W.O.O.M., particularly the *Older Men* part, bother you?" His reply has been, "As long as she looks as good as she does, treats me as well as she does—I have no problem."

In our marriage there's no room for one taking the other for granted. The sexual attraction is that we both look good to each other—are proud of one another. But the more alluring enticement is that we challenge each other and feel special together. We joke, but there's a ring of truth when I say: If I don't live up to his expectations, he might look for a younger model. In turn, if he doesn't return the favor, I'll be checking out the eligible *older* ones! Neither one of us wants to be with an ordinary person. Knowing where we stand makes it a lot easier to get on with simply loving one another.

During my interviews with older husbands and those dating younger women, I often ask why they are attracted to younger women—why they don't date or didn't marry women closer to their age? Aside from the obvious superficial reasons—"she's so pretty...fresh...smart"—they talk about women of all ages in general, their expectations and attitudes toward men.

The gentlemen in their fifties and sixties complain that many single women, close to their age—especially those who were jilted—are bitter men-bashers. They gripe that these women complain incessantly about their divorces and what rats their former husbands were. One muttered, "Doesn't make me feel she's going to think I'm much better."

Other men are turned off by older "bra burners." They feel that women in the feminist movement have spent years reducing men to regard women with confused ambiguity. "I don't know whether to hold the door for her, help her with her coat—pay the bill," said one. "I get the feeling they just want to be one of the boys."

Some of these women are suffering the consequences as older men retaliate by marrying younger women who are more comfortable handling their femininity, sexuality, jobs, and families. They have less of an ax to grind. Men in their late thirties and forties grumble about competition and jealousy. "My wife would constantly one-up me." Others feel they are young for their age. Younger women help them hold on to that image.

This rebound is a reality with which women across the ages have to deal. And quite candidly, with a divorce rate well over 50 percent, we have to appreciate something's wrong. Additionally, women have to comprehend that very little has changed when it comes to their appeal. Men want feminine, sensual, and adoring wives for spouses. If a wife can successfully prosecute an alleged felon or access Cyberspace, that's icing on the cake.

Women as a whole have to wake up and realize the man they married and all men, for that matter, take of this very seriously. They enjoy bringing home the bread, but it had better be worth it! Even more important than good looks, they want women who offer mental stimulation and intellectual insight.

Charlie Chaplin had several very young lovers and even younger wives, but when he met eighteen-year-old Oona O'Neill, he was smitten. She was young, attractive, well-bred, and privately educated. Her father, playwright Eugene O'Neill, disinherited her when they fell in love, but Charlie was perfect for Oona. She willingly gave up her family and privileged life to indulge him. It was apparent to all that he had met his match, and their marriage lasted thirty-four years, the rest of his life. Oona knew just which buttons to push to keep Charlie, thirty-six years her senior, from straying. She plugged into his visions. She understood his tirades and together, they made *his* dreams come true. In turn, she was blessed with a beautiful family, an exciting, international social life, and the opportunity to stand side-by-side with a cinema legend.

If you think it's awkward only for the younger woman in a relationship, think again! Initially, an older man may feel embarrassed and self-conscious dating a younger woman. But on the whole, it takes a great deal of self-confidence to marry someone a couple of decades younger. Men have to muster up a lot of courage to deal with society's icy stares.

Rusty Shaffer, a steelworker from Clarion, Pennsylvania, is often asked if his wife Marcy, twenty-three years younger, is his daughter. If he is greeted with a curt "oh" when he says she's his wife, Rusty just smiles and says, "Eat your heart out." Marcy might be embarrassed by her husband's smug retort, but she knows Rusty's boasting comes from his recognizing what he wants in life. She says, "He's getting older and knows he has to look out for himself in the years to come."

❧ *The Pride Factor* ❦

Sometimes, pride can make an older man shoot himself in the foot particularly when a younger woman's youthful stamina challenges his masculinity and is a physical reminder that he isn't as young as he used to be. Still, most older husbands and male friends have high self-esteem. To those who are self-assured, their younger wife's superior physical endurance is only a tiny obstacle because being surrounded by vitality and excitement is worth the few occasions when they might not be able to keep up.

As an older man survives each hurdle of the relationship, his ego is being fed by the adoration and possession of a younger wife. But other men, less secure, may not find that enough. Some need to prove themselves and will push their physical capabilities. Aside from looking foolish trying to perform the latest dance craze or competing in a sports match that's way beyond him physically, a man could wind up with dislocated bones, or worse yet, in intensive care!

Some sedentary older mates get a kick out of their wives' activities without needing to get off their sofas. One fellow I know encouraged his wife to trek in the Himalayas while he stayed home. They exchanged faxes, and he bragged about her to his friends.

However, all older men who think they have to keep up with younger women, associates, and jobs should be forewarned. Marrying a younger woman is an enormous commitment—even a burden. Unless he's prepared to push himself and dip into savings because he will literally be starting over (babies, a new house, white-on-white kitchens, tuition for his young bride to get her Ph.D., alimony and child support payments), he shouldn't even *think about* attempting an exhausting relationship with a younger woman! This is why you see so many older men having a fling and running back home, blaming a midlife crisis for their silly behavior.

❧ *Midlife Crisis* ❦

*I*n recent years, there have been numerous articles in popular magazines blaming a midlife crisis for men's midlife peccadilloes and wife dumping. This is a quasi-affliction which provides Oprah and Donahue with sensational chatter. However, I am often confused by what it *really* means clinically. Is it a coined phrase conveniently used by wives and former wives who refuse to look at what's wrong with the marriage and their contribution to its decline? Or, is it a reliable term that has psychological and/or pathological importance?

Marc Levin, a psychiatric social worker from Little Silver, New Jersey, said he, too, was baffled. "I don't quite understand what it really means either. I often cringe when I hear the term because it's a bothersome expression used to describe almost anything, any type of anguish a middle-aged man might go through that has potential disruptive capabilities for his family. I have a hard time giving it universal credence. Personally, I think some of the men that make decisions to somehow uproot their life and turn it into a different direction may be doing the healthiest thing in their life; while others may be acting out of incredible narcissism, or almost antisocial or self-destructive behavior."

When men are younger, they tend to bury their problems in their work and daily routine, but as they age, preexisting conflict issues surface and demand attention. In midlife, the stakes seem higher; anxiety is elevated. Levin elaborated. "The stresses that are threatening their self-esteem, power, dependence, and difficulty coping with intimacy may be different, but the responses are the same. What men do in midlife is probably consistent with how they've addressed other developmental issues in adolescence and adulthood, yet it manifests itself in radical behavior changes as they get older and are less able to cope with frustrations and disappointment." Thus, midlife crisis.

❧ *Erotic Savior Faire* ❦

Older men often make better lovers! The ones who have continuously flirted with, have had affairs, dated, and even married younger women really *like* women. Whether they are single, divorced, widowed, or married-but-not-happy, oldsters are deliberate in their selection. After years of finding out what they don't want in a woman, many fall instantly and incautiously in love when the right "Ms. She" walks into their life.

In 1917 William Randolph Hearst went to see Ziegfeld's *Follies*. Even though he was married and had no intention of leaving his wife, he fell madly in love that evening with one of the shows exquisite dancers, Marion Davies—thirty-four years his junior. Infatuated and determined to make her a big star, Hearst attended the show every night for the next eight weeks. Smitten as well, she became his mistress and princess of Ocean House, a luxurious California mansion he built and deeded to her. Although Marion wasn't Hearst's first mistress, their relationship lasted until he died more than thirty years later.

Sexually, older gentlemen are considerate and worry very much about pleasing their younger lovers and mates. Younger women accustomed to "wham bam, thank you ma'am" younger guys will find older men unselfish, compassionate, thoughtful, and in no rush. What the men may lack in athleticism is more than compensated by their gentleness—a powerful turn-on. To an unpracticed younger woman, an older lover's experience gives her the confidence to learn erotic and arousing techniques. His skill combined with an understanding of a woman's emotional and physical desires is an incredible combination.

Decembers take pleasure setting the stage for their enchanting Mays, starting with dinner by candlelight and the courtliness that follows. Forty-five-year-old French publisher Bernard-Henri Lévy is married to Arielle Dombasle, an actress ten years his junior. In his best-selling book, *Les Hommes et Les Femmes*, Lévy states that he prefers the strategic game of seduction to the contact sport of love. Journalist Sheila Maloney*, a newly married W.O.O.M.ie from Seattle, agrees. "From the pursuit to the evocative capture, quality lovemaking is all very elaborate, artistic, and unhurried with older men."

Several years ago, *Cosmopolitan* published an article, "The Joy of Sex With an Older Man." In the story, Pat, a travel agent, insisted, "Tenderness can be extremely erotic and far outweighs any shortcomings." Barbara, a paralegal, said, "A man in his twenties or thirties has such an urgent drive for his own pleasure that he can't pay enough attention to satisfying you." Likewise, W.O.O.M. members rarely have love-making complaints.

The vast majority of our husbands are sexually active. Of the few who find their performance waning, many still try to meet their wives' needs. Just lying near their wives, admiring their youth, can be fulfilling to an older man. This is very satisfying to couples who approach lovemaking with appropriate expectation. Thus, over the years, as frequency of sex may decline from twice a week to once every other week to once a month or less, couples learn how to satisfy each other with alternative techniques.

It would be wise for younger wives to educate themselves about men and aging so as to adjust their goals. For instance, as a man ages, he may get a little slower and will not always reach an orgasm. This is not necessarily something negative for women having experienced young men's quick-ejaculation-and-then-off-to-sleep style of lovemaking. The book *Love and Sex After 60* written by Robert N. Butler, M.D. and Myrna I. Lewis, M.S.W., offers a vast amount of insight. They mention, "Younger wives of older husbands frequently express concern about male potency as their husbands reach their sixties. Sometimes the anxiety is unfounded and reassurance is all that is necessary."

However, some men do experience erectile dysfunction because of physical reasons. Often it is because the vascular system isn't as healthy as it should be, or they suffer from diabetes or illnesses associated with aging and related medications.

In these cases, a urologist may suggest a variety of measures that offer a more active and fulfilling sex life: oral medications, vacuum constrictive devices, or penile prostheses. However, the most popular treatment today is the penile self-injection program, a relatively painless procedure where a vasodilator substance is injected into the penis.

Assistant professor Dr. Ridwan Shabsigh, a urologist at Columbia-Presbyterian Medical Center, who subspecializes in sexual dysfunction, finds these injections more than 80 percent effective! However, he said, "It is too bad that some men, and that includes those in their fifties, are often too embarrassed to even go to the doctor to discuss their problem."

The bulk of the age-disparate couples Dr. Shabsigh sees in his office are often there because of the wife's encouragement. Generally, she's the one who makes the appointment. While his practice deals mostly with sexual problems, he contradicted malicious jibes ridiculing older men's libidos in general. He points out that we should not assume a man's chronological age has anything to do with his sexual performance. Dr. Shabsigh sees men in their eighties who are functioning far better than those in their fifties. He said, "Numbers don't mean anything. However, if there is a problem, and as long as a man wants to pursue this, help is available. I can offer him hope. I have a high success rate. Many of these men can confidently return to a reasonably normal sex life."

A few years ago, at an *Oprah* taping, we got into the subject of how fabulous sex is with an older man. Sitting in the audience was a little old lady vigorously waving her hand wanting to comment. She shouted out, "Ladies, just you *wait!*" Implying that our spectacular and fulfilling sex lives would soon turn into one big snore. Quickly I became aware she wasn't the only one who believed that!

During an appearance on the *Joan Rivers Show*, Rivers asked, intending to poke fun at me, "Well now, what *about* the issue of prostate problems?" Unschooled in this area, I didn't have an answer but realized this was always going to be titillating bunk for most of the talk shows on which I appear. I decided to find out real fast about the inner workings of the male sex organ—particularly what a prostate problem really is and if it affects sexual performance.

I called Princeton-based Dr. Stanley Rosenberg, a clinical professor of surgery (urology) at the Robert Wood Johnson

Medical School. He said, "It's a very common misconception that men with enlarged prostates are impotent. However, prostate cancer surgery, where the nerves to the penis are interrupted, and radiation therapy may very definitely cause dysfunction." But he added that these men can be implanted with prosthetic devices, inflatable or rigid, or they can use an exterior vacuum-pump suction method that can allow them to enjoy sex.

On the other hand, Dr. Rosenberg went on to point out that there are lots of other ways to enjoy sex and get around the impotency issue. He mentioned oral sex, fondling, holding, and cuddling. Aware that quality sex is not all about a penis entering a vagina, I added to that massages, erotic movies, and mechanical arousal devices. "As a matter of fact," Dr. Rosenberg chuckled, "I treat a man whose beautiful wife is quite young." Actually, she was a college roommate of his daughter's. "She told me once, 'I don't care about his penis, as long as he has his *tongue!*' "

Nevertheless, there can be emotional pitfalls having sex with an older man who experiences frequent disappointments. His fear of sexual dysfunction can be very upsetting to him. If it is long term, the man could develop psychological symptoms such as depression and turn inward, which can destroy an otherwise positive relationship. Dr. Rosenberg said, "A lot of older men don't think they're allowed to fail once in a while. They have a couple of unfortunate episodes and assume it's all over. They have to get over that before we can help them."

Sometimes, younger wives of men experiencing trouble can't deal with the responsibility of lifting their older husband's or lover's spirits. Sadly, "The subject is so touchy that often nothing is said," says Dr. Carol C. Flax, a psychologist in Manhattan who works with younger women/older men couples. She has found that the wives tend to internalize this issue and assume they have to mend this. She said, "Women feel as if they have to be the great fixers." But Dr. Flax is adamant that a woman must be told, over and over again, his problems are *not* all her fault. "It is not

her responsibility to deal with this," she said. "It's a couple problem that becomes *our* problem and has to be addressed in couple
therapy."

Not all potency problems are pathological. An older husband
may experience trouble when he becomes anxious about generation differences—particularly when a younger woman matures
and begins to assert herself, producing a power play. Dr. Flax
explained, "She may unexpectedly not defer to him anymore and
speak up. He may not be able to deal with that, especially if he's
been treating her like a little doll for all those years. And if he's
out of touch with a lot of things his younger wife does and thinks
about, he's going to be upset in the bedroom, too."

Lovemaking can be extremely unsatisfying when the older
husband's difficulty performing becomes the focus of the relationship. A younger woman will have a hard time dealing with
her lover's withdrawal of tenderness as his self-esteem sinks to its
lowest ebb. Dr. Avodah K. Offit, a New York psychiatrist and
author of *Virtual Love* and *Night Thoughts: Reflections of a Sex
Therapist,* says, "Often the older man's only real problem is not
diminished potency itself but the fear of it." Unfortunately, this
apprehension may destroy a marvelous relationship. If the couple
wants to remain together and everything else is good, this is the
time the *couple* should seek professional help.

A younger woman will need a great deal of patience and
understanding. In return for her helping him conquer his anxiety, their love affair will take on a more meaningful dimension.
He will love and appreciate her more. Sex therapist Offit points
out, "A warm, supportive, understanding woman can deepen the
man's love for her." Passion will take a new turn—devotion.

On the lighter side, W.O.O.M.ies tell me a lot of their older
husbands changed wives because their lessening sexual desires
didn't satisfy their husband's sexual appetite. Sometimes, these
men are so vigorous the young wives have a hard time keeping
up. Like me!

❧ *Chivalry* ❦

In general, older husbands are far more attuned to women's needs because they have enjoyed spending a great deal of their lives obliging them. They are acutely aware of menstrual period depression and PMS symptoms, the feminine mystique, and reading between the lines. For a traditional woman, an older man is the answer. He's the kind of man who is offended if you want to split the tab. He'll help you with your coat and open your car door. Experience has taught him how to get a positive reaction.

You can't beat an older husband's pride in his younger wife. There's nothing he won't do to make her happy. I remember Sam freezing as he watched me train, hour after hour, for the 1976 World Professional Figure Skating Championships in Jaca, Spain. Never complaining and always encouraging, he drove me to Lake Placid and all around to work with the best coaches. He was so proud of me. Because many older husbands feel positive about themselves and the changes that have made their lives happier, they are a lot more giving.

The right older husband is excited to share in his younger wife's good fortune. He'll encourage her to reach for goals she may not have had the courage to try alone. John Crocker, an older husband who prints my newsletters, boasted to me that his wife, Anita, thirty-one years his junior, had recently completed a master's program in communications. He laughed, "I want to quit, and she's just beginning. There go my retirement travel plans! That's okay. I'm investing in my future. Someday, my wife might be supporting me!"

One of the most charming and special older husbands I ever met was retired United States Army Colonel Lou Reinken. Lou, a West Point graduate, divorced his first wife and married Renate Haas, a West German couturiere, while serving as an aide-decamp to the chief of staff in Stuttgart. It was truly a match made in heaven as Lou doted on Renate, seventeen years his junior. He was her biggest fan and encouraged her to start a dressmaking business when they moved to New Jersey in 1975. Over the years, she became very successful, outfitting some of New Jersey's most prominent women.

Everyone knew how much Lou worshiped Renate. They enjoyed an affectionate love affair that lasted until Lou died unexpectedly, in January, 1993, at the age of sixty-five. Renate was devastated but will always remember the kind and devoted years she shared with Lou. During a W.O.O.M. television taping, Renate was asked by Geraldo Rivera if she was a trophy wife. She said, "No, I don't think so. I have a trophy husband!" And indeed she did.

At times, there may be some confusion relating to the generation gap, but in general such problems are minor. Many men brag that they have newfangled wives who are out and about doing their own thing because they know her energy stokes the home fire and keeps him alert and interesting. Older men who are successful in their relationships with younger women like being a part of the new scene. They want to share in everything she does. However, the tricky part is that at times, their caring can smother a young wife. Wanting desperately to hold on to their lucky break, many get caught up in a power and control issue.

❧ *Control* ❦

Older husbands are generally more self-centered than husbands nearer in age to their wives. Often the older men overstep boundaries. While they do encourage their younger wives to express themselves, they also hold her back with excessive control. At their stage of life, they are not shy about verbalizing what they want. Additionally, it's going to be up to younger wives to compromise to keep the relationship on an even keel.

Younger wives are also expected to handle the emotional issues of the relationship just as the first wife did, but tack onto that the unfriendly excess baggage that comes along with the divorce and remarriage and the future can look ominous. Many oldsters use their age as if being older gives them the right to wield power over their younger wives.

"Both Bob and I are very strong-willed people," says Linda Smith, a twenty-year-younger wife from Manhattan Beach, California. "We're both chiefs, so when one of the chiefs is a lot older, guess who gets to be the Indian?"

Yet, as these May/December marriages progress, sometimes, there is a reversal of roles or a shift in power. The man, who initially was the leading character and planner of the family events, can find himself after a few years with a very confident wife at his side. No longer in awe of him, she now speaks her mind and makes her own decisions—and decisions for him, too. This change in the balance of power may make our husbands anxious. And that may have him pulling in the reins of power.

In the back of a lot of men's minds is the fear that their younger wives will leave them for a younger man. And take his money with her. Or worse yet, kill him for his insurance policy! As in the case of wealthy, fifty-four-year-old, Brooke Lennon whose twenty-three-year-old topless dancer wife, Michelle, and her tattoo-adorned boyfriend, Robert Tomassi, twenty-five, were arrested and charged with bludgeoning him to death with a baseball bat. Of course, this is the extreme; but Lennon paid the highest price to keep watch over his wife. Knowing she was fooling around, he was planning to move in with them just before they allegedly killed him.

One of my employees who sold my cosmetics at Bloomingdale's is a woman in her late fifties. She has been married for many years to a very powerful executive twenty-five years older than she. Now that he is bedridden, Myrna* occasionally goes out with girl friends or to local charity events by herself. When

I saw her last summer, she mentioned that as she leaves the house, her husband frets so much about the dangers of driving in their exclusive neighborhood that she's developing a phobia. Instilling fear is a control tool that many men use when they see their younger wives becoming independent. It's especially prevalent among those who recognize their lives are nearing the end. Clawing possessiveness, wanting to be with their wives every minute, is another control mechanism of a senior older man.

Younger older men have control agendas, also. There are those who are used to getting their own way when their partner is a capitulating younger woman who feels less powerful and assertive because she is inexperienced and in awe. He suppresses her assertiveness with negative opinions. This is particularly obvious when she expresses her desire to have babies, redecorate his house, get a job, or simply pay a visit to her friends.

Then there are wealthy, demanding older men who pay for the privilege of being married to a beautiful young woman who was attracted to his position. They expect a high-quality return— and don't want to be disappointed. These women are treated as badges to be worn frequently and kept highly polished at all times. They're expected to attend to his every beck and call.

Older men regard catching, dating, bedding, and marrying a younger woman a ticket to longevity. The thrill for many is molding an impressionable, but quick learning, younger woman into their version of the ultimate woman. Having a perpetual protégée is exhilarating, however the thrill can fade quickly. For some older men, once the challenge has been met, and he finds he's created another version of himself, he ends up hating it and goes on to another. Actress Linda Day George, who appeared with the late Telly Savalas, a notorious womanizer of young ladies, in a 1973 television movie observed, "When Telly finally finds it isn't necessary to conquer every woman he meets, he'll begin to enjoy life."

❧ Trading Up ❧

According to Sally Cunningham, a demographer at the National Center for Health Statistics, there is a slight trend toward the younger bride–older groom marriage. About 15 percent of 1986 marriages involved a man at least eight years older, up from about 13 percent in 1976. Remarriages are up, also, and as grooms get older, the age difference between spouses grows because many men like to cast in a pool of sweet young things the second or third time around.

Trading up is even more evident among those who were nerds in high school, those who couldn't get a date and metamorphosed years later into successful, powerful individuals. Many of them feel burdened by what they consider to be boring, presuccess wives who remind them of the days when things weren't so wonderful. She lived his shortcomings, and this guy wants to drop her like a hot potato! Particularly now that his money and status can buy the homecoming queen who wouldn't give him a second look twenty years ago!

It's a real ego trip. Judi Wolf, the "generation" younger, second wife of Marvin Wolf, owner of Denver's Wolf Energy, told the *Rocky Mountain News*, "A successful man often looks for a woman who makes him feel like a king."

During my interview with Sheldon Linz, he said, "In high school I was a pimply kid with a big nose. No one would give me a second look. When I was twenty, I married a woman that I met when I was fifteen. She was right for me then, but once my pimples cleared up and my nose grew into my face, I discovered women were attracted to me."

For Sheldon it was a new adventure. He was rediscovering himself and liked what he saw. He said, "I couldn't get enough of that, and that's when the affairs began. My former wife was no longer stimulating to me. It wasn't her fault, it was mine."

❧ *When At First You Don't Succeed...* ❦

Sam serves on the New Jersey State Board of Dentistry with Dr. Arnold Graham, who has had a succession of young wives, girl friends, and fiancees. He is a distinguished and handsome black dentist—a respected professor at the New Jersey College of Medicine and Dentistry and is well thought of by his peers and the community.

Being an exceptional catch, it's easy to see why each woman Arnold dates is more beautiful and younger than the next. One day, I jokingly asked him what was the attraction? Arnold bashfully laughed and said, "I often ask myself that same question. In the beginning, they were the aggressors, and the attraction is that they were attracted to me. Not that once started, the feelings weren't mutual, but they pursued the relationship."

However, I wondered, why the high failure rate? It intrigued me that such a stable individual couldn't get his marital act together. After all, his first wife, only a couple of years younger than him, was a successful superintendent of schools. Selecting progressively younger wives thereafter, Arnold's second wife was a psychiatric social worker, the third a beauty queen and lawyer. Not so bad.

Delving further, I wanted to know if searching for a nonexistent perfect woman broke up all these love affairs. He said, "I need someone who is emotionally in my corner because that is what I give and demand in return. I had two exceptional situations in my life—my mother and my father's marriage and my sister and brother-in-law's marriage that let me know what it could be. It made me want to search out the very same thing for me until I got it right."

Curious, I wanted to know why he continually chose wrong. I asked Arnold if he was looking only on the outside of the package rather than seeking a woman with substance. He said, "With one or two of them, it was emotional, maybe superficial. With the other two, it was hard cold figuring. I sized her up. Good family plus nice upbringing equals good wife. But I figured wrong. In each failing situation, I thought my younger wife understood my needs, but she didn't. After I was married, I felt as though I was thrown in the corner when they paid more attention to their children from earlier marriages or careers."

He said, "You know, people change after you marry them. It's not always for the better. What I divorced was what I wound up with, not what I married." It was obvious to me that Arnold wanted these younger women's undivided attention and just couldn't get his point across.

Later on in the conversation, I asked Dr. Graham about the younger women he didn't marry. He told me that after his initial two marriages failed, he was committed to raising his son and didn't want to subject him to any more emotional hassle. He remained single for seventeen years. But his devotion to his son cost him personally. During those years, he cast away one or two women he was more in love and deeply involved with than some of his wives. But he stuck to his personal pledge and purposely dated women he never intended to marry. He explained, "They were usually young, mostly white, and not interested in marriage. In fact two of them were Playboy bunnies! Because I was busy raising my son, I only had a certain amount of time to be with them. I was only interested in playing—going on the boat, fast cars, etc."

Sometimes Arnold's honesty became a challenge. Even though he made it perfectly clear to many of his girl friends he wasn't playing games about not wanting to get married, some of them thought they could change his mind. They heard his warning, but they didn't listen. In one situation, he was dating a woman, fifteen years his junior, with whom he was very much in love; but she wanted children and he didn't. He felt he was too old for that, and most of their arguments were about his not wanting babies. At one point, she gambled the relationship. She went off the pill and became pregnant. Knowing he didn't want children, she got an abortion without telling him. What broke up the love affair was not that she became pregnant but that he was deprived of being involved with the decision. He thought he was intimately in love, and even if they ended up with the same result, she did all of this behind his back.

A few months ago, Arnold married his fourth wife, a thirty-five-year-old woman, twenty-five years his junior, who majored in business. She is the daughter of a good friend who asked Arnold before he died to look after her. Arnold remembers, "In the beginning I looked upon her as a kid, but when she entered her thirties, I saw her in a different way and fell in love when she asked me to marry her."

I asked him, what do you think is different with this marriage? He said, "I don't need a woman to cook, to clean, or look after me anymore. I can do all of that for myself—maybe even better. I need a woman who will take care of the other things— the emotional stuff, keep me young and stimulated. She seems to understand that."

❧ Sometimes It Can Backfire ❧

Being involved with a younger women can have its downside. Restauranteur and philanthropist, Joe Amiel, owner of the Spring Lake, New Jersey, Old Mill Inn says, "I've been involved in a lot of those relationships. None of them have really worked out well for me."

He pointed to one reason why. "Above all, I don't think I gave it a chance to work." He explained that he felt safe with these women, knowing he wasn't likely to marry someone so young. Almost as if just realizing it himself, Joe said, "It wasn't a conscious decision. I kind of subtly led them on without literally leading them on." Feeling badly, he admits, "This was totally unfair on my part. They went into it much more open-minded and reasonable about it all than me. I just didn't emotionally give them a chance."

A few years ago, Amiel was quite serious with a younger woman, twenty-two years his junior. In fact, they lived together. He told me that at that time, he was vulnerable and felt he was ripe to nurture someone. "I'm not sure why it happened. I knew it wouldn't work. And it was my fault for letting it continue."

When he tried to break it off, his girl friend wouldn't let him. Even though he was bored with the love affair, he said, "Her will was so strong, I felt it necessary to give it a chance." In a way, he felt he was being taken advantage of—manipulated and used. "It was perplexing, I felt I was more like a father to her." Despite the paternal undertone, he said, "I can't say there wasn't a lot of feeling there, because there was, but I was more angry with myself for continuing a relationship where we didn't relate to each other."

Joe realizes, now, that he enjoys his freedom of being single and doesn't feel threatened by being alone—because he never is alone. He has also come to the conclusion he is more comfortable with women in their mid-thirties and forties who've seen a bit more of life. "I can handle a ten-year, maybe twelve-year difference in age," he says. "However, I don't have the same needs to be taken care of as many other men." He explained, if he is hungry, he goes to his restaurant to eat. His secretary pays his bills and schedules his appointments. When he is lonely, which is seldom, he goes to his restaurant where he finds people he knows and is always meeting new people. In Joe's opinion, "A lot of people get married because they pursue life as if they should be married." In contrast, Joe, a handsome, extremely desirable bachelor, who just turned fifty, admits having so much available to him makes being single much easier.

When I asked him about children, he said, "That's the rub." Admitting that at some point in his life, he would have liked to have had children, Joe said, "You give up something. You give up other things, too."

I suggested that in time, when he was ready—had partied and played enough—perhaps he would find a wonderful woman, younger or maybe not so young. For a moment Joe was pensive, then he said, "I think you may be right. That sounds about right."

Statistics show that the chance of divorce is greatly reduced when men marry for the first time over the age of forty-five. Perhaps taking the time to know themselves, know what they want in a woman, and not feeling pressured to marry at a young age would lower the divorce rate.

❧ *"The Johnny Syndrome"* ❦

*A*s some men age, I find it increasingly more apparent that they confuse their fantasies with reality in searching out the perfect mate. Some want a demigoddess who will stop the age clock, but find it difficult to comprehend that physical perfection does not guarantee emotional devotion. I worry when some trade in wives continually, others seek out lover after lover while still married, and a few bachelor diehards leave a trail of unhappy candidates in the wake of their quest. Could it be the pinup, dream-girl expectation makes it impossible for these men to ever find a woman to fulfill their needs?

While they were just barely in their thirties, director John Derek divorced two beautiful younger wives—actresses Ursula Andress and Linda Evans—before he created and directed his perfect "10," Bo Derek. She was twenty-two, thirty years his junior. However, his age-defying, still-gorgeous Bo worries fifteen years later, "He's never been with a woman as old as I am. He likes me to have opinions and talk back, but sometimes when I do, he'll threaten to go down to the high school and look around."

Years ago, I coined the expression "Johnny Syndrome." It came to mind when I realized that men like John Barrymore, whose third wife was less than half his age and fourth wife was just nineteen, Johnny Carson, and John Derek sported around with new, younger wives seemingly at regular intervals.

The syndrome describes men who are never satisfied with present wives and continually trade them in for younger ones. "Johnny Syndrome" is a label I use for men who have no notion of what is best for them when selecting a mate. Or, it could cover those who may not be able to emotionally handle the intimacy it takes to make a marriage work. Once their spouse gets to know them too well, they flee the coop.

Recently, I was touched by the poignancy of an article written by *Vanity Fair*'s Elizabeth Richardson on pop artist, Roy Lichtenstein. She said a lot about what I think is happening to men in search of feminine excellence and why their relationships fail.

She wrote, "Lichtenstein's women seem to get more perfect every year but even more detached." As Lichtenstein reaches seventy, and his women come of age, "None of that beauty that appears in his work is real." Richardson describes it as the classic twentieth-century artists' malady, the inability to express feelings directly. "These new women don't say anything. It is an evocation of an entirely fictional femininity, drawn secondhand from a presentation of beauty so common and codified that it's lifeless and cold." We might ask, is it an affliction that describes what is happening to some twentieth-century older men who are attracted to a certain type of woman for all of the wrong reasons?

This article prompted me to call West Los Angeles psychologist Dr. Stephan Tobin. He treats successful Hollywood film and entertainment folks who have a really high profile. Knowing that a high percentage of these people's love affairs end in disappointment and marriages in divorce, I questioned him as to what motivates them to be in constant search of the perfect woman.

Tobin said, "This type of man is usually somebody who feels very imperfect himself. As children, I find a lot of them never got a lot of praise, even when doing well. Even though this kind of person is usually very perfectionistic himself and generally quite successful, he is encumbered by his feelings of inadequacy. So in order to feel good about himself, he seeks a beautiful talented woman—an icon—who will make him feel okay. However, in many cases, he's disillusioned in a very short time."

Dr. Tobin said these men tend to go from woman to woman. Because the bulk of them are rich and powerful, beautiful women are at their disposal. It doesn't give them very much motivation to look inside themselves. He told me they seldom give up because they would be very depressed if they did. However, if they faced their feelings of shame and inadequacy, he said, "They might get over this and enjoy a good relationship. The unfortunate thing is that many are equally as perfectionistic about their therapists, and they are tough to work with. It's a big challenge for me to treat a guy who is on a pedestal."

❧ *I Found Her!* ❦

A few pages ago, I briefly introduced you to the former Sheldon Linz. Later in our interview, I met the new Sheldon Linz.

"Do you believe in love at first sight?" he asked. I said, "Yes, but it's dangerous because it is so compelling." He laughed and said, "You got that right! From the first moment I was introduced to Jennifer, and she put her arm on mine, I couldn't believe the warmth. It didn't matter that I was with someone else or that I was in the process of dating four or five other women. I fell in love with her that moment...I couldn't get her off my mind...I was oblivious to anyone, anything except to my thoughts about Jennifer. About three months later, I called her. We went on our first date. Afterward, when I kissed her, bells went off. They still do!

Nobody else mattered, and I never dated another person. Her bub-bliness, enthusiasm, and freshness was so exciting. And it hasn't changed, and it's been eleven years."

But Sheldon, you were such a womanizer. Remember the woman in every port? The guy who cheated on his wife for twenty years, and she didn't care as long as you came home? The man who needed a secretary to sort out his love affairs around the country?

"Oh, but I've changed," came his response. "I would never ever, ever, *ever* cheat on Jenny. The thought has never entered my mind. I'll never find anybody like her again."

I chuckled in disbelief. "R-e-a-l-l-y? Tell me about it."

And he did! When he was finished, I fell in love with his compassion and caring as well. Just talking with Sheldon gave me a positive feeling about love and deep commitment. When Sheldon and Jennifer, who is twenty-two years younger than he is, were married for a few years, she started changing. Sheldon said, " I didn't know why. I knew she was a survivor and that she was sexually abused as a child, but I couldn't relate to that. I'd never been around anyone whose father had ever done anything like this. I came from such a nice family."

The relationship got to the point where it was affecting them sexually. Sheldon said as much as he tried, he didn't know how to sympathize with Jenny's problems. Things got pretty tough. So much so, they both thought they might have to break up. Sheldon explained, "When Jennifer would start to have flash-backs, I didn't understand. I couldn't comprehend that someone would ever hurt a child. Therefore, I wasn't able to handle the deep-rooted hurt, emotional pain, and distrust she was experi-encing. It was over my head."

After awhile to save the marriage, Sheldon and Jennifer decided to go to couple therapy. They had to learn how to dis-cuss this problem.

"But you don't realize what I had to go through to get myself to that point," said Sheldon. "I was very macho and thought only sick people went to therapy. But I loved Jennifer so much that I was willing to put one-hundred-and-ten percent into this relationship—something I have never done before with any woman."

During couple therapy, Sheldon realized he had a lot of things inside himself he had to work on and began to see the therapist alone. He says, "I've been going about a year now. It's been great. It's unreal—the healthy thing to do when things aren't all right. Before Jennifer, I never would have considered it. Never.

"I used to pull rank," says Sheldon. "I thought older men should dominate and be in control. I was an unbelievable male chauvinist pig. I tried to do that with Jennifer, but she would never let me get away with it. Before seeing a counselor, that bothered me. Now in looking back, I should have realized she was no ordinary woman."

I smiled as Sheldon rattled off Jennifer's list of accomplishments. He was like a little kid with a new toy. Proudly, he told me she had straight As in college and was first in her class. "In fact, after an internship at NBC, they created a job for her upon graduation. That's how badly they wanted her." Continuing, he said, "She's bright. But I had to learn how to deal with that kind of woman. Now, when she tells me like it is, I listen and ninety-five percent of the time, she's right."

Sheldon told me if I had spoken to him a year ago, before he began therapy, I would have found him a totally different person. He talked about how couple therapy has brought them so much closer. He said, "Just the fact that I was willing to do it has helped me so much."

Their relationship has taken on a new dimension. He pointed out, "I was always a workaholic. I never took time off from work. Now, I can't wait to go on vacation and be with Jennifer. The other night I was watching a Mel Gibson movie, *Forever Young*, the one with Jamie Lee Curtis. I shocked even myself, I was crying like a baby. I used up two handkerchiefs! Before Jennifer and therapy, I would never have cried at movies. I wouldn't have felt secure enough to show my emotions."

You see—it's never too late!

A Compendium of May/December Marriage Issues

❧ Your Mom Won't Speak to Him, Your Dad Won't Let Him in the House ❧

No matter how old we are, how successful we are in our jobs, or how secure we are with others, every child seeks parental acceptance. Even when we are grown and become parents or grandparents ourselves, our moms and dads can reduce us to sniveling nitwits with their disapproval. Under normal circumstances, we quickly get over it. But, when daughters marry older men, their parents' negativity toward the relationship can permanently damage the parent/child bond.

Younger women involved with older men confront their parents with a strange set of circumstances. A few parents will be delighted, while other moms and dads have mixed emotions. After all, in traditional pairings, our children marry people similar in age to themselves. The parents are the *older* generation.

Here is a situation where the child's mate may be as old—or older—than the parent!

Many parents find the age difference confusing. This man is not a child, but to them, their daughter is. All kinds of strange things go on in their heads. Some women say their distressed parents deny the relationship. "You can visit, but don't bring him!" Others say that a cold war is their parents' way of dealing with it. "Don't come back until you get rid of him!"

Rather than cope with it, a lot of parents choose to ignore the older male friend. Thinking the affair is a passing fancy, those upset parents will not allow the older male friend's name to be mentioned in their presence. They will never ask about his well-being. Younger women, in this situation, tell me their parents pray to God it's a phase—a bad dream that will go away if there is no interaction. Unfortunately, their rejection disrupts family harmony.

Some parents worry their parental doctrines will be undermined by a suitor who is similar in age or older than they are. It can turn into a real power play if this man usurps their influence. Margo Johnson*, a flight attendant from Phoenix said, "My mom and dad didn't find it just unacceptable, they were hateful. I fell in love with Jimmy* while I was married to another man. Even though my parents knew I was miserably married, they were despondent that I had left what seemed like to them a perfectly good marriage to marry someone thirty-three years older. I had embarrassed them in front of their church and friends by marrying this *old* man. We didn't talk for years."

A lot of W.O.O.M.ies tell me their parents have refused to attend their weddings. Others say if they do show up, their disapproving body language ruins the day for them.

Christine Parker*, a schoolteacher from Des Moines, said, "Chuck* and I were married twice." After many attempts to convince her parents how much she and Chuck, a high-school principal, twenty-eight years her senior, were in love, Christine's parents still refused to accept their engagement.

She said, "Knowing we couldn't change their minds, we were married in a judge's chambers, without family and friends, on Valentine's Day." Two years later, her parents realized they had made a big mistake and had lost their daughter. Brushing pride aside, Christine's parents turned around and made a church wedding and large reception for her and Chuck.

"I didn't know until two weeks before my wedding if my parents would come," says Anna Carson*, a pediatrician and twenty-three-year younger wife from Philadelphia. She was distraught. This was her wedding day! Her brother intervened and convinced their parents they would live to regret it if they didn't go. Reluctantly, they went. But even the morning of the wedding, they refused to speak to Joseph*. Anna said, "During the reception, they slipped out of every photo being taken if Joseph was going to be in it."

"But why?" I asked.

"Joseph and my father, a Holocaust survivor, just didn't hit it off from the very beginning," Anna said. "Joseph believes the Holocaust was a despicable ordeal to endure. However, one should live for the future, not dwell in the past. My dad, who talks about it on a daily basis, felt Joseph belittled his pain."

Anna told me her father created all kinds of conflicts. Her dad was so hurt by Joseph's lack of understanding, it was tough for him to even believe Joseph was Jewish. "His gentile last name troubled dad," says Anna. "But more bothersome to him was Joseph's involvement with alternative spiritual philosophies."

Anna met Joseph at a yoga center in Los Angeles and really got into Mahikari, a spiritual energy group. Her dad thought this older demagogue was taking advantage of his young, impressionable daughter. "He thought Joseph was diluting my Jewish upbringing and messing up my head," says Anna. "He also thought that at Joseph's stage in life, he should have been a lot more successful." Anna further explained that her father really wanted her to marry a doctor.

"It wasn't until I asserted myself that we started to get somewhere," says Anna. "I also realized I had to tune into my parents' life for them to understand me better. I refused to allow any more 'How's the weather?' conversation. I began to take a bigger interest in their daily routine. But I was firm and insisted my parents inquire about Joseph and accept the fact that he's my husband in return."

For a moment during the interview, Anna was quiet, then revealed, "Although we have reconciled, and my parents are trying harder, weeks before Joseph and I plan a visit to them in Wisconsin, I still get butterflies and stomachaches."

When Nancy Murphy*, a registered nurse married her husband, Robert*, a surgeon thirty years her senior, at Tulsa's county courthouse, she wore a white gown, carried a bouquet, and went to the photographer—like all other brides. The difference was that no one came to the reception. She and Robert were all alone at a table for two. A week later, she called to tell her mother she was married. Her mom's remark was blunt. "I'm so sorry to hear you married him. A bullet is too good for Robert's head!"

Sam and I made our parents very unhappy future in-laws. I delivered my mom and dad a triple whammy. Not only was Sam older and unimpressed by my parent's age superiority, he was divorced with two children and Jewish. None of which was something mom wanted to brag about at bridge club! Twenty-three years ago, interfaith marriages weren't as commonplace as they are today. When I told my mom I was going to marry Sam, her first words to me were, "What will Dr. Meister [our minister] say?"

I hadn't given it much thought. And frankly, I didn't give a damn! However, by the time our wedding day arrived, it was obvious, both sets of parents had given it a great *deal* of thought and neither family was very happy.

Sam's father, Sol, an unbending, old-school physician, was totally impossible. He treated me as if I were a child. Unable to control his emotions and loss of authority over Sam, he verbally attacked us at our reception. Sol reduced me to tears, and I spent most of my wedding crying. No one had ever married a gentile in his family. It was the judge who married us that was the kicker. Because of his full beard, he looked rather rabbi-ish to me. And we intentionally chose a Jewish judge to lessen Sol's anxieties; but to no avail. Worse, what we *thought* would work for one set of parents, created problems with the other. It was a Catch-22.

Even though she didn't say it, I knew having a judge officiate bothered my Protestant mom. She kept referring to him as the rabbi. But I give her credit. She did manage to curb her feelings. Although my parents did not participate in any of the wedding plans, I'm luckier than most wives of older men. My parents didn't burn bridges. My father walked me down the aisle, and my whole family, in whatever state of mind, was with me for my special day.

Needless to say, it would be much nicer if I could look back on our wedding as a happy occasion. It did have a bittersweet twist though. Sam's dad eventually turned around. He deeply appreciated how I cared for Laurie and Jill, and we developed respect for each other. By the time he died, several years later, he felt really positive about our marriage. In fact we named our son, Sean, for him.

As for my family, for several years, I never felt comfortable around them when I was with Sam. Because I had lived away from my parents' influence for so long, I always deferred to him. There was an evident, but unspoken, undercurrent of competition. A few years after we were married, Sam and I went to an eightieth birthday party for my Grandmother McMaster. We felt like outsiders. Even my brother Bing and his wife, Ann, were distant.

I realized I was forcing Sam and me on these people. Sam was upset, but I decided to sever the relationship and stopped all communication. I was so torn up over their attitude that I felt like an alien. I sought professional help to cope. I learned that I had to be happy for me. And while my parents' and family's acceptance was important, I couldn't control how they felt and shouldn't even try. They were entitled to their opinions. However, holidays were especially lonesome, and I missed my dad terribly.

Five years later, when Ashley was born, I sent an announcement to my entire family. Much to my surprise, they were very excited and came to a party Sam and I gave to show off our new baby. Since then we have developed a lovely relationship. Our children's grandparents are proud as punch, and it's nice that we're together again.

But this was only after I came to the painful realization that I had to distance myself from my family in order to accept their shortcomings, intolerance, and reproach. I needed to become a separate entity—a Furman. During that time, I even changed my, never-used, first name from Margaret to Beliza. For professional reasons, I was advised by a publicist to find an upscale, foreign-sounding name for my cosmetic company that could also, be adopted by me, similar to what Estee Lauder had done years earlier. I changed my first name, without as much as a glance back, emphasizing further how important it was for me to live a life of my own.

My experience taught me that children and parents shouldn't take each other for granted. We may be related genetically, but we're not joined at the hip. For me, time was a great healer.

On behalf of W.O.O.M., Sandy Grappel and I appeared on the *CBS This Morning* show with another W.O.O.M.ie, Jamie Johnson, whose husband was twenty-seven years older. Sandy and I were describing to Erin Moriarity how much fun the support group had been for all of us. Not that each one of us didn't have a reason for joining. But we considered ourselves to be part of an elite club. Jamie took it much more seriously and interjected, "I come to this group from a different standpoint. I come with a lot of pain. My husband and I were in a situation of being ostracized."

My heart went out for Jamie. You could see the anguish in her eyes when she said, "For instance, no one came to our wedding. No one wished us happiness—they thought it wouldn't work. I *need* the support I have received from W.O.O.M. It has been tremendous."

Julie Reinhart*, an accountant from Oklahoma City, took a great deal of abuse from her parents when she announced her pending marriage to Scott*. Knowing her parents would be upset, Julie, who was twenty-four, lied about her fiancé's age. He was thirty-eight; she told them he was thirty-six. Even with the lie, they felt he was too old. On top of that, he was divorced with two children which in and of itself would have made him totally unacceptable.

Julie responded to a questionnaire I sent out to W.O.O.M. subscribers that asked, "Did your parents have a problem with (or are they still upset with) your relationship or marriage to an older man?" Choosing to write it all down, Julie replied, "I can't tell you how often my mother cried about this. She constantly repeated her disappointment by telling me I would never be happy with Scott. That we would never have anything of our own, and all of his money would be spent on child-support payments."

Julie and her mom went round and round. As hard as she tried to persuade her mom that Scott didn't pay alimony and that *she* respected the fact he paid child support in lieu of all the deadbeat dads around, her mom was unyielding. "Particularly because," says Julie, "I wouldn't tell her why Scott and his wife divorced."

"For a while," Julie wrote, "I kept my mother (my father wasn't happy, but not as distraught as my mother) at bay by telling her it was none of their business why Scott and his wife got a divorce. Reflecting back that was probably a mistake because the reason was easy to understand: they simply grew apart and stopped communicating. My obstinacy probably piqued her curiosity because she made stabs in the dark. In fact, at one point she was so frustrated she surmised Scott was gay!

"After we were married," continued Julie, "my mother tried as hard as she could not to like Scott. She told me I was breaking her heart." When it came to choosing between Scott and her mother, "Mom lost."

I called Julie and asked how her husband felt. She said, "Scott hung in there. He was really supportive. And never said anything bad about my parents."

Eventually, Julie's mom started to come around. "Slowly but surely, my parents recognized how good Scott was for me," says a very relieved Julie. "They saw that he was a sweet person and had a very likable personality. Scott won them over completely. Now, when we visit my mother, she often kisses Scott before me!"

Julie feels any rift that came between her and her mother has healed. She assumes her mom still harbors some doubts but is happy she can get on with her marriage without the tension of parental disfavor. Assured, Julie said, "My mother loves Scott now, and we're developing a good relationship."

After speaking to several W.O.O.M.ies about their parents' reactions, I wanted to find a mother who would be honest and talk with me about her misgivings. I called Abigail Hayden*, a cosmetic buyer for one of the department stores I dealt with in Southern California. Her daughter, Lindsey*, thirty-three, married a man nineteen years older than she.

Abigail said, "At first, we were worried because we knew Peter* had two sons from a previous marriage. We thought he wouldn't want to have any more children. But on the other hand, we were concerned that he would die and leave her alone to care for a family by herself."

I asked Abigail if she liked her daughter's husband? She said, "Yes. Oh yes, we liked him, but we just didn't think he was good for Lindsey. He was a born-again Christian, and we are Episcopalian. The religious difference didn't upset us so much, we were just unsure he would fit in."

I asked Abigail if she tried to persuade Lindsey to break up with Peter when they were dating. She said, "At the beginning we did, but we learned from a younger daughter, whose husband is Mexican, that had worked against us, and she married him anyway. So we didn't push too hard."

I was really proud of Abigail's sincerity. She seemed able to cut the apron strings, curb her opinions, and maintain a loving relationship with her daughter. She admits to being worried but realizes her children have lives of their own.

At the end of our conversation, I asked, "Now that your daughter has been married for the past seven years and she has a new baby, how do you feel about the marriage?" She said, "Lindsey has matured very fast. She used to be funny and outgoing—now, she appears more serious. I am concerned that she and Peter spend a lot of their time together alone. They don't seem to have many friends. I think the age difference makes it difficult for them to fit in."

Jennifer Stanfield*, a W.O.O.M.ie from Dalton, Georgia, is an articulate woman, mature beyond her years. She fell in love with her forty-six-year-old high-school teacher, a widower, when she was nineteen. The attraction started while she was still in school, but the love affair took place after her graduation. Three years ago, she and Allen* became engaged but have never discussed it with her family. Allen is forbidden to visit Jennifer at her home; his name is not allowed to be spoken under her father's roof. She says, "My father refers to me as the family whore!"

"It's a happy but unhappy time," says Jennifer. "No one talks about our engagement around my father, who thinks if everyone ignores the affair, I will eventually come to my senses, it will fizzle out."

Jennifer regrets that her dad doesn't trust Allen's intentions. She told me her father thinks Allen has stolen her from him and regards their love affair as immoral. To point out just how upset her father is, Jennifer said, "My dad's a real macho man who was raised in the tough part of town. Despite that, when I mentioned Allen once, he cried—real tears! When I tell him we have set a wedding date, he's going to come crashing out of denial. I can just picture him shackling my ankles...restraining me!"

I found all of this hard to believe. Jennifer made her dad sound like he was W.O.O.M.'s worst case of parental disapproval. But as she continued, I realized she wasn't exaggerating.

Out of respect for her strict Southern Baptist upbringing, Jennifer has chosen to remain living with her parents. She said, "I don't want all of this to come back to haunt me. It's also giving me the opportunity to work on my relationship with my mom who is coming around to accepting Allen."

Her dad ignores the engagement ring, the dozen roses she received on Valentine's Day, and the many phone calls. After work, weekends, and holidays, Jennifer visits Allen at his home. Once or twice a year, they go on vacation but going away together only adds fuel to the fire. Jennifer chuckled, "When dad sees me packing my bags, he says, 'I can't believe you're going to go shack up with that *old* man!'"

With everything going against them, Jennifer and Allen have spent many hours in couple therapy dealing with the age issue and her parents' rejection. They have resolved many of their concerns and feel ready to pursue their future. It hasn't been easy for either of them. Each has paid a heavy price to be together. Read on, this saga only gets worse!

From the very beginning, Jennifer's father, an archconservative, has been unrelenting. Initially when he learned that Jennifer lied and wasn't dating Allen's son but him, he went to the school board and insisted they take Allen's job away. Jennifer was so frightened, she called the superintendent and went through an inquiry assuring them that Allen hadn't violated her. When her parents were unsuccessful in getting Allen fired, they had their attorney draw up a document for Allen to sign that stated he wouldn't see Jennifer anymore. "Of course," Jennifer says, "we tore it up."

"I've put Allen through a lot," Jennifer lamented. "He's had to deal with my phases of misgiving. It's been quite a journey. I've grown up a lot, though." She confided, "I'm going to have butterflies when I tell my father that I'm getting married. And I won't believe everything will be all right until I have every last article of mine out of that house. I know my dad won't come to the wedding, but years later, if he wants to see his grandchildren, he's first going to have to show respect to their father. If he doesn't, he's never going to see them. I'm going to make that very clear."

Susan Snyder's* father cost her a baby! At nineteen, she and Jonathon*, her optometrist and lover, eighteen years her senior, were careless, and Susan became pregnant. She and Jonathon wanted that baby more than anything, but Susan feared for Jonathon. Her father hated him. He was too old, the son of an arch rival, and she was in college.

She said, "I'm not sure what violence my father was capable of, but I knew I couldn't carry that baby to term. My dad has a really mean temper; I was just too frightened."

Susan and Jonathon decided to have an abortion. She told me that they both cried but knew if there was any chance of her father's acceptance of their marriage plans, this was not the way to start off. Suppressing tears as she spoke to me, Susan admitted, "I was scared and resentful. I don't think Jonathon and I will ever get over it."

So what do you do? You've fallen in love with a much older man. You've thought it out, weighed the pros and cons. You can't imagine life without him. Do you elope? Or try to persuade mom and dad it's going to work? Although I am not a psychiatrist, I've consulted with enough disappointed younger women whose parents are somewhere between despondent and repulsed by their relationships with older men to know a young woman has to assert herself and stand her ground when telling them about her older male friend.

It's a matter of, "Mom and Dad, I would like you to meet, so and so." Or, "Mom and Dad, I am so happy, I want you to be the first to know, John and I are getting married."

Expect a bit of shock, tons of advice and perhaps, an aftermath of rejection, but don't whine. You'll play right into their hands. It's your life and your future. Over time, they'll probably come around. If not, you'll feel guilty for awhile, but losing you will be their loss. And bear in mind, you could miss out on the love of your life.

❧ Friends' Reactions...Prejudice and Isolation ❧

When a younger woman plans to marry an older man, friends of both the bride and groom display a gamut of emotions—positive, negative, angry. Some are even repulsed. How much an age-disparate couple is accepted or rejected depends greatly upon their age difference, the prestige of one or both of the people engaged, and often for the older groom, the circumstance under which the couple met.

I remember explaining to Regis Philbin and his audience that friends aren't terribly delicate nor ashamed to express their feelings. I was somewhat passionate when I told him, "Sam's friends dumped him, and my friends dumped me."

In Sam's case, the bulk of his friends, including one in particular who was his next-door neighbor when they were growing up in Jersey City, sided with his ex-wife, Joan. Knowing they would be the first to admit that his marriage wasn't a happy one, Sam was really hurt that his friends wouldn't accept his divorce and marriage to me. We both realized a lot of their displeasure came from their wives being threatened by Sam's affair with me, but that didn't ease the sting of their rebuff.

On the other hand, my friends regarded Sam as a dinosaur. He just didn't fit in. As a practicing dentist, he had absolutely nothing in common with those still in graduate school bucking the establishment—he *was* the establishment! Fine dining to my unworldly pals was eating at a Chinese restaurant on upper Broadway. It was a tough adjustment for Sam to find himself selecting spicy or mild egg rolls from column "A" rather than quenelles at Lutèce.

Even after being cleaned out by his divorce, he still had more money than my twenty-two-year-old buddies. That made some of my female friends jealous. But it wasn't just the money that cooled our friendships, it was the fact that I had landed a sophisticated, older man. A few resented it was me and not them. After all in their eyes, "What could she have that I don't?" Others simply felt Sam was too old and wondered what I possibly could see in him. This led to Sam and me spending a lot of time alone, together.

More than 50 percent of the women who write to me for solace and advice complain they have no friends. They feel very isolated, lonely, and rejected. Mary Friese, from Huntington, Long Island, said she only has one colleague at work that she dared to tell about her engagement to Ken, a fifty-year-old widower, thirty years her senior.

Judy, a registered nurse from the West Coast, said, "I couldn't accept LeRoy's friends vanishing. I didn't want to believe it was our twenty-two-year age difference that caused the rift; but all of a sudden, we weren't accepted either socially or professionally in the circles we very comfortably moved within before our marriage and LeRoy's divorce."

In some cases, it takes years for younger women and older men to find a social niche. I know of one W.O.O.M. subscriber who was so hungry to find a group of friends with whom she and her husband could socialize as a couple that she called every couple on a networking list I provided her the day she received it!

Ilene Hochburg, New York City author of parodies *Catmopolitan* and *Forbabes*, told Rene Hanley, of *People Are Talking*, that when she and her husband Irwin, twenty-five years her senior, first started dating she found their friends' reactions fairly negative. She said, "A lot of Irwin's friends didn't take us seriously at all. They thought he was going through a midlife crisis, some sort of phase that would be very short lived. A number of Irwin's friends wouldn't even socialize with us." Bluntly put, many age-gap couples get to know who their friends really are. And who is going to give the marriage a chance.

Lucille Colantonio, who appeared on the same show, empathized with Ilene. She said, "Most people thought I was a fantasy for Ralph. I would give him his youth back." She said his friends who were in their late fifties and early sixties thought their affair wouldn't last, that it also was a short-term thing. Lucille said, "Ralph's friends were angry; they couldn't understand what we could have in common."

Many W.O.O.M.ies have had similar experiences. The majority say friends find the love affair or marriage atypical and controversial. Siding with this couple, if there has been a divorce or disputed circumstances, could also affect friends' standings among their social groups and demean their status. Ilene summed it up by appealing to the *People Are Talking* audience, "It would only be fair if people would just judge us by who we are, rather than the facade we represent."

Although the prejudice is disconcerting, there is an upside. The loneliness and isolation strengthens the relationship. Because initially age-gap couples spend most of their Saturday nights as a twosome, the older husband and younger wife get to know each other very well. Since they meet resistance from both sets of their friends, they become comrades with a common feeling of alliance; each is very defensive of the other. But being together day in and day out without the variety and humor friends bring to one's social life can get boring. And it doesn't take very long before younger wives become despondent.

Older husbands need to realize that alternating and compromising on attending age-appropriate entertainment, types that attract crowds such as concerts, pro games, art shows, etc., can be a quick fix. Such activities will help diminish the feeling of isolation often experienced by younger wives. They won't replace a best friend but will offer a reprieve from a young woman's loneliness.

Forlorn younger wives trudge along in frustration as they search for a confidante who will understand the intricacies of her marriage without prejudice. Often, they haven't even one friend with whom to discuss everyday, common marital tiffs. In most cases, friends immediately blame their marriage to an older man as the problem. It may even be the reason he doesn't turn his socks right side out before putting them in the hamper. A shoulder to lean on appears inaccessible when the majority of one's friends and even family come back with "I could have told you so."

Sandy Grappel, wife of Hy, a wealthy widower nineteen years her senior, said, "At the beginning, I spent a lot of time with Hy's friends. There was no question about it, some of them viewed me as a gold digger. I felt insecure with these people who were all friends of wife number one."

She said she would worry about what to wear, what to say. Often, younger wives do move into whatever is left of the older husband's circle of friends because older husbands make no bones about the fact they don't want to spend too much time with her friends. And especially not her friends' younger husbands who are still learning the art of making the deal, when he has successfully exercised it for the past twenty years!

A young wife will have to be flexible. Often, she will have to swallow her dissatisfaction and put on a happy face as she finds herself spending the bulk of her social time with her husband's older business associates and friends. Marcie Thompson*, an elegant fifty-two-year-old W.O.O.M.ie from Chicago, married for seven years to a seventy-six-year-old former company president, told me that health problems, medication, and blood pressure conversation just gets on her nerves. She said, "I feel like I'm dining out in an infirmary!"

However, in many cases, when younger wives are given the chance, very special relationships with confident older women can help a younger wife learn the ropes. When Sam and I were first married, one of the couples that stayed with him were Lita and Alvin Melser. Lita, a consummate hostess and doyenne of the community, propelled me into social maturity. She taught me how to entertain—which wines to serve, how to cook, how to set a formal table. Having a daughter Laurie's age, I conferred with Lita about everything from the common cold to after-school activities. She even shopped with me for expensive dresses, shoes, and accessories. Lita was thirty-eight when I was twenty-three. She was the big sister who was as determined to have me accepted as I was.

Yet, to sustain the marital relationship, a compromise must be made. Either the younger wife goes out once a week with her same-age friends, or an older husband is going to be married to one unhappy camper. On the same evening, he could schedule a poker game with his cohorts. Together, the couple should enroll in courses or activities that aren't necessarily age related such as working out at a local gym, taking dancing lessons, or a computer course.

Living in the same community as Sam and his first wife made it difficult to ease into friendships with people who may have heard from others about what an ogre Sam was and what a gold digger I was to marry him. I ameliorated this problem by helping charitable organizations that Sam and his first wife weren't involved with. Soon after, I opened my own business where I could meet people and develop a set of professional friends. In addition, over the span of our twenty-four-year marriage, I have taken French and ballet lessons, become an avid gardener, and joined a tennis league.

For the past sixteen years, Sam developed a great group of friends who have served with him on the New Jersey State Board of Dentistry. This gubernatorial appointment has given him the chance to meet dentists and consumer advocates of all ages with whom we both socialize and enjoy.

I was a bit intimidated the first time we met these people because they were much older than me—and even Sam. Many were very successful and prominent. One summer evening in 1976, Sam and I were invited to a cocktail party hosted by Walter Sloane, president of the board. At that time I was almost thirty but looked nineteen. We drove up to Dr. Sloane's impressive home. Sam helped me out of the car, and just as I stepped out, a young teenager hanging out a window yelled, "Hey mom, some guy brought his daughter!" I seriously considered turning around and leaving. However, within minutes everyone was laughing with me, it broke the ice for all of us, and we have remained good friends ever since.

Little by little, you will develop a set of friends that span both your ages. Most of them will have an activity in common with you, rather than age. However, every once in a while, you will both feel the need to be just with your own-aged friends. Making time for outings with them will give each of you a chance to participate in age-related discussions and provide a positive balance. Seldom, but on occasion, older husbands need to moan, groan, and act old; younger wives need to giggle, be silly, and act young.

Ironically, and much to our surprise, Sam and I attended a party recently where many of his pre-me, erstwhile friends were invited also—including his ex-wife! I purposefully wore a very short, bright red suit with a hint of black lace bra peeking out. Both Sam and I looked around the room and realized we had absolutely nothing in common with these once-forbidding people. Sam has a seven-year-old daughter, most of them have seven-year-old granddaughters. Our life-style is different. We're in overdrive; they are retiring. We're building, acquiring, pumping iron; they're slowing down and playing shuffleboard. We can't possibly relate to them. Funny, after all of these years of animosity and rejection, I detected a hint of envy.

❧ *The Consequences of Living with a Prenuptial Agreement* ❦

*H*idden away, but handy enough to be found when the younger wife doesn't live up to her older husband's expectations, is the ominous prenuptial agreement.

Ashamed and demeaned by it, many younger wives (and a few husbands) live daily with its disagreeable implications. Yet, with less than a 50 percent chance of marriages surviving these days, prenuptial agreements have become a necessary evil. According to *Money* magazine, prenups are now signed prior to roughly 5 percent of all marriages and 20 percent of all remarriages. In W.O.O.M.'s case, 87 percent of our husbands are remarried, while this is the first marriage for 45 percent of the wives. Consequently, the bulk of our older husbands and their lawyers think a prenup is a sound idea. Conversely, about half of their younger wives think it stinks! Which makes for a serious conflict of opinion.

Nevertheless, the no-guarantees-anymore attitude has made marriage a very tenuous institution. And you can't blame the party with greater assets for taking precautions, especially if they have been burned before. What I question instead is the lack of sensitivity with which the contract is sometimes presented. Rather than broach the subject as "We must protect both of us," some self-centered men take the position that "I need to cover my butt."

Younger wives from twenty to forty are much more intimidated by the prenuptial agreement and less likely to know their own self-worth than older women. Caught up in romance and love, they can easily be taken advantage of—and often are. On the surface, it appeared, thirty-nine-year-old Jacqueline Kennedy, former first lady and something of a world icon, received a fair shake when she married sixty-two-year-old Aristotle Onassis. But in reality, her prenuptial agreement was unfavorably balanced—sources say she agreed to less than 1 percent of his net worth. One must appreciate that to younger wives the prenup treats them as a commodity and insinuates the older husband has an even-more powerful upper hand. Joan Braden, longtime friend of Jackie's, told *People* magazine, "To Onassis, she was just another bauble."

Younger wives over forty seem more confident and are often bold enough to make demands—maybe require a marital contract themselves if they have been married before or are personally successful and come to the marriage with considerable assets. These older younger wives are aware that a prenup can work both ways and are emotionally equipped and experienced enough to negotiate a better deal.

Robert C. Novy, a Toms River, New Jersey, lawyer who specializes in elder law, draws up prenups for retired newlyweds. He told the *Asbury Park Press* that often oldsters specify the spouse can live in the house after they die. There's only one catch: The survivor can't remarry. If you're eighteen to twenty years younger than your deceased spouse, that's a mean restrictive stipulation!

Some marital contracts are fair; others are generous. A few are petty. And there are those that are unjust and downright degrading. Furthermore, they are no longer reserved for the very rich. Roger Bamber, a matrimonial lawyer who practices in Cambridge and London told *The Times,* "During the last twelve months, more clients have asked for prenuptial agreements than in the previous nine years combined." Men (and a few women) in every social stratum, all over the world, are jumping on the bandwagon to protect their premarital, worldly goods.

When I talk with some W.O.O.M. subscribers who are married with prenuptial agreements, I'm surprised by their insecurity. Usually they are the prettiest, brightest, and most desirable women. The type to whom any other man would sign over *all* his money. Yet, when it comes to their marriage, I detect an undercurrent of low self-esteem.

Because the prenup interferes with working things out, I am not an advocate of such contracts. I feel if you love someone enough, you should take the risk. I'm not alone in this opinion. *Even* Geraldo Rivera, who has had three former wives, says he is appalled by prenuptial agreements. How good can these contracts be if many men are so defensive about them that rather than do it themselves, they have their lawyers approach the subject with the younger wife? Some husbands seem to squirm when I address these financial agreements. This makes me wonder how much actual input they offered. Or, do many of these prenups reflect an overly ambitious lawyer who has intimidated or influenced what would normally be a very fair man?

However, prenuptials are here to stay, and the women and men who sign them are, too. So let's take a look at how living with one affects the marriage.

Most wives feel the preparing and signing of prenups have a negative impact on the marriage. John Carnahan, a matrimonial lawyer and former president of the Ohio Bar Association echoed their sentiments when he told *Money* magazine, "When you get right down to the nitty-gritty, you're throwing cold water on the romance." Norman M. Sheresky, another matrimonial lawyer told *The New York Times*, "They're like tiny poison pills: they infect a marriage from the beginning. The marriage can fail for the very reason you might have expected—simmering cynicism."

W.O.O.M.'s first-time, younger brides often regard it as the divorce before the marriage. When they make love, they feel used. One W.O.O.M.ie said, "I'm good enough to be a bed companion but not worthy enough to be offered a full partnership."

In all fairness to their husbands and their original families, many subscribers understand their husbands came with a marital history and appreciate that legacies have to be provided. But the issue becomes considerably more complicated when you discuss property settlements, the wife's contribution and sacrifices (jobs, careers, the hours they devote to his children, not having babies—

time, personal, and emotional constraints that are difficult to put a price tag on) and his and her after-marriage acquisitions.

I often suggest a woman, marrying a man who is well off, broach the subject of the prenuptial agreement first. If she's really clever, she might even convince him it was *her* idea. Essentially, it will confirm to him that she is not a gold digger. The older male friend will appreciate her concern and be relieved by her reasonableness. It will also give her more power during the drafting of the document to include some of her demands and modify some of his.

Each state has its own marital laws. California is a community-property state. So are Arkansas, Idaho, Louisiana, Nevada, New Mexico, North Carolina, and Texas. That means that everything the couple accrued during their marriage (excluding inheritances) is considered to be owned equally by both spouses. However, other states mandate that property be divided equitably, not necessarily equally. To thoroughly protect herself, a prospective bride must know her state's law—INSIDE and OUT!

Even though prenuptials are considered ironclad contracts by the lawyers who write them and by their clients, each agreement may be handled differently by family court judges in each locality. Invariably they hold up, but Peter C. Paras, a lawyer from Eatontown, New Jersey, told the *Asbury Park Press* that he had never been involved with a case where a challenged prenuptial agreement was 100 percent enforced. But, he said, the pacts provide more protection for couples wanting to separate their assets than if no agreement existed.

Disagreeing, Robert Stephan Cohen, attorney of the very, *very* rich like Henry Kravis and Mrs. David Merrick, told *W*, "If done right, a prenuptial agreement is bulletproof." On the flip side, another lawyer, Stan Lotwin, stated in the same article, "All agreements can be challenged." (All these conflicting opinions makes me a little nervous—what about you?)

In *W*'s feature, entitled "Dividing the Spoils," authors Despin and Reginato decided: "Challenging a well-drafted prenuptial agreement almost always fails. Rich husbands are generally deal-makers and know how to use savvy lawyers and accountants. What starts off as a straightforward divorce case, ends up as a high-stakes game of cat and mouse—with the wife having little or no chance of finding her husband's true worth."

Attorney Richard Golub concurred. "It's all a big game of fraud. It's the world's best board game, and everyone knows it; it's hide 'n' seek."

Yet, remember "The Donald"? Wasn't Mr. Trump the ulti-mate dealmaker? Media sources say Ivana received the estimated twenty-five million dollars in property and perks (*Time* magazine says the agreement offered her ten million dollars) believed to have been the amount stipulated in their prenuptial agreement. But Trump still had to sweat it out for four months before their final court date when Ivana was going to try to break the prenuptial and ask for 40 percent of his total assets.

And what you read is not always what people get. According to *Forbes*, sources who know the score say Patricia Kluge's bally-hooed divorce settlement of interest on one billion dollars for the rest of her life was a fabrication. Other sources say she's actually getting a flat fifteen million from her thirty-three-years-older, billionaire, Metromedia boss ex-husband, John. Appreciate that he is the third richest man in America, and she received only one quarter of one percent of his $5.9 billion net worth. However, Patricia does have the right to live rent-free with the couple's eleven-year-old son at Albelmarle, John's twelve-thousand-acre estate. Matrimonial law experts *Forbes* spoke to were confident the marriage had been sealed with a prenuptial agreement.

On the other hand, according to *W*, Francis Lear got $112 million, and Anne Bass received something between $200 and $500 million, $87 million in Disney stock, and $12.4 million in American Medical International, plus, plus. Even if some say these astronomical settlements are on the way out—Lear and

Bass were married when prenuptial agreements were the exception not the rule—it's apparent these women mastered the game of hard ball in the big leagues. And if they can do it, so can you!

One lawyer I interviewed, who wanted to remain anonymous, warned, "When a couple splits, their worst enemies are their lawyers, the judge, and *lastly*, the spouses. It's a shame the couple couldn't have evaluated their assets going in, made a marital pact, and saved the money that gets eaten up by legal fees and hassles." He continued, "I refuse to work with prenuptial agreements. When a couple signs them, I'm looking at one great big, possible malpractice suit." After reviewing all of this, it appears both the husband and wife, and undoubtedly their lawyers, should rely on crossing their fingers as much as their attorneys' abilities.

A prenup's power is pervasive. The younger wives I have interviewed were fearful of provoking a fight or showing any disgruntlement. This forbidding contract brings shivers to one's spine as it tends to devalue and control a wife's every marital move. In some cases, this even extends to what weight a wife must maintain, how many times she has to exercise per week, and the number of times per week they are expected to have sex! Jenny Natale*, a W.O.O.M.ie from San Diego says, "It can make a woman feel like she's a leased vehicle. He'll take real good care of you until you're not new and shiny anymore. Then he'll pay off the lease and get a new model."

For many W.O.O.M. husbands, the average of whom are eighteen years older than their wives, a prenup becomes a bargaining chip. Some are sensitive not to lord it over their wives; others are abusively cognizant of the impact: "If you do this, I may tear it up...After we're married a certain amount of years, I'll change it—you'll get more and more; or I'll get rid of it."

When Nancy D'Onofrio* became pregnant with her second child, her husband told her if she would have an abortion, he would tear up the prenup. Devastated, but afraid he would divorce her if she didn't terminate the pregnancy, she complied with his wishes. That was in September. The following Christmas, an infinite year-plus later, he put the torn-up agreement in a pretty gift box under the Christmas tree. But was this a gift or a sadistic manipulation and show of power?

For younger wives, the prenup's existence is a reminder of the power of the age difference. Daddy is giving the little girl a pat on the head. Be a good girl, follow my rules, and you'll get your allowance. It affects how she will act and react. She can't move around her marriage comfortably; it's tough for her to assert herself, love freely, mature, and grow.

Very few younger wives can call the financial shots with their older husbands. Many just haven't lived long enough to compete financially unless they inherited their money like the late heiress, Doris Duke. There may be a handful who received large divorce settlements from a previous marriage. However starry-eyed and idealistic, few said they would have required their husbands to sign a prenuptial agreement if their parents and lawyers hadn't insisted upon it.

Most younger wives, fearing they'll lose a fiancé or that no one else will marry them, feel pressured to sign prenuptial agreements. Ironically, if their marriages dissolve, a number of them will be worse off than the couple's children!

Many W.O.O.M. subscribers found the prenup situation hard to talk about. They tell me they live with the humiliation for years. But a few are so quick to get it over, they don't even hire a lawyer. Fortunately for them, in most cases, the courts take a very hard look at the conditions surrounding the signing of the agreement.

Attorney Gary Skoloff, chairman of the family law section of the American Bar Association, cited two such cases during an interview with *Forbes* magazine. In one, a New Jersey bride saw the prenup agreement for the first time on the night before her wedding. She refused to sign it. Her about-to-be husband persisted, and two hours before the ceremony, he threatened to go on the honeymoon alone unless she signed—which she did.

When the marriage ended in divorce a few years later, the prenup was thrown out by an angry judge. The last-minute agreement not only failed legal scrutiny, since it was signed under duress, but it also destroyed the marriage. The husband said his wife talked about it "at least once a week."

A prenup that is considered too lopsided may also have trouble sticking. Skoloff referred to a case where a schoolteacher, who owned very little, was married for ten years to a wealthy man twenty years older than herself. The couple had one child, and she was pregnant with a second. They had signed a prenuptial agreement in which she had waived all alimony and equitable distribution of all assets, except for what her husband put in her name. Her name wasn't on the deed to their $1.5 million home. Even though her husband was worth $20 million, the judge told the defense counsel that the law was against her, but the facts were for her. The case was then settled out of court, with the husband setting up a substantial trust fund for her and the children. She did not, however, get any of his capital.

Second, third, and fourth wives have to appreciate that some older men have been taken financially by women. And once bitten, they're going to be a lot more cautious about the financial ramifications of remarriage. If a man suggests a prenup, give it some thought. Many women are so insulted, they walk away from what could have been a beautiful relationship and marriage. If the agreement is fair and incrementally weakened, with the exception of legacies for a husband's existing children, accepting it could demonstrate a grand gesture of her love for the man.

When subscriber, Allison Detwiler-Jones*, forty-three, became engaged to her fiancé, sixty-two-year-old Robert*, he deposited $150 thousand in cash in her bank account and gave her three certificates of deposit valued at $300 thousand dollars each. When they decided to get married, Allison agreeably signed a prenuptial contract that gave her one third of Robert's estate after the first three years of her marriage, half after seven years, and the entire estate after ten years of marriage. Not only was that better than fair, he promised to set her up in her own cosmetic business, had a vasectomy and a facelift!

When Lyle Stuart, the older husband of my publisher Carole Stuart, sold his business a few years ago, the first thing he did was present her with a check for one million dollars—and he paid the tax on it. He told her he was impatient with insecure men who had to control the purse strings in an attempt to control their women.

Dentist Ira Zohn told the *Geraldo* audience, "It's to protect my children's future." His gorgeous, sixteen-years-younger wife, Lynette, said, "You better tear it up." Which he eventually did.

Many guys come up with a myriad of reasons why they require a prenup. Essentially, they don't want to lose their shirt for the sake of marriage. When an older man announces his intentions to marry a younger woman, everyone wants to get in on the legal picture. Even if the male friend doesn't want a prenup, his company partners may insist upon it. Randall Whitmore says, "My last wife wiped me out! I'll never let that happen again." But that only adds fuel to the fire, and very few new wives want to be put in the same category as an ex-wife who walked out or was dumped.

Many W.O.O.M. subscribers think the real reason their husbands pursue the prenup and drag their feet when they have promised to tear it up is because it implies power and most of all, control. They say that numerous older men silently think "I love you a lot, but I want to keep my hold over you." Deep down, a husband may be insecure about being older. Uncertain his younger wife loves him for him, Gerald Murray*, twenty-one years older than his third wife said, "How do I know this young woman won't walk off with a younger man, take my money, and leave me hanging! At my age, I couldn't survive that. I'm too old to rebuild my life." Obviously, he has little confidence in his selection of wives.

Seen from the woman's point of view, younger wives fear that at any moment their husbands could kick them out and leave them with nothing but a mere pittance. But they can't, if she does her homework.

Lawyers I spoke to suggested a young woman seek good legal advice and be aware of her own net worth. Giving up a job to marry a guy and being available to play golf all day or travel at a moment's notice sounds great, but the availability she brings to the marriage is an asset for which she should be compensated. She shouldn't forget to include her car, furniture, grandmother's cuckoo clock, the George Michael CDs he hates, and anything she can think of that she is contributing to the marriage. Although it is rather petty, she can also stipulate that her husband can't gain more than a certain number of pounds, will do a hundred sit-ups per day, will quit smoking, and won't become a couch potato. (If men can make demands, why can't women?)

As trivial and miserly as it sounds, the agreement should include the cost of visits to her family he promised, the business he agreed to purchase, her college and/or career aspirations, the furs, oil paintings, and big home. Remember, the prenup was probably *his* idea.

Money magazine suggests as a guard against inflation, women should ask for percentages of her husband's salary, not fixed figures. If a younger woman has been married before, she should protect her personal assets. Both parties should see to it that the agreement is fair and equitable for each of them. And the legal fees should be covered by the person who requested the prenuptial agreement. One should seek second and third legal opinions if they are uncertain. And even if everyone is happy, pick a date you'll adhere to and *revise* the contract *annually*.

In closing, my husband Sam has a word of advice for all younger women whose older husbands have died. Insist upon a prenuptial agreement if you remarry. I know that Sam has worked too hard to protect our children and me in case of his death not to heed his advice.

❧ The Generation Gap ❦

A few years ago, a forty-year-old friend of mine, married to a man only a year older than herself, joked, "Can I join W.O.O.M.? My husband *mentally* acts like an older man!" The request was funny but pertinent and shows that a *generation gap* is in the mind and not necessarily age related. Which is why you'll find men in their sixties who are more responsive and up-to-the minute than those in their forties. A lot has to do with attitude.

In operating W.O.O.M., I have discovered the *generation gap* is troublesome when the younger wife is in her mid-twenties and her husband is fifteen to twenty or more years older. Just entering adulthood, the wife is "green" and compulsive. Wishing to protect his younger wife, the husband will lord over her, attempt to influence her every decision, and suppress her ingenuity. It's not surprising that the younger wife might come to resent his overbearing approach.

If their marriage has seasoned, and the couple has made it to middle age or a couple has dated and married while in their middle ages (thirty-five and fifty respectively), the couple sees more eye to eye. Individually they are secure, busy with their careers or family life (if he lets her have children), and more accepting of each other's point of view.

However, it is certain age-gap couples will find their greatest challenges occur at the opposite end of the age spectrum, when the older husband or male friend reaches sixty-five to eighty and beyond. Dr. Georgia Witkin, clinical psychologist and professor of psychiatry at Mount Sinai and news reporter for *WNBC*, told me "age-disparity problems at this time are more obvious because men are moving from maturity to elderly."

"At the beginning of their marriage," says Dr. Witkin, "the older husband absolutely loved having his younger wife focus on him. Then, while his younger wife comes into her own in her forties or fifties and is smart, self-reliant, and independent, the focus shifts to her. And any marital problems that exist are intensified as these men's careers take a downswing."

If an older husband hasn't planned a course for after retirement—albeit golf, a college course, consulting, or refinishing the basement—so that he is retiring *to* something, he may resent his younger wife's job and busy life ahead, his feeling of being alone, and a power reversal.

"And often," says Dr. Witkin, "the relationship changes from a father/daughter situation to mother/son dependency. If he was married to a similar-in-age wife, they would be going through this together. It would be easier to face."

Often, I find that couples misconstrue *generation-gap* problems with power and control confrontations. It is very easy to do because often the reactions are the same, but the cause is different. To me, a generation gap is created by a subliminal, subconscious aura developed by growing up and living in a different time period with different values and ideologies. In our situations, it evolved from experiences that happened years ago (before we were born) when our older husbands were most impressionable—creating a frame of mind that is difficult to alter and accept change years later. Older husbands are often bewildered when their younger wives aren't able to relate to their way of thinking and vice versa. Power and control issues, which we will address in greater detail later, include personality traits which may be easier to approach and change.

Uppermost, husbands—especially those married to much younger women—have a responsibility to stay in touch with current happenings, act young, and cope with change. If he wants to remain happily married, an older husband doesn't have a choice but to continually revise his way of thinking by associating with younger people and/or active retirees.

During an interview with Mia Oberlink, a research assistant for *Reader's Digest's*, *New Choices*, I recited this mantra and took her by surprise. She said, "I would think that a man's feeling young is a woman's responsibility. But, why should it be?" Most fifty year-old, fixer/mender, younger wives do feel obliged to keep their husbands fresh, lively, and stimulating. Mia was just realizing that the liberated thirty-year-old younger wife doesn't have the same attitude.

Women, born after 1960, expect their older husbands to leap over the age hurdle like role models Sean Connery and Clint Eastwood. And as feminist as it may sound, these youngsters have no room in their lives for healthy, grumpy, old men who use their advancing age to attract attention and threaten those around them with "Just wait 'til your *my* age!" (For corroboration, take a look at the chapter in the book, *Love and Sex After Sixty*, entitled "The 'Old Person' Trap.") Clearly more independent than her middle-aged counterpart, who percolates privately as she copes with a barrelful of missed youthful opportunities and begrudgingly slows her pace to accommodate her older husband, the young younger wife won't put up with it.

Erma Bombeck agrees. "Men have to shape up to bag a trophy wife," she warned one of her unmarried sons. "The way the trend for the 1990s is headed, my advice to you would be to get a terrific job, make a bundle, go to a tanning salon, lift weights, and buy a good hairpiece. Your trophy wife is about to be born." Not bad advice. Except, she failed to include maintaining a youthful outlook.

I'm a die-hard Republican, but it was evident to me early on that incumbent George Bush couldn't win the 1992 presidential election. I felt he was out of touch with the times. He separated himself from many of the voters with a generation gap, and his old-fashioned attitudes cost him his political career. And as capable as he may have been, he lost the election because of his unwillingness to see change was needed.

It didn't help his cause that he was married to a grandmotherly type—even if she was more up-to-the-minute than he. And worse yet, he was too chauvinistic to listen to her when it came to relating to the majority of the American population. As fit and young-looking as Bush is, his thought processes regarding America's youth are over the hill. Some older husbands lose their younger wives for the very same reason.

Literally, a generation gap is a span of about thirty years. But we often use the term loosely to define a discontinuity that the majority of us blame on an age span. Many W.O.O.M. subscribers are married to generation gaps, but most are married to decade gaps. (Eighteen years is our average age difference.) As the decades broaden, they shake up an age-disparate couple's relationship. New York City psychologist, Dr. Carol C. Flax, told me that when older men criticize and belittle (because they can't relate to) their younger wife's music, taste in art, dress and her philosophical attitudes, there is bound to be trouble on the home front. Unless, the older husband updates his way of thinking, paradise will soon become a frigid iceberg.

A perfect example of what might appear unimportant to an older husband but is darn important to a younger wife surfaced when Sam and I were first married. Sam was thirty-eight; I was twenty-three. We would go to parties, and enviously I would watch the young couples gyrate to my favorite songs. Sam made it very clear to me he wouldn't be caught *dead* wiggling his hips in public! Since I love to dance, it wasn't long before I was a *real* unhappy younger wife. Eventually, I balked at even going to parties where there might be that type of dancing. They frustrated the heck out of me!

Then one day, Sam and I were at a party having a really great time. When the music moved up a notch beyond a fox trot, Sam began to escort me to our table. I took the bull by the horns and said, "Why should I be miserable? NO—not this time, bubbie!"

Sam and I made a pact: Until he learned how to dance, I would dance by myself or with others. He could simmer with jealousy on the sidelines, but I wasn't going to feel guilty. It worked! He learned to have a good time watching me have fun.

But it's not just dancing that gets a younger wife's dander up. Fossilized mannerisms, old-fashioned prudishness, chauvinism, not keeping up with the times, flab, flamingo-pink-and-kelly-green jackets, giving in to old age, and thinking one has all the answers because they were effective in 1958 are the real relationship coolers.

Last year, Joan Kelly Bernard, a staff writer at *New York Newsday* and younger wife, said in her article, "Love Across the Ages," "If a man was in a more traditional marriage the first time around, he may have expectations his younger wife finds difficult to fulfill."

In other words, older husbands married to younger wives can expect to hire Servicemaster, eat out almost every night, and pay soaring dry-cleaner bills! On an emotional level, I was quoted: "Younger women don't want as much protection as, let's say, his [first] wife may have wanted. And they're much more independent. They're very career oriented, so it's a whole different woman than what he was brought up to think he was going to marry. He likes it—it keeps him humming. But on the other hand, he doesn't know what to do with it."

Another woman in her late forties, who recently left her husband who is in his late sixties, told Bernard, "I felt confined. The biggest difference is in agendas. I'm much more focused on the job; his are on self-satisfaction and pleasures."

Manhattan-based marital and family therapist, Laura Singer-Magdoff, sorted it out for those of us involved with the story. She said, "Partners come to the marriage not just with different expectations, but with very different experiences. In an era of such rapid change, you get discrepancies."

Partners can enrich each other by sharing their disparate experiences, but they may have to accept that they lose something that couples who have lived through the same periods of social and political history do not. "You lose the buddy relationship." A bond that suggests, "We've been through this together."

The forty-eight-year-old divorcee agreed. She said she prefers dating people her own age now. "It's much more a peer relationship rather than a relationship from which I was essentially taking."

The generation or decade gap creeps up on younger wives married to older men. Neither of them see its impact when they are dating because, at first, the "gap" is a novelty. He's expending energy acting young; the younger wife is adopting a more mature attitude. At the time, it feels right—you are so much in love. But little by little, you and your husband may start to notice points of reference that appear to come from left field. In addition, incidences and philosophies can crop up that are completely foreign to each of you.

Your husband may mention an historical event that seemed like it happened yesterday to him but is ancient history to you. You probably studied the milestone he's talking about in high school, but he *lived* it! Your music grates on him. His music puts you to sleep. You're more comfortable in a disco; he prefers a ballroom. New-look colors and a more modern decor are your cup of tea. He might have trouble parting with his more traditional, timeworn objets d'art. One day you disagree, but you're not sure why. Then comes the *look* as if you have two heads when your convictions and decade gaps thunderously clash!

Neither of you are wrong. You're simply from contrasting cultural, social, and philosophical time periods. And it's not just a cerebral variance. Physically, you look different to each other. He's older, you're younger. Your energy levels vary. You may be jogging a 5K run while he takes a walk in the park. He's lost his invincible carelessness. Thinking you're going to live forever, you may be a bit reckless. Your husband is probably counting his pennies; you've maxed your credit cards. Depending upon where your age gaps begin and end, the age stretch will determine just

how much you're going to have to get to know one another—
adjust, compromise, and modify your thinking.

In the younger woman/older man relationship the age span
is a significant concern when trying to relate to one another. In
many instances, it can work to both the husband and wife's benefit, but at times, the age difference can cause periods of consternation. If the couple views their marriage with open minds, the
time warp offers a profound advantage for both the younger
woman and older husband. Personally and professionally, you can
play off each other's eras offering a well-rounded, in-depth
approach. But it requires a great deal of compromise by both
sides.

Dr. Evan Longin, coordinator of Allied Mental Health
Training at Salem State College in Massachusetts who also has a
private practice, says, "If we look at the physiology of development, older men don't have the capacity for adding to their
understanding of the world in their twilight years—the last quarter of their life. These older men have constructed an entire emotional life-style for themselves—especially those who have been
single for some time. What they do have, though, is the capacity
to utilize what they have learned."

This complicates the age-disparate marriage because while
he is entrenching, the younger wife is adding new concepts and
nonchalantly adjusting her way of thinking to adapt. Author and
journalist Sally Quinn told Vanity Fair, "There are ways in which
I am different than Ben [Washington Post editor Ben Bradlee],
maybe partly because I'm who I am and partly because I think it
ought to be done differently than he did."

"Older husbands," says Dr. Longin, "know where they are
going. They offer a younger woman a safe, controlled, and dignified life—completely different than what she has experienced
with her father and age-similar relationships with other men. But
the majority of older men build an impenetrable fortress that's
unmovable and often they are intractable. So on one level, the
safety and tranquillity an older husband provides is appealing but

becomes confusing on another level, because it is also confining and restricting." At this point, we exit the generation-gap issue and cross over to a power and control predicament.

A younger wife has to be aware that if she wants to move into an older man's emotional compound, she'll have to accept that he isn't going to budge too far from *his* timeworn, fail-safe ways. And, "In order for their marriage to work," insisted Dr. Longin, "younger women are going to have to opt for a very, very autonomous life apart from her husband. Which should include independent relationships via support groups, work, or community service where she can be herself." But that's easier said than done when most older husbands find all kinds of reasons why their younger wives shouldn't be independent.

Fifty percent of the women who call the W.O.O.M. office for support complain that the imbalance is overwhelming, that it requires someone backing down from their dreams, career goals, and ideologies—generally the younger wife. Dr. Longin was adamant and repeated, "An older man has to be *flexible* to allow his wife to leave his fortress. To leave that defined experience— or the marriage will fail."

"On a more positive note," I said to Dr. Longin, "I have seen older husbands, including my husband Sam, who also works alongside sixteen women under the age of forty, assimilate into their younger wives' worlds and successfully make a paradigm shift. They are the happiest couples."

"I believe that is possible," said Dr. Longin. "But that is why this book of yours is so pertinent—because it is so frequently *not* possible."

To conclude our interview, I asked Dr. Longin, "When an older man and younger woman are dating—romantically in love and unable to see the pitfalls that lie ahead—what should they look out for?"

Dr. Longin said a woman has to fully understand that this may not be as wonderful as dinner at Le Cirque and trips abroad. "She has to be really, *really* sure she wants to go on a defined journey to a very specific location." She will deplete a great deal of energy adjusting to his life-style. Her life will not be spontaneous.

If a couple can cope with all of that, there is a very special side to the dynamics of the age difference. Nancy Dunnan, a writer in her forties married to a man in his sixties, wrote a piece several years ago for *New Woman* magazine entitled, "In Praise of Older Men." I've never forgotten a very poignant paragraph that seems to calm the torrent of my younger-wife restlessness.

She wrote, "[Being married to an older man] means he has experienced enough illness and tragedy to know the importance of living each day to the fullest. By sharing in his knowledge, you add a new dimension to your own life; you begin to cherish your own friends a little bit more, you begin to reorganize your priorities, putting people and love before things and achievements. Materialism takes a backseat to life."

Ideally, if a couple can deal with age-gap related issues and learn from each other, their marriage will provide a positive bond, full of growth and admiration—completely free of ennui.

There will be times when a couple can't work things out because the generation gap is such a strong influence. It's disappointing to me because I often see two people, very much in love, who are frustrated by each other's era-related, contrasting attitudes. And even though sources say the divorce rate for age-gap couples is low, these marriages will most definitely fail if they don't respect their age-related differences.

But there are ways to work around the problem. If it's a philosophical difference, allow each other to express beliefs without criticism. And don't just hear what the other person has to say, *listen*! Be flexible to allow each other space as an individual to grow, change, and expand or alter horizons. Lower your demands and expectations. Age-gap couples tend to put a great deal of pressure on each other to succeed. By following this formula, immediately, each spouse is a winner. If it's a physical difference, appreciate that your good times *together* will revolve around less-strenuous activities that don't necessarily have to mimic a couch potato.

❧ *Dealing with Power and Control Issues* ❦

Power is the spellbinder that attracts many younger women to older men. Although at times, it can be their archenemy. Because power refers to authority and command, its axle is *control*—an action that disciplines, restrains, and limits. As has been noted throughout this book, many older husbands are very powerful people. In the May/December relationship, seniority prevails.

The question is: Do older men marry younger women because they feel the need to control, guard, and dominate at home, as well? "Yes—for them, it's inherent," says me, Beliza Ann Furman, founder of Wives Of Older Men. And, do others think they have been henpecked by an overbearing, similar-in-age, first wife and feel the need for role reversal? Donald Trump said that when Ivana ran the Plaza Hotel, she became hard. He didn't like *his* wife giving orders.

At the beginning of their relationships and subsequent marriages, I am told by younger wives that they confuse control as concern for their welfare. It's easy to understand why. Few men, if any, have ever paid this much attention to her before. The older husband's experience puts her on track. It feels wonderful. But in the long run, *some* find the dominance suffocating and restricting—thereby developing a love/hate story line.

"Why should she complain?" asked a popular media shrink who had second thoughts about our telephone conversation being on the record. "She's not a victim!" Considering this a valid point, however strong, I listened on (I couldn't get a word in edgewise anyway).

"I think," blasted the shrink, "that younger women with older men behave like teenagers with their parents. They want the rights, and yet they haven't necessarily earned the ability to take responsibility. They take input from their older husband as some kind of insult—and that's when the fight begins."

The shrink called for an immediate attitude adjustment on the part of the younger wife, suggesting that she should draw from her older husband's experience—listen, absorb, and query him—then do as she sees fit. *I'll buy that.*

The shrink, who was blowing me away with this Boot-Camp-for-Younger-Wives mentality, then pontificated that "These women wanted older men so they didn't have to take responsibility...so they could work under the umbrella of his power." *Whew!* "He wanted someone he could feel heroic with. Someone to control, rescue, and feel wonderful."

Brace yourself, there's more. "Younger wives want an older guy to fulfill whatever daddy needs they have. They want someone to take care of them and be ultimately responsible—get them off the hook." Thinking back to my days of being on my own at seventeen—and surviving—I got my back up when the shrink said, "These men went out and took on the world—she didn't. She found somebody who did it so she could ride on his comet and be protected and successful by association. They have the accoutrements of being successful by virtue of his own efforts. Then when she grows up, she's still under the umbrella of his protection but resents the very protection she sought. Ultimately, they don't want to give up his daddying, they just want him to daddy the way they want him to daddy."

Wrapping up, the shrink said, "These younger women don't take responsibility for their own lives which is why they marry a richer, more powerful older guy—then react like a child with a parent, who knows they are dependent. She does not want to let go of the dependency but rails against the order. Then, she doesn't want to take responsibility for having done that! *That's* a bad hairdo."

Well! 'Fes up, this point of view does demand immediate attention!

Six years ago, I met the vivacious Kathi Travers, director of exotic animals and animal transportation for the ASPCA. (Remember Tabatha, the cat, versus Virgin Airways? Kathi supervised her rescue.) I remember her telling me that her twelve-year marriage was the best thing that ever happened to her—that her husband, George, a racehorse trainer, was her mentor and biggest supporter. Their life revolved around animals, and each derived great joy from each other.

After she took the job with the ASPCA, George would stay up many nights to help her bottle-feed baby monkeys and other exotics. She laughed, "He never even changed a diaper for his *first* wife!" Counting her blessings, she said George, twenty-four years her senior, brought a profound sense of history and experience to their marriage that made her feel very secure. Today, she is divorced.

"*Please* tell these ladies to *not* let their husbands retire!" begged Kathi when I spoke to her after the breakup. She said, "George was always controlling but never too bad. Then four years ago when he turned sixty-two and retired, he became a wicked control freak."

Here was this man who was used to getting up at five in the morning and going to work—he was very active and respected in his profession. "Then all of a sudden," Kathi said, "he found himself sitting in front of a television set, alone with his remote control. George had no place to go." Kathi said he was impossible.

"In all fairness, I'm not the easiest person to get along with," Kathi confessed. "I'm mouthy and very, very Irish. And George was very good to me." It seemed to her they started having problems when her own life was taking off. "I'm always on TV or the radio or traveling around the world for the ASPCA. All of a sudden, his life was at a standstill. And George started to get on my case! He got very nasty. He wanted me to quit my job and move to Florida. When I refused, he controlled me financially."

George began to complain about little things. He was upset Kathi didn't make dinner for him. She bellowed, "I can't imagine why that was such a problem! It never bothered him before." She said he became threatened by her business trips and book offer. "I think he was jealous of all the media attention I was getting. I was no longer in his shadow."

Intimidated by the people attending, George refused to go to ASPCA cocktail parties and galas that were part of Kathi's job. One time, she was getting on a plane to go rescue some lions in Mexico, and he forbade her to go. She screeched, "Are you kidding!"

By now, talking a mile a minute—emphasizing her Boston Rs—Kathi blurted, "I can still remember the very spot at Tampa Downs where I fell in love with George. I went nuts over him. George was the most handsome man I ever saw—he still is!" Slightly embarrassed to admit it, she said, "I was his midlife crisis."

Yet now, nineteen years later, she is exasperated and defeated. "We went through so much together," she winced. "His divorce, stepparenting, the murder of his daughter when she was twenty-four, maintaining the strength to hold four grieving children together afterward, and the pain of never knowing who the murderer was."

On top of that, she admitted the stress of dealing with her crazy hours took its toll. Additionally, George convinced Kathi she would be a terrible mother and intimidated her enough to remain childless. "*This* has always remained a very sensitive issue," exclaimed Kathi, "but we survived it! It's hard to believe after all of that, we couldn't make it through George's retirement."

"For the past four years, since George retired, I've been confused," said Kathi. "He was the one who said, 'If you're going to work with animals, you better do it right. Not 98 percent, but 100 percent.' He instilled in me that there were no shortcuts. He put me in the right direction. And yes, I was married to the ASPCA, but he was right alongside helping me. I learned all of this from him!"

Grateful, Kathi admitted she never would be what she is today without him. "I was his best student." But defending herself, she said, "Don't you think he should be proud of what I did with the Travers name? All this crap happened after he retired."

"I hate him now," Kathi sighed. "He was such a coward. It was his way or no way." When Kathi suggested they go for counseling, George wouldn't go. Aggravated, she said, "He never even *tried* to make it work."

One day, she came home from work, and George was gone. Reflecting back, Kathi said, "At one time my husband was a nice guy. And he's *not* stupid. But I am devastated by the way he acted towards the end. I didn't deserve that."

Power and control issues creep up when W.O.O.M. subscribers are in their midtwenties to early thirties. The relationships are awkward because younger wives believe they can't spar on equal footing because of their youth, inexperience, and awe. What confuses the spousal role is this woman is this man's wife, yet her marriage resembles a student/teacher relationship. At the outset, the young younger wife regresses. I see many deal with confrontation in a whiny manner, almost resorting to teenage manipulation to get their way. But sooner than their older husbands think, many of these women develop confidence and come into their own. With maturity and age, they take advantage of the knowledge (which is often significant) learned from these older professors in their lives and wham—an oppressive power play ensues!

You can't imagine how money of her own, prestige, business trips, respect, and her own power threaten an older husband when his young wife's professional life (be it paid or voluntary) soars. Often threatened that her world isn't revolving around him anymore, an older husband doesn't know which way to turn. It's troubling when he realizes he's lost his favorite sports partner, that he can't take endless trips, dinner isn't on the table when he gets home, and *he* is the one visiting Johnny's teacher at school. Making matters worse, the younger wife is not asking permission anymore.

An older husband could almost kick himself for launching this capable creature! But what did he expect? Remember

W.O.O.M.'s survey indicating most younger wives met their spouses in the workplace? Our older man didn't fall in love with his young associate because she was an airhead—she was his right-hand woman in business and otherwise! Crediting himself, he's sure he taught her everything she knows and now look— she's off setting the world on fire, and he *assumes* she doesn't need him! Nevertheless, it's only human nature that the older husband begins to grumble, restrict, and confine. His younger wife simmers in disbelief.

Power and control issues are most prevalent and damaging to the marriage when wives reach their forties and fifties; their husbands, fifty-five plus. The pot boils over because all the emotions festering over the past several years finally surface. Some younger wives have a devil of a time realizing that their newfound confidence and maturity may be a threat to their older husbands. The confusion creates a sore spot in their relationships because these women are being pulled in opposite directions by the same force.

At the outset, the older husband was attracted to his younger wife's independence, assertiveness, and personal successes. Dr. Evan Longin said, "This is a very, *very* special woman." Moreover, throughout the marriage, the younger wife is expected to adhere to an unwritten rule to make the most of herself. Yet, as if she has one hand tied behind her back, she is restrained by her older husband's misgivings, including his fear she may be independent enough to leave him—and not to be discounted, his self-centeredness.

Case in point: Marcie*, a paralegal with a prestigious law firm, is thirty-four years old; her husband Jerome*, a successful attorney in Sacramento, is fifty-six. Marcie wants to go to law school. Jerry is all for it but puts up a real fuss when he realizes she can't join him at their vacation home, one week a month in Palm Springs. When she quits school to placate him, he's disappointed in her, and she blames him for her disappointment.

The power play is complicated to work out. The very traits that were the real *turn-ons* for both the oldster and the youngster when they fell in love, have *turned* on them. Today's new woman who is confident with or without her older husband and secure professionally may not put up with it. Like who the *hell* is he to tell me? Yet, if she is deeply in love, she may find herself compromising even her own values to make a go of it. But she'll be real quick to set the record straight.

Jan Johnson, a California marriage, family, and child therapist and wife of a sixteen-year-older husband, said, "When a husband and wife disagree and don't get their way, they have to put down their arms and talk and listen to each other—face to face. They very definitely have to stop using 'always' and 'never.' And they have to stop using primitive statements such as, *Mommy never took care of me, and you're not either.*"

Jan advised, "People have a right to own their own feelings. Yet, they have to develop the confidence to express their feelings from an 'I' position." People have to take responsibility for how they feel. "Couples battling with a power struggle need to work towards nonblaming." In the age-disparate marriage, there is a lot of projection like, "He's your daddy, and he's going to give you all the things daddy never gave you," Jan said. That's a big order. Sometimes he can't.

"When husbands retire," Jan went on to say, "husbands have a tendency to micromanage their wives like: 'Why are you washing the floor like that?' On an ongoing basis, it can drive a woman up the wall!" Simply rephrasing a sentence and taking a more positive approach can make all the difference in the world.

I mentioned that many older husbands might start therapy with their younger wives but often quit just when it comes time to expressing how they feel. They can't open up. Jan said, "I never knew my husband, Pete, was such a controlling person until I stopped being so controlling. When we were first together, it was the passive man/controlling woman situation. He grew up in a strong Swedish Midwestern family. They were never allowed to express feelings at all—especially, feelings of anger. So when he

got angry, we went through a passive/aggressive behavior conflict. He'd do things like leave the house.

"When I stopped being so controlling, and went through
therapy myself, he stopped being passive and has switched over to
being more controlling—so now we get into these power struggles, but they are healthy power struggles. Like he'll say, 'It both-
ers me when you say that to me.' I'll say, 'I don't like the way you
just said that—say it again.'"

When Jan and Pete learned to have a more conscious marriage, he opened up and learned he could express his feelings. Jan
smiled, "After twenty-two years of working at our marriage, we
banter; but don't have to fight anymore. I feel really good with
Pete now."

Judy*, a fifty-two-year-old divorcee, has been a buyer at
Nordstrom's department store for the past eighteen years. She
supported two children and struggled to make ends meet.
Recently, she was promoted and became a divisional merchan-
dise manager, a position she deserved and desperately wanted.
Into her life walks Hal*, a sixty-eight-year-old retired police captain. They fall madly in love.

Hal wants to take Judy on a two-month-long dream trip to
New Zealand and Australia. Judy insists she can't take that much
time away from work. Hal boasts, "You don't need to work anymore. I'm going to take care of you!"

"At first, it was like a dream come true," says Judy. "I worked
my butt off all of these years! I was alone and scared most of the
time—afraid I wouldn't make it. Hal's offer was so tempting, but
I would *never* give up my benefits and security."

At present, Hal and Judy are trying to work it out. But they
are spending more time arguing about her quitting work than
enjoying each other's company. (Some of us might wonder why
he doesn't seek out a sixty-eight-year-old woman who would be
damn pleased to accept his offer!) Judy said, "Hal is in a position
to compromise. I'm not—but he won't. What if I do quit my job

and we become disenchanted, or he dies unexpectedly—where am I then?" Younger wives spend a lot of time delving into Catch-22s!

I went out to St. Louis to visit my stepdaughter, Laurie. While there, I looked up an old friend who is engaged to an older man, eighteen years her senior, and invited her to join me for an after-dinner drink at my hotel. Lorraine* is very talented. She's written a couple of books and is respected as a fine art appraiser.

After a few minutes of catching up, she stared nervously at her watch. I said, "Are you in a hurry?" "No! Well, yes," she sighed. "Brad* expects me home in a half hour, and I need to watch my time." I suggested that Lorraine call Brad, tell him that she is having a great time, and she'd be a little late. But she groaned, "He'll be mad at me because I'm not with him, and I'll be upset all of the way home."

Lorraine is forty-eight years old, but cowers like a two year old when it comes to her relationship! She constantly gives in to Brad's possessive hold on her. We talked it over and both came to the conclusion that she had allowed this to happen. She said, "Brad has always dominated me. In a lot of respects, I kind of like it." Yet, when she is appraising a Monet or a Miro, she is well respected and admits she would be embarrassed if her business associates ever saw that side of her.

Typical of many women her age, Lorraine grew up at a time when husbands were the boss and it was okay. But now, she is torn between his demands and keeping up with the pressure society places on women to perform equally. She's caught between a rock and a hard place. It's a long way from May to December when the younger wife and older husband have to cope with the peculiarities of their own, particular age group.

The unfortunate thing is that many of the younger wives I deal with, ages twenty to seventy-plus years old, aren't secure enough to state their position when dealing with older husbands. They allow themselves to be subjugated by their older husbands and begin to rely on their dominance. Many are torn because often they like being taken care of (who wouldn't at times?). However, this impedes intellectual growth and accepting responsibility.

Awhile back, I was talking to one of the few gentlemen who initiated the call and subscribed to W.O.O.M. He said he was worried that his younger wife, twenty-one years his junior, wouldn't be able to take care of the house and finances when he died. He said, "She doesn't know the first thing about balancing a checkbook."

I asked him how their finances were handled thus far. "Oh of course, I always took care of that," he bragged. "But when my cataracts started to act up, I had Susie* help me. What a disaster! I lost control for two months and now, I've got to clean up the mess!"

I explained that W.O.O.M. didn't offer courses in bill paying but suggested that perhaps he should give her another chance. But I cautioned, "This time don't challenge her. Help her—be a team player!"

At first, he was taken aback by my assertiveness. But on reflection said, "I realize a lot of this is my own fault. I never trusted her to do as good a job as me. We've been married over thirty years, and I always felt I needed to take care of Susie. She was just a young girl when I married her." In essence, Arthur* stifled Susie's development with a half-the-age, half-the-brains perspective. He has always dictated her life.

One February, I was sitting on the beach in St. Thomas reading *The New York Times*. When I opened the "Wedding section," dated February 21, 1993, I noticed three of the thirteen brides—thirty years old and under—had married older men. "Well...well...well," I thought, "we've really come up in the world!" This, after all, was the *Times* not the *National Enquirer* which used to be the only journal that covered age-disparate marriages.

I read each announcement closely. Patricia Wagstaff, a stockbroker in Stockholm for Marsh and McLennan, married Mr.

Dohrmann, the company's managing director and chief executive of the Stockholm office, twenty-one years her senior. "Good luck," I chortled. "She's marrying her boss! Their power adjustment is going to take some time getting used to."

Scanning the page, I came across Claudia Dumschat, director of music at Trinity Evangelical Lutheran Church and Broadway United Church of Christ, both in Manhattan. She married Richard Olson, twenty years her senior, a playwright who graduated from Princeton University and received a master's degree from Yale. "This guy's venerable. She's too young to be venerable—yet, from her job description, I can't see *her* taking a backseat to seniority."

Then at the very bottom of the page was Alexis Robinson. She was married at the ritzy Church of Bethesda-by-the-Sea, Palm Beach. The announcement mentioned Alexis was an advertising coordinator at Sotheby's International Realty in New York. She married John Waller III, fifteen years her senior. He's the founder and chairman of the Waller Capital Corporation, a cable-television investment banking company in New York. He's *real* successful, and she appears to be really rich and successful. Clash!

Silently, I quipped, "Just take a look at all that male/female power!" Then thought, "Who is going to give in, compromise? Let's call in Woody Allen! He loves and *lives* relationship follies!" Kicking it around, I smiled and thought, "These guys are in big trouble. Each of their previous marriages ended in divorce! They have married the American dream for older execs, but wait until these ladies want to have a baby, a nanny, a house in the country, a Range Rover, and their career!"

Throughout this book, I have discussed the huge responsibility it is for a man to marry and cope with the predilections of a much younger woman. By now, some of you may be wondering, "Is she for this marriage or against it?"

Of course, I am all for it but would be remiss if I didn't help open the airwaves for both the younger wife and older husband to vent misgivings. Appreciate that my flippantness in describing the futures of our *New York Times* brides is a reaction to the tug-of-war situations I hear about from W.O.O.M. subscribers and their husbands on an ongoing basis.

At the outset, the age-disparate marriage has all the trappings of a fairy tale because while dating, both parties only see what they want to see. The older lover sees that his paramour is young, pretty, and will give him a new lease on life. She sees that he is handsome and sophisticated and will watch out for her. However, the very things that appealed to the couple in the beginning can create an enormous clash later on—when they really get to know one another and maybe find out that he or she is not what they were looking for in a spouse at all.

The tough part is that often the couple can't or refuses to comprehend each other's age-related goals, dreams, and commitments. They get into a power and control struggle. To obtain an upper hand and take responsibility for each other's happiness means that both the husband and wife will have to face their differences head on. Unfortunately, sometimes they don't want to.

❧ *Surviving Stepmotherhood* ❧

*O*ne of the most common, difficult-to-answer questions asked about the younger woman/older man union is exactly what is the new wife's responsibility in raising his kids? Will she be expected to quit her job and stay at home if he is the custodial parent of young children? What if he has older children who have moved back with him after college? Their coming and going, interference and inferences, friends and late hours could drive a wedge through any happy relationship.

How will the new stepmother feel about giving up her weekends and vacations to be with her husband and his family if he only has limited visitation rights? Will her husband help her with cleaning up after them? What about dinners, homework, and other parental responsibilities? How much time will *he* devote? How traditional is this man? Considering he is older, he may not be accustomed to pitching in.

A black cloud looms overhead when an age-gap couple blends two families. Most often, the wife's children are considerably younger than his. Expect more than pillow fights! The majority of older stepsiblings will resent the attention younger half- and stepsiblings require and receive.

Subscriber Kathleen Doucette, a thirty-six-year-old stepmother of three children in their early thirties, appreciates any bitterness that comes between her husband's and their kids. She surmises, "Second-time-around dads are older and have learned that family is more important." She said a lot of men ignore their family when they are younger because they are struggling financially and are often too exhausted at the end of the day to spend time with their kids. "I think a lot of older, second-time-around dads are more secure and probably try not to repeat mistakes they made with the first family."

The truth is, when dad remarries a woman with or without kids, everyone is pulled every which way. The generation gap between stepmom and dad may clash with her modern discipline standards and his conventional family values. Most devastating, though, is how a younger wife handles her resentment of taking care of his kids when her husband won't let her have a child of their own.

These are just a *few* of the stepfamily scenarios I hear about regularly that interfere with the blended family's well being. If not worked out, each on its own creates havoc. Combine a couple of them, and you're headed for certain disaster! When I conduct a W.O.O.M. meeting and mention the stepchild issue, loud groans far surpass the positive reactions. Angela, a forty-year-old subscriber who has two stepchildren in their early thirties, says, "Hope for short visits." On the whole, subscribers who are stepparents feel as if they and their marriages are on thin ice. Younger wives are torn between a husband who wants it all to work out and his children who want it all to go away.

All of the professionals I interviewed for this chapter concurred: Unless you both have established your position—what you're going to have to personally give up, your level of involvement and expected parental duties—*before* your marriage, the situation can get stormy. Don't wait for your husband to talk about it. For your own sake, you should initiate the dialogue. Use a mediator or professional experienced in stepfamily situations who understands what lies ahead if the going gets rough. Fathers won't be able to foresee the demonic behavior their precious darlings are capable of exhibiting. Bear in mind: Under the best of circumstances, marrying a man with kids is one *colossal* commitment!

FOR BETTER OR WORSE—Most of us, one way or another, are abruptly initiated on our wedding days. As luck would have it, many stepchildren turn into the worst of monsters just when it's too late to duck out. Even when the stepmother and stepchild enjoyed a friendly premarital relationship, after the marriage, there is almost always some degree of resentment that comes from the competition for dad's affection, time, and even money. The rivalry can undermine any positive feelings that once existed. The son's or daughter's loyalty to their mom is also a serious consideration. In some cases, the ill will is short lived; in most, it's an ongoing bellyache.

Subscriber Jody said she has a congenial and friendly relationship with five of her husband's six children, some of whom were older than she. However, she senses her stepchildren liked her more before the marriage. She said, "Inheritance rights may be an issue." She feels like an outsider when the kids reminisce about "the good old days."

Before her husband died, Martha thought she had a good relationship with her stepchildren. After his death, they dragged her through court and tried to take away the business she and her husband built together.

Some stepmothers are dismissed as "dad's wife." With good reason. Stepmother is practically a dirty word. Judith Winckler, a family well-being agent for the Cornell Cooperative Extension of Broome County, New York, publishes a newsletter, "Building Strong Stepfamilies." When we spoke, she mentioned that some children will go to great lengths to dissuade dad from bringing home a wicked stepmother. Subliminally or consciously, a stepmother connotes evil, bad, and mean. Winckler noted, "Fairy tales, like 'Snow White,' have done stepfamilies a great disservice." They portray the stepmother as the wicked witch of the west who will interfere with the good relationship children enjoy with their dads.

The reality is you have married a package—for better or worse. One that will include the children's mother and her family (even if she is deceased) as well. With respect to the continuity of the marriage, the younger woman, in love with an older man with children, really has no choice but to accept some type of motherly role. Some do it with more grace than others. Nevertheless, it is startling how quickly the anticipated romantic beginnings of newly wedded bliss vanish in the wake of addressing stepchildren's needs, hostility, and insecurities.

THERE WILL BE TIMES WHEN YOU DON'T FIT IN—As you are confronting problems dealing with his kids, bear in mind that your husband is dealing with his own dreams, goals, conflicts, and disappointments. The guilt in leaving children behind after a divorce or remarrying and replacing a mother after her death is too emotionally charged an issue for a father to always be rational. At times, you'll feel helpless. At others, intrusive—like a third wheel. It will be very difficult for you to penetrate the family bond, their language, and history. Complicating matters further, Mrs. Winckler said, "The less contact fathers have with their children, the more common it is for them to side with their children and close out the stepmother when they visit."

In the book *Stepmothers*, authors Merry Bloch Jones and Jo Anne Schiller discuss upsetting and traumatic first experiences. They quoted one stepmother who said her first memories were of being overwhelmed by the realization that her stepchildren's needs will forever compete with, and usually take precedence over, her own.

The authors warn, "Don't expect your husband to understand your feelings about his children. Where his kids are concerned, you and he will probably always have different perspectives. When you can, let his feelings prevail. Assume his needs about his kids are greater than yours."

Subscriber Kathryn says, "I have a lot of repressed anger toward my stepchildren. While I know it is not right for me to hold things against them that their mother caused to happen, I just can't seem to help myself. I saw my husband go through hell for them, and I sometimes feel they don't deserve his love. Now that I am a mother myself, I understand this love a little more."

Recently, Kathryn called and brought me up to date. She admitted she is still having a great deal of trouble getting over the pain of what she and her husband have been through. "It's been an awful ten years," Kathryn lamented. "And it's not over! As much as I wish I could say an emphatic '*No*,' my husband insists his grown son who lost his job move back in with us." She quipped, "Fasten your seat belts, this could be interesting!"

LOYALTY BACKLASHES—The parameters are different for a younger wife who has stepchildren too close to her in age to be her own children and more difficult still, if they are older. In a W.O.O.M. survey I conducted entitled "Your Relationship With Your Husband's Kids," 24 percent of the 112 subscribers who completed the questionnaire have stepchildren older than they. One would think dealing with children old enough to reason, who have been around long enough to appreciate the ups and downs in relationships, would make it easier, but it isn't. Stepmothers violate continuity. They usurp mom's position which divides loyalties.

As a vivid reminder of the discord between the biological mother and stepmother, many subscribers added various comments to the survey that indicated the children's mothers and her family pumped their kids' minds with venom and bile. Stepmothers constantly feel defensive.

Older adolescent and adult children have as much trouble dealing with loyalty as younger stepchildren. Many are just meaner and more apt to verbalize or act out their disdain. Teenagers and adult children who no longer live at home pay a visit, wreak emotional damage, and then leave. Because they are not in the home on a daily basis, it takes longer to work things out. Accustomed to an order that has prevailed for many years, older stepchildren disrupt the efficacy of a new wife's discipline and ideology. Because she is young, older stepchildren tend to mock her abilities.

A real power play develops when, all of a sudden, this complete stranger walks in and has some different ideas about how a household should run. Judith Winckler acknowledged, "Teenagers experience a great loss of power. If they had a single parent for any length of time, chances are that parent used them as a sounding board and that child assumed many more responsibilities than she might have had in a two-parent family. The new stepmother tips the rules, roles, and responsibilities. It's going to cause chaos."

STEP BACK AND WATCH WHAT HAPPENS—Stepmothers have been given a bad rap since "Cinderella," but Kevin Richer, president of the Stepfamily Association of America based in Lincoln, Nebraska, says, "Some stepmothers, in an effort to be accepted, come on much too strong—too quickly." Sure that they love children because all their nieces and nephews love them, stepmothers who haven't had children assume their relationship with their husband's kids will be similar. Richer says, "Out of the best of intentions, they try too hard." Stepmothers are often disappointed when their stepchildren aren't quick to respond positively.

Mr. Richer advised, "This sets in motion some of the rejection a stepmother feels. She needs to back off and let her husband's children get to know her—take a very conciliatory position—a *one-down* position." He suggested that stepmothers try to stop being a stepmother and become a friend. And not set herself up with expectations. "She's a Johnny-come-lately to that family. The stepmother is going to have to let the family set the pace." He also warned, "Stepmothers should be very, very careful not to try to establish a parental role. They're never going to be able to pull that off."

Suzanne is only nine years older than her oldest stepchild. She said, "It has been a long haul. The boys have blamed me for their parents nonreconciliation. Despite the fact their mother and father were separated before I came along, all three children believed their parents would end up together again. [They thought] I was the culprit preventing this."

Suzanne assured her stepchildren that she was not trying to take the place of their mother. She said, "I took a complete backseat. Letting them come to me when they were ready was especially helpful." Suzanne confided it has taken a long time, but now, she and her stepkids have a fairly stable relationship—the sulks and tantrums are practically nonexistent.

ADJUSTING TO DIFFERENT SETS OF RULES—When stepchildren are younger, the disciplinary change in command is confusing. It's even tougher when it's on an every-other-weekend basis. Young children find themselves bogged down trying to adjust to different sets of rules and values at selected intervals. Actions that don't disturb their mother bother their stepmother. And vice versa. The young stepmother becomes an easy target for abuse. Out of earshot, she's the bimbo. Many stepchildren act out when they feel their turf has been violated by shocking physical and emotional changes. They refuse to accept new decor as strongly as new family values. This can continue even when they are grown, married, and living on their own.

PART-TIME DAD—Many stepchildren feel shunned by dad when he divorces their mother. No matter who is at fault, he is often the one who leaves. Not just the house but them. He is no longer a part of the daily happenings in their life, putting a Band-Aid on the scraped knee or giving driving lessons. He is often not there at the moment of crisis to buoy deflated spirits. Even if he calls regularly, the telephone is a hard, cold instrument that can't replace an arm around a bruised child's shoulder.

Children's weekend visits are contrived affairs. Dad becomes a tour director shuttling kids from the movies to McDonald's while packing in a couple of weeks worth of missed parental opportunities. In essence, he's not a *real* dad anymore. When he marries a much younger wife, mom's injured ego can often turn her into a raging maniac. The children are the victims of her self-centered scorn. Many W.O.O.M. subscribers complain that the ex-wife's interference with the father's visitation with his child(ren) was particularly damaging to a healthy relationship with his kids and irritating to their new marriage.

When dad is a widower, the deceased mother is enshrined. There is an exact recall of her disciplinary patterns, which were, of course, perfect. The stepmother is locked in by an aura of remembered past sensitivity and is often undermined by the dead mother's immortalized standards. Those words "Mom would have let me" can leave a new stepmother powerless.

RESENTMENT—Stepchildren continually resent the wicked step-mother who in their eyes is the perpetrator of their humiliation and loss. In reality, it is a no-win situation. The empty black hole caused by the abandonment of divorce will never be filled by her. Lashing out at the innocent, usually much younger than their father, second, third, or even fourth wife is a sure bet. It's safe. "I don't love her—she means nothing to me—this airhead's not *my* mom!" Unfortunately and almost always, the pain for both the children and the stepmother has almost irreversible consequences because of the enormous effort and energy it takes to make the relationship work. However, for those with fortitude it can have a happy ending—sometimes.

Connie Ruggiero* has a thirty-eight-year-old stepdaughter who constantly compares her to her mother. "Paige* also seems to be jealous of everything I get—even if I pay for it myself!" Connie revealed that Paige, who is thirty-six, doesn't go out of her way to see her father, but when she does, she's all over him. "As soon as he walks out of the room, Paige passes off sarcastic remarks which offend me and my children." Obviously, Paige has gotten her message across. Connie wishes she had broken off the relationship with her husband before committing to marriage.

Tennessean Kim Campbell-Dunn, twenty-three years old, had a very strained relationship with her twelve-year-old stepson, Brandon. During the two years she lived with her husband, Joe, before they were married, there were lots of bad feelings. Kim blamed the child's manipulation of his father, who undermined her discipline. She said, "We went through many hard times, and each of us wondered if it was worth it."

Kim, who has no children of her own, said Joe's son was her biggest obstacle in deciding to get married. She confessed, "I would not accept him, and he absolutely did not like me. We were both fighting for his dad's attention." To make matters worse, Joe was granted full custody of his son. Kim thought, "Surely this will be the end of us!" But shortly after her stepson moved in with them, things changed for the better. Kim says, "We both realized we just had to get along for his daddy's sake."

Brandon, like so many children, believed Kim broke up his mom and dad's marriage. Trying to put herself in Brandon's shoes, Kim thinks, "Brandon was afraid I was going to split him and his dad up, too."

Concerned that Brandon might feel left out at their wedding, Kim and Joe bought him a simple wedding band of his own. They also asked the judge to include him in the ceremony. Kim said, "Brandon cherishes that ring. It made all the difference in how he accepted our marriage." Happy and relieved, Kim said, "I gained a wonderful new husband and a new stepson, whom I think of as my own now." She advises giving stepchildren a chance to adjust. "If it can work with me, it can work with anyone."

If the new wife can be objective, she'll understand that there is a real basis for her husband's children resenting this alien addition to their household. To maintain their status quo, children usually manipulate and attack at every given chance. The stepmother is the interloper.

Family therapist Jamie K. Keshet, author of *Love & Power In The Stepfamily*, writes, "A new adult member of the family is not a part of your child's agenda. The child (including those who are grown) is a step or two behind you in accepting the changes brought about by the divorce. When you finally let go and are ready to enrich your life, your child may still be letting go of the former family. You try to explain that mommy is still your mommy, but the children may find it hard to understand this concept. They have no intellectual framework in which to place this new idea."

SOMETIMES, IT'S HOPELESS—One W.O.O.M. subscriber said she has never met her husband's son. Others wish they never had! Ayline Richter* told me that her stepson stole checks out of *her* personal checkbook and cashed them to subsidize a drug habit. Weeks later, her husband asked her to rescue the stepson from a lower Manhattan drug hovel and arrange for him to enter a dry-out center. She cries, "Randy's* brain is fried, and he is near death. His mother has washed her hands of him."

A subscriber from Pennsylvania said her two thirtysomething stepchildren tried to taunt and scare her out of her inheritance. Within a few days after her husband's death, she had to arrange for police protection! Fortunately for some, the stepchildren survey indicated that only 7 percent of the stepmothers interviewed said their stepchildren lived in the father's home.

"The stress is taking its toll," says Susan*, a forty-year-old W.O.O.M. subscriber from South Bend, Indiana. "I can't find a decent therapist who can understand what I am going through. I've been marching from shrink to shrink begging for help, but it doesn't do any good because my husband refuses to go with me." Susan's stepchildren ranging in ages from thirty-four to forty-nine years old treat her like dirt! When they visit, at least half of them walk right past her without so much as a greeting. "The others aren't as kind," says Susan. "They come prepared to give me a hard time."

Susan told me she goes to work, has a good day. "But the moment I hit the house, I get severe headaches and abdominal pains. I feel worthless, used, and unloved."

When Susan tries to discuss the problem with her sixty-eight-year-old husband who was a widower before their marriage, it falls on deaf ears. Once Susan told Joe, "I can't hold out much longer. He as much as said, 'There's the door.'"

I asked Judith Winckler for one piece of advice she could offer a woman in Susan's situation. She said, "Her best bet is to send an 'I' message. '*I* am feeling very left out...not a part of things. When you and your children are together, I don't feel like I have a place.'" She cautioned, "He can choose to do something or not, but let him know, 'we can cooperate just for today, but I won't put up with this tomorrow.'"

Kevin Richer said, "Stepmothers are dependent upon the role the father sets up for her. She can't make a role for herself. The stepmother can be the sweetest person, but unless her husband makes a place for her and insists on it, she's without a country." The inability or unwillingness of the biological father to take a stand will leave his young wife hanging out there. Richer also said, "Some fathers tend to kiss ass, just so they won't lose contact with their kids. That's so damaging for the stepmother."

GUILT, ANGER...DISTRUSTING LOVE—Children take divorce very personally. According to several professionals, stepchildren become consumed with guilt because they believe that they caused the divorce. Many have a low self-esteem and can't accept or return love. It can take years for them to trust the love of others.

Stepchildren need to express their feelings about the divorce. This will help them to not feel responsible. Defensive and caught in the middle, it's too painful to blame their parents and risk losing their love and affection. When the stepmother comes on the scene, she's an easy scapegoat for all ills. She's also a constant reminder mom and dad will never be together again.

Even adult children are often embarrassed about their father sporting a young chick on his arm. All kinds of sexuality issues enter the picture. It is kind of tough for the close-in-age or younger-than-them stepmother to command respect, particularly if she has been one of many live-ins or wives the children have seen in their father's life. Sometimes she is caught in the cross fire when Junior is secretly in love with her, too!

There isn't a quick solution for the anguish and hurt a stepmother goes through when she marries a man with kids, especially those close in age or older than the insecure, often unprepared, younger wife who wants to put her best foot forward. Their hostility can be brutal. Only time can help.

To make way for a happy marriage, the father and stepmother have to be sympathetic but not give in. If both the wife and father respond to unfounded criticism with, "I'm sorry you feel that way... I hope in time we can work it out," they'll present a united front that the children will eventually see is impenetrable. Uppermost for the stepmother is that she concentrates on her marriage and makes sure it is working.

Sherrie, twenty-seven years younger than her husband, describes her relationship with her stepchildren as, "One good, one tolerable, and two nonexistent!" She complains, "They never really befriended me. For the first four or five years of our marriage, I sent all the girls presents and cards or money for various holidays and birthdays. Never once did I receive a thank-you note or a birthday card for me or their father."

After awhile, with her husband's blessing, Sherrie decided, "*The hell with this!*" She stopped cold. "It seemed they didn't know the difference," says Sherrie. Under the best of circumstances, at the outset one can only hope to have a civil relationship when she is with her husband's children. Unfortunately in some cases, hostility lingers for years.

George Wilson* divorced his wife when his daughter Carey* was three. Twenty-three years later when she was planning her wedding, she invited her dad, her stepmother who was twelve years younger than George, and half siblings to attend but never asked her father to walk her down the aisle or to join her stepfather in giving her away. Insensitive to his feelings, Carey ignored him and the subject completely.

George was heartbroken because he had never abandoned this child. He had picked her up every other weekend, took her on vacations, paid for her college education, and was there for her at any time. George said, "At first I was going to tell her to go to hell! But I went to a therapist, and he helped me sort out my feelings. With his help, I mustered up a lot of emotional strength and courage and went to the wedding. I didn't want to lose her completely."

However, he was emotionally unprepared for the slap in the face he received when he arrived at the church. He got through his daughter being escorted down the aisle by her stepfather. But as the minister, who was never told Carey had a father present and a concerned father at that, offered his congratulations to George's daughter, her new husband, and her parents, he referred to Carey's stepfather as her father. Devastated, George was in tears. He remembers not being able to breathe.

Sadly he recalls, "What added salt to the wound was the woman sitting behind me. She whispered to her husband, 'I wonder if her *father's* here?'" At that point, George said, "I had to run out of there." Moments later, even friends who sided with George's ex-wife after the divorce came to his side to express how appalled and upset they were over the terrible slight.

Despite it all, George, encouraged by his wife, Jennifer, waited in the vestibule to ask his daughter, "Why?" She just stared at him. Carey, unable to understand the hurt she caused, was confused by George's anguish. Children are so used to having their feelings attended to, they too often grow up without a clue that their parents have emotions, too.

Stung by the destroyed relationship, George says, "I didn't know what to do. How to cope. I never realized how much Carey hated me." A few days after the wedding, Jennifer, upset for her husband, sent Carey a letter telling her how hurt they felt. Carey sent a return letter that explained her position. The letters vented everyone's frustration and deep-seated hurt feelings. They all realize the damage is irreversible but are attempting to start over.

Jennifer admits, "I am not certain we will ever be able to discuss the past. Both of us are afraid to rock the boat. But just knowing that we are a family—that everyone is trying—makes every effort worthwhile."

I WANTED TO PULL THE COVERS OVER MY HEAD AND SLEEP THROUGH IT!—More than 90 percent of the W.O.O.M. subscribers who are married to men with children complain that their husband's children put a tremendous strain on their marriage. There is no quick resolution. I remember times I wanted to pull the covers over my head and sleep through it. On other occasions, I found I was babbling incoherently to myself.

It was especially bad when I was planning my stepdaughter's wedding! Laurie was caught between a power play with her mom who came out of the woodwork and dad who was paying the bills. Then there was me with whom she had lived for the past sixteen years! Fortunately, the groom's side was pleasant. Their only concern was "How could a Christian pick a decent rabbi?" Don't ask—Martha Stewart doesn't know the half of it!

In retrospect, I realize time, patience, consideration of everyone's feelings, not undermining everything their mother does, and not blaming oneself for what happened in your husband's past are effective paths to follow. Holding one's tongue over trivial matters, deep breaths, lots of Tylenol and Tums, and *especially* professional help, are good antidotes

It took me many years to understand that I wasn't responsible for Sam's unhappy marriage, his ex-wife's contempt, Laurie and Jill's sibling rivalry, or any of the unhappiness that happened before me. *Sam was.* I spent year after year fixing, mending, healing, testifying in custody trials, deferring having children of my own. And I was only in my twenties! I made myself sick over trying to develop a sense of stability out of this chaos. Instead, I should have concentrated on my marriage, my children, and Sam's and my love and happiness. All of the rest would have fallen into place as it has anyway.

In *Stepmothers,* authors Jones and Schiller described me to a "T" when they so deftly state, "In fact, most stepmothers are so focused on gaining the approval of their husbands, stepchildren, and stepchildren's mothers that it does not occur to them that they have the power to take control of their own emotional lives."

Years have passed and despite their parents' and stepparents' squabbling, Laurie and Jill are now both well-adjusted, happily married women engaged in their homes and professions. And Sam is a proud grandpa. As a family, we're all eager to put the past behind us. Relieved, we are picking up the pieces—sorting them out. And just maybe, taking a look at each other as individuals for the very first time. Our past grievances will always influence how we act and react, but it's a tremendous relief to shed the baggage. Deep down we all really love one another. We just have to develop the confidence to express it.

Recently, we had a family reunion at our vacation home in St. Thomas. I hadn't seen Sam so happy in many years. He was—*unconditionally*—Laurie and Jill's dad again.

DEEMPHASIZING THE STEPMOTHER'S ROLE—W.O.O.M. subscriber Jan blames her husband's overinvolvement with his adult son who gets into trouble for any strain on their marriage. At times, they sought professional guidance, but in the end she realized she had to stop getting involved with her stepson's difficulties and concentrate on taking care of herself and her husband.

Sometimes when the children are older, it is best for a stepmother to remove herself from her husband's relationship with his children. It's more productive to play up being dad's wife and deemphasize her role as their stepmother. When they visit, it might be best if she did some errands or see a friend—just not be there all the time. Dads and their kids need time to be together without her around.

STEPDAUGHTERS' ANGUISH—I once had a conversation with Robin, a beautiful and lively forty year old, who told me that for years she was the one who tried to work at the relationship with her impenetrable father. But his new, younger wife was jealous of the time they spent together and would vie for his attention when the children were visiting. Sadly, she sighs, "At times when we were little, my stepmother would race to the car so that she could beat my sister and me out of sitting next to dad." Over the years, the relationship has deteriorated. "We haven't spoken for two years now."

Stepmothers in general try very hard to keep the family together despite resentment and hard feelings. When Karen Handler* was in her late twenties, she wrote a letter to her stepdaughter when she turned fourteen explaining that the love a dad has for a child should not have to change with the addition of the love he has for his new wife. Unfortunately, the child, who is now twenty-four years old, hasn't been able to cope with the rivalry and almost as if out of spite, has turned to alcohol and lying.

LOVE AND ANGER—Linda, the forty-four-year-old stepmother of forty-five- and forty-eight-year-old stepchildren, mentioned that it took fourteen years to develop a "great" relationship with her stepson. "The turning point came several years into our marriage when I finally forced him to tell me why he disliked me. He would not come up with a reason but said, 'Just habit, I guess.' I explained how his father and our daughter were hurt by his behavior toward me." Gradually, Linda said her stepson changed entirely. "We are finally happy in each other's presence. Holidays and visits are very pleasant."

Keshet explains in *Love and Power in the Stepfamily* that anger and conflict are tough for most of us. She says, "We dread conflict because it can lead to anger." Often, "We think of love and anger as opposites," when in fact, "Love and anger can go together. Similar to when you and your husband have a good fight followed by passionate love making."

She continues, "Anger is frightening because it is a powerful emotion. Dangerously, it can lead to violent feelings and violent actions. But anger that is recognized and controlled is also a sign of personal power and an expression of the depth of our caring."

ANGER AND SABOTAGE—For years Linnea Berg* curbed her anger, held her tongue, and brushed off the rude remarks and cruel and damaging antics of her fourteen-years-younger stepdaughter, Helene*. The worst of which was when Helene went to her father's best friend and convinced him that Linnea and her husband Sandy* were alcoholics. And he believed her.

On a roll, she didn't stop there! Helene went to her dad's office and pulled the same thing with his partner who fortunately didn't believe her and told Linnea and Sandy. It took them months to convince Sandy's friend that Helene was lying, but it took years for them to get over her sabotage. They couldn't understand why she was so desperate to hurt them.

Naturally, Linnea and Sandy no longer trusted Helene. They tried very hard to return to the love and concern they had before, but it was tough. Helene went to college, was married, and had a child. Things improved but were never the same. Helene acted as if she were the injured party.

One afternoon years later, Linnea went to the airport to collect Helene and her baby. As she waited by the gate and thought about their relationship and how it had deteriorated over the past twenty years, she couldn't help crying. The strain this woman/child had placed on her and Sandy's marriage had been brutal.

A few minutes later, Helene came up the ramp, laden with baby in arms, carry-ons, and a stroller. Linnea offered to help, but Helene recoiled. Aware that Helene didn't want any favors, Linnea let her struggle. After several hundred feet of watching Helene drop things and run out of steam, Linnea blew. She screamed, "What is your problem?" Helene spun around. Her scornful eyes said, "I don't want to owe *you.*" It was frightening to Linnea that her stepdaughter could detest her so much. But the confrontation gave way to some dialogue and soon after, Helene and Linnea were at least able to politely talk to one another.

GIVING-IN DADS—Guilt-ridden about the divorce, some fathers tend to be overly permissive, unnecessarily generous, and often proprietary when it comes to *his* kids. They may or may not say it, but some operate within a *"That's mine!"* mode of defense. On many occasions, they undermine the stepmother's discipline. After all, she's just a kid, too!

Often, a father is caught between a rock and a hard place. Does he please the stepmother whom he loves very much or his kids whom he loves very much, also. Many only see their children every other weekend and a couple of vacation weeks throughout the year. Some share joint custody or have physical custody.

Because their time together is precious, dads tend to overlook poor behavior and bad manners as a trade-off to not losing his children's love—even when he knows they are wrong. For convenience, and because divorced parents compete with each other, children from broken homes usually have two sets of everything. And if both parents have remarried only once, stepchildren have at least four pairs of grandparents and assorted extended aunts, uncles, and cousins to dote on them. They seldom want for material items but confuse gift giving with love and continually need more. Dads tend to fall for that trap, also.

Linda Osprey*, thirty-one, said her fifty-one-year-old husband feels so badly about abandoning his children when he divorced sixteen years ago that, "He throws money their way to ameliorate his guilt feelings." These things are perceived as a quick fix, but in reality they are a poor remedy when a hug would be far more potent.

Thirty-six-year-old Susan Dorsey* went to a therapist to help her cope with her stepchildren's efforts to interfere with the happiness and success of her new marriage. Her sixty-one-year-old husband reacted to his ever-present guilt by being, "Too permissive in setting limits when his two youngest children lived with us," she says. At other times, "It led him to being overly generous with me. Against my wishes, he cosigned for loans for his late-twenties sons who are consistently delinquent in repaying. Now, *we* receive the notices from bill collectors and have to pay to protect our *own* credit rating." Susan said her husband seems afraid to ask his sons to repay the money. "When I mention it, I become the bad guy or wicked stepmother."

Oh yes, keeping it together with your husband and his kids requires the utmost endurance. And as W.O.O.M. subscriber Terri Rosmarin Zestar suggested, "Perhaps the following chapter should be 'How To Find a Good Lawyer To Get You Off Attempted Murder Charges.'"

There will be times when you can't make it alone. At those moments, reach out for support—it will make all the difference! In the meantime, try a couple of these exercises I have compiled from my experiences and the various professionals with whom I have spoken:

> Be there, listen and care but don't interfere or compete with the mother's role. Ask continually, "What would your mother think?"
>
> Find something positive about each family member and build on that.
>
> Step aside. Let dad assume some of the responsibility for his children. Mom, too!
>
> Take a stand. Insist your husband hear how you feel.
>
> Understand stepchildren need space to mull it over. If they have gone through a traumatic divorce, it will take a great deal of time (years!) for them to sort out their feelings.
>
> Don't pry.
>
> You will most often have to make the first move. Let them know, "I'm here for you when you want me."
>
> Always invite, always include. Let your stepchildren accept or decline.
>
> It *ain't* easy, but don't take it personally. They probably wouldn't treat any other stepmother any better.

Note to Dads: Two weeks to very young children is an infinite amount of time away from their father. If distances allow it, opt for shorter, more regular visits or preferably, continue the every-other-weekend schedule and add dinner out during the week. You'll see a drastic change in behavior for the better. Moms, I hope you read that, too!

214 ❦ Beliza Ann Furman

❦ The Issue of Wanting a Baby of Your Very Own ❦

Elizabeth Murray and I sat together at Lou Reinken's funeral. After being diagnosed with cancer, he died quickly, at the age of sixty-five. We grieved and cried for his wife, Renate, who sat next to her two grown stepsons. Most of Renate's family reside in Europe and only a handful of family members came to comfort her. Nineteen years Lou's junior, Renate was all alone—childless. One half of a loving and devoted, twenty-year marriage that began and ended with Renate and Lou.

What upset Elizabeth and me, particularly, was that we had something we so desperately wished Renate had. A child to hug her...chatter away the endless, solitary hours. A living legacy to remind her of the precious moments and memories she and Lou had together. Fingers and toes—smiles—and sparkling eyes that would keep Lou alive, forever, in Renate's heart. A son or daughter to care about Renate when she gets old—a child of her very own.

Only a mother can appreciate the devastating sadness Elizabeth and I felt for Renate who had commented on *Geraldo* that at first she didn't want a baby. Then, "*Yes.*" And after awhile— "*No again.*" Yet, as if she was echoing her older husband, Renate reminded herself as well as us, "You knew from the very beginning what you were getting into."

Unlike Renate, Elizabeth and I had been certain of what we wanted. We fought hard for our babies! Elizabeth and her older husband, Larry, waited out eleven years of heartache trying, failing, and then at last, finally delivering their precious son, Michael.

Sam asked me to put his children first. At the beginning, it wasn't a problem. I was in my early twenties, training for figure-skating shows, working in his office, and helping him rebuild his life. But later, I realized how very much I wanted and needed *our* child. The love and affection I had for Sam's daughters just wasn't enough. I was desperate for a bloodline to connect me to the marriage—to make me a part of the family. A baby who looked like Sam and *me!*

When Sam saw how upset I was becoming—that I was beginning to resent the time I spent with my stepdaughters, Laurie and Jill, the never-ending court battles, the frenetic weekend visitations—he backed down. He realized just how much having a child meant to me—to him—and to the future of our marriage.

Eight years after we were married, I delivered the little boy I wanted so badly to carry on the Furman name—our son, Sean. By then, I was president of Beliza Cosmetics and was sure that one child would be enough. But on my thirty-eighth birthday, I decided it wasn't. It was a little harder convincing Sam the second time around, but seven years after Sean was born, I got my own little girl, our beautiful Ashley. Two little redheads. My greatest accomplishments!

Of course, the effort for both Elizabeth and me was worth it! And never did we count our blessings more than that tragic day when we realized how terribly alone Renate would be.

The baby issue drives an unsolvable wedge between younger women married to older men. For W.O.O.M., this *is* the Number 1 issue! My subscribers tell me that no other age-disparate problem causes such emotional anguish and endless remorse. And anyone who has been through the arguing and the agony of rejection knows this is one issue, no matter how much it fragments the relationship, on which no compromise exists. Either you have a baby or you don't. And all the money in the world can't replace having a child—if you want one.

Often, young younger women who fall in love with older men are so busy with their careers and growing up themselves that they feel confident they can fulfill their promise to their older lovers that they will not have children. Yet, an older husband, who often has children of his own, has to comprehend and appreciate *even more than she* that his younger wife may not be able to stick to that pledge. If he's fair and concerned about his younger wife's happiness, he has to offer her the opportunity to change her mind and let her have a baby naturally or through adoption when her maternal urges strike. If he doesn't yield to her wishes, he'll place a kiss of death on their relationship. The younger wife will seethe with resentment—cynicism—and the marriage will flounder and may eventually fail.

Nancy* and her fiancé, Mitchell*, twenty-eight years her senior, went to premarital couple therapy to resolve many issues. Yet afterward, Mitchell still insisted Nancy would have to give up the idea of having a baby. Standing firm, Nancy told Mitchell, "That's one condition I am not agreeing to." However, without the baby issue resolved, they quietly married. Nancy and Mitchell avoided putting an announcement in the newspaper and shared their good news with a only handful of friends. Because Mitchell is a physician in a very small, provincial midwestern town, he was concerned about how his marriage to a younger woman would affect his practice.

Nancy feels playing down their May/December marriage is spilling over and influencing Mitchell's decision not to have a baby. "He's very worried how the community will react," says Nancy. "I have argued that I am only thirty; he is fifty-six. He's my employer. When he's gone, I won't even have a job. I'll be alone most of my life." Nancy went on to protest that she felt Mitchell is being self-centered and thoughtless. "He doesn't want to share me with a baby."

During our interview, I rooted out another, perhaps, deep-seated reason why Mitchell has cold feet: His kids. To anyone listening, Mitchell says, "I'm too old. I can't start over. I don't want to pay for children and have to work for them the rest of my life." Yet, Nancy told me Mitchell has called his twenty-eight-year-old daughter to ask her opinion. Or, in reality, is he asking for her permission? Fortunately for Nancy, Mitchell's daughter reassured her dad that she thought it was just fine. "Now," says Nancy, "he's going to call his son." In view of Mitchell's misgivings, I suggested Nancy wear a good-luck charm.

In November of 1993, I waited out election-night results of Christie Whitman's gubernatorial campaign with a charming man who is a successful financier in Manhattan. We were talking about my book, and he mentioned that several top brokers in his company had divorced their similar-in-age wives in search of a younger one. He asked me about some of the issues that crop up.

When I mentioned the baby issue, he said, "Yes, these guys refer to it as the ultimate wrinkle! They just don't want to have one." "Yet," I responded, "they continually seek out a young lady who will promise them the best of both worlds." I assured my friend that any guy who gets involved with a younger woman has his *head in the sand* if he thinks she's going to be happy for very long placating him by suppressing her longing to have a baby.

World-renowned artist, Georgia O'Keefe told one of her friends, "I'll die if I don't have a child of my own." In the book *O'Keefe and Stieglitz* by Benita Eisler, the author describes O'Keefe's quixotic infatuation with children and writes, "There had never been a time in her life when Georgia had not wanted to have—and assumed she would have—a child. Wherever she lived, she had *adopted* little girls of friends and colleagues."

Eisler goes into O'Keefe's maternal obsession and quotes one of O'Keefe's letters to an old boyfriend, "There must be a little one in my life someday." And Eisler adds, "Georgia felt enriched by her engagement with young children."

This longing manifested itself in her art. "She tried to retain the direct perception of a child," writes Eisler. However, when she fell in love and married illustrious photographer, Alfred Stieglitz, twenty-three years her senior, her dreams of motherhood were shattered.

Eisler felt the baby issue was so important between O'Keefe and Stieglitz, her adulating mentor and indefatigable promoter, that she dwells on the topic. "During their first months of their life together, Alfred seemed receptive to having a child." Knowing it would be easier for Georgia to continue her career, his niece, Elizabeth, offered to care for the baby Stieglitz and Georgia would produce. On hearing this, Alfred said, "I'm beginning to see the possibility."

But according to Eisler, "Early in 1922, there was no more talk of possibilities. Alfred had either changed his mind or, never intend[ed] to have another child. He had preferred to appear undecided. In the heat of passion, to declare his adamant refusal to allow Georgia to have a baby would have seemed a failure of love; it was easier to equivocate with *perhaps* or *someday*." Even though Georgia ultimately supported Stieglitz and he was emotionally—almost childishly—dependent upon her, she felt, "A baby agreed to under duress would be her child, not his."

The decision for Georgia to remain childless, Eisler feels "Bore the burden of other broken promises, of unmet needs, unspoken resentments, betrayals like internal injuries that weaken as they bleed unseen." Knowing the decision was set, Georgia's life became riddled with chronic depression. At one point, she spent months in a sanitarium. Yet she was completely dependent upon her older husband's approval—as if she would be nothing without him. She said, "I don't like being second, third, or fourth. That's why I get on with Stieglitz—with him I feel first."

For many younger wives very much in love with their husbands, a baby truly consummates their marriage. And as we discussed earlier, age-disparate couples feel isolated and alone. At the beginning of their marriages, they have a hard time making friends. Young children will help them integrate into the community—give them an opportunity to meet other married couples with kids. Another plus is that parents, siblings, and friends may accept them less unfavorably as a couple.

Elizabeth Hirsch told Diana Williams of ABC's *Eyewitness News* that at first she promised her fifty-four-year-old husband John, a successful Wall Street executive, that she wouldn't have children. She said, "John made it very clear to me that his time meant a lot to him." A baby just wouldn't work. But a few years after they were married, Elizabeth realized, "I lied to him and I lied to myself."

Luckily, John had a change of heart. He remembered putting himself in her shoes and realized he couldn't deny her a baby. He admitted to do so would have been "pretty selfish." Yet, he was adamant about his role: limited diapers and *no* PTA meetings.

When you think about it, power, control, rejection, parental overtones that you can't have—or do—and selfishness are involved when denying a young woman of her right to motherhood. If an older man doesn't want to have children, his best bet is to find a woman his age who has had her tubes tied and get the young, beautiful plaything notion out of his head!

Susie Friedman* wrote me that her to-have-or-not-to-have-children issue is an ongoing change of minds. She and her husband, Jay*, a father of five, have been going round and round for five years! "We are wrought with strife," she cries. "I remember calling counselors to help," yet confesses, "I would hang up the phone when the secretary answered." Susie admits to being confused over pleasing her older husband and pleasing herself. However, as she reaches forty, she feels, "The decision is coming to its own natural conclusion."

When Jay and Susie were dating, she brought up the baby issue during premarital counseling. She remembers Jay saying he was open to the option. Yet, after they were married, he decided definitely not to have children. However, baby fever consumed Susie. Eventually, Jay suggested she leave him and start life over with a man who wanted kids. "But I just wasn't motivated to do so," says Susie. "I wasn't sure I wanted children badly enough to hurt him. So now my feelings about offspring are of surrender. It is a sacrifice not having children, and I am, in my own way, griev-ing my loss."

Susie, who just received her college degree, said that she feels there are pros and cons to not having children. But at present, she envies women who have happy healthy families. She says that she is content with her life-style with Jay and savors their time together, but laments, "I will never know that special bond that a mother and child share nor the challenge and responsibility of raising a family."

"Couples are often reluctant to talk about it with each other because it's such an explosive issue," says Peter Schild, an Old Bridge, New Jersey, psychologist. "It can tear their relationship apart. It's particularly frightening when there's been a longtime silent understanding that they would have children, or when there's been an actual agreement—then one person changes their mind."

Recently I received a letter from W.O.O.M. subscriber Vickie Hill, who wrote, "Unfortunately, Jerry and I are divorcing after twelve years of marriage. We were unable to resolve the baby issue. There was no right or wrong; we could see each other's point of view. He did not want to start over with a new family, and I couldn't imagine my life without children."

Vickie felt depressed living in a no-win situation with this issue. If that could have been resolved, the marriage would have been a happy one. But not being able to come to terms on it exacerbated what would have otherwise been run-of-the-mill, workable marital problems.

Reflecting back, Vickie realizes, "It was an incredible struggle to reach this decision; we both feel so badly—but relieved. We're not hurting each other anymore. Unfortunately, divorce was cer-tainly the better conclusion for both of us." Vickie can't stress enough the importance of discussing and resolving this all-important issue up front—before marriage.

There are a lot of *reasonable* reasons why an older man doesn't want children. He may not have enjoyed fatherhood the first time around. It may have interfered with his job, career aspirations, and free time. Some fathers have been through an awful divorce. Perhaps, his children don't talk to him. He may be afraid of rejection, anxious about failure. Or he may not want to offend his original family.

Some men can't see how they are going to pay for college tuition with social-security checks. A lot of older fathers take a look at the thirtysomething fathers changing diapers on television and can't possibly relate. I mean, What's Lamaze? Others want their freedom to come and go without the hassles of babysitters, car seats, and breast pumps. Let's face it, Sam and I were potty training Ashley and planning a wedding for his daughter Laurie at the same time. *That's* parental commitment!

But take a look at the physical, erotic side of it. Finally, an older man has the wife of his dreams. He's aroused by the Victoria's Secret lingerie, the firm, smooth skin. A swollen belly, stretch marks, an episiotomy—midnight feedings—a baby who will divide his wife's attention aren't on his agenda. Perhaps, they are unfriendly reminders of a previous marriage that went awry. Once the playmate of his lifetime gets pregnant, he's *married...* committed...his illusions have vanished.

Additionally, there is the embarrassment of being too old. "What if someone makes fun of me? God forbid...mistakes me for this child's grandpa?" That's a real ego crusher that only a man with a great deal of confidence can deal with.

"George was afraid when the baby came," said food authority, Jenifer Harvey affectionately about her older husband, "that it would take away all of his toys." George Lang, is the owner of the celebrated Café des Artistes in Manhattan and an international food consultant.

On the other hand, during their interview with *Metropolitan Home,* writer William L. Hamilton discovered, "The birth of Lang's son, Simon, taught the man who has been called 'the experts' expert' an unexpected lesson: how to relax." To

Hamilton, "Jenifer and George's home is the best of both their worlds: A clear harmony of new and old rituals."

On many occasions, I have had young women call me to say that their weddings were canceled, just as the invitations were ready to be sent. Often the cause is the baby issue. Karen*, a sales representative, told me her fiancé, a sixty-three-year-old politician, twenty-eight years her senior, decided after many heated discussions that he would let her have a baby. With his promise, she went ahead and bought a wedding gown and planned her wedding. The day after the invitations were mailed, he said he couldn't live with the decision.

"It was such a dirty trick," says Karen. "He knew all along what he was doing. He wanted to embarrass me in front of my family and friends into marrying him on his terms." Which she did. Fortunately, his conscience got the better of him, and they did have a baby. But a young woman can't count on this always being the case. And don't even think about having a second child. Many W.O.O.M.ies are escorted, by limousine, right to the front door of the abortion clinic!

Jan Bohren, seventeen years older than his wife, Debbi, compromised, and the couple's six-year-old son, Jonathan, will probably be their only child. Even though Debbi might like to have more children, she says, "You have to look at the practical side of it—putting a child through college on retirement." Jan admits, "I'm not real good at [parenting], but I'm a lot better at it this time around."

What perplexes me is that younger women who really want babies are incredibly intimidated by their older husbands. Some are so uncertain they can make it in life without their husbands that they relinquish their hope and make this extreme sacrifice. They allow one of the most important decisions of their life to be made by someone else! Many live in constant denial. Nevertheless, if I hear one more time from an older husband who brags about how much *his* children fulfill their stepmother's baby needs, I'll run to the nearest toilet! Because often, it's *his* younger wife who is on the phone calling me weekly to find out if she can live with the agony.

Furthermore, some older husbands also overlook how inconsiderate it is to expect his younger, child-denied wife to jump up and down over the birth of his grandchild. Many of these women bemoan the obligation of accompanying "gramps" to the hospital for a first-time visit. Often this puts her over the edge. Word of caution—don't ask her to buy a baby gift!

In the view of Jeffrey Berger, a Metuchen, New Jersey-based psychologist, "Couples don't necessarily have to agree on everything. But," he told Ruth Padawer, a staff writer for *The Record* of Bergen County, New Jersey, "if they disagree on this one [having a baby], one person feels rage, pain, and embarrassment. The other feels suffocated and backed into a corner. On top of that, they both feel an overwhelming sense of fear that if they stick to their positions, they could lose each other."

On a trip to the Caribbean, I spent some time talking with Lisa, a Continental flight attendant. I mentioned that I was writing a book about younger women marrying older men. Surprised, Lisa said, "Oh I just read about you in this month's *Mademoiselle!*" She said the article interested her because she was engaged to a neurologist, sixteen years her senior.

With this chapter on my laptop back at my seat, I was eager to enter Lisa's feelings. I asked, "Do you plan on having children?" Lisa responded, "It's something I really have to think about—I'm not sure it's fair to him." After dealing with so many women who regard not having a baby a matter of not being fair to *them*, I asked Lisa what she meant by that.

Lisa explained that after she and John had dated for about six months, he mentioned he would like to marry her someday. Excited, but a little concerned that John might not be interested, Lisa brought up the issue of children. She was straightforward and wanted him to know from the very beginning that she required the option of having at least one child. She even discussed the possibility of she and John having a baby with his thirteen year-old son. Lisa said, "He wasn't that thrilled about it and took it as a threat. Shortly after we talked, he insisted I start sitting in the backseat of the car so he could sit, up front, next to his dad."

Weeks later, Lisa's birthday and Christmas came and went, but John didn't give her a ring. Then six months after they started dating, Lisa and John, who had been single for ten years, broke up.

Missing her terribly, John contacted Lisa four months later. They got back together again. But Lisa said, "John wasn't sure he wanted to get married anymore. He told me, 'I think I may be too old to have children.'" Yet after being without her, John realized Lisa was very important to him. When their relationship became very serious, John and Lisa made an appointment for premarital counseling. During the three sessions they attended, John accepted that marriage to Lisa would mean he would have to accept having a child. Last October, Lisa and John were married with a full understanding of each other's concerns.

Mary Beth Hartley* is engaged to a divorced man, twenty-two years older than she. Unlike Lisa, she's afraid she'll lose her older fiancé if she makes a point of how important having a baby is to her. She reasons, "I know it's wrong, but I'm scared. Robert* has told me over and over again, he doesn't want to have a baby. If I push the issue, I'll lose him."

I warned Mary Beth her problems may be bigger than she thinks, adding "Wouldn't it be best to find out before it's too late?" She then revealed her secret wish. "I am hoping, after we're married, he'll see what a wonderful wife I am and change his mind." To many of the W.O.O.M.ies who rely on this optimistic approach, I have responded, "I wouldn't count on it!"

Edward Monte, a family therapist in Moorestown, New Jersey, who specializes in conflicts over parenthood, asks couples to switch roles. He suggests, "The one who doesn't want children talks about the positive side of parenthood. The one who wants kids talks about the disadvantages."

Many professionals agree this is a very constructive approach. It opens the door to communication and alleviates the threat of personally revealing one's innermost fears. Objectively speaking, someone else has done it for you. It also will help each partner ascertain if their images of parenthood are realistic.

In the book, *Who We Are*, author Sam Roberts uses census figures to judge our nation's proclivities. He points out that "There are more families now without children than with children." Today, society is more accepting of couples who opt not to have children. For women who are career bound and don't want a family or for those physically unable to bear children, marrying an older man who doesn't want any kids or to extend his family could be very fulfilling.

Others who have given up on the idea, for whatever reason, but feel the need to be around children could volunteer their services at orphanages, hospitals, and schools. One of Edward Monte's therapy clients, who gave up her dream of motherhood, demanded that she and her husband take in foster children for short-term care. Monte said, "She wanted to feel needed, like she was giving back to society."

A few older husbands are secure and happy having children later in life, albeit, not always without obstacles. Many will reverse vasectomies to please their younger spouses. Others go through stringent fertility programs, including a few subscribers who fly great distances, back and forth, to visit reproductive specialists not available in their areas.

Steve Miles, from Clarion, Pennsylvania, was forty-two years old when he married Pam, seventeen years his junior. Married once, without children, he really didn't care one way or another if he ever became a father. But he knew it was important to Pam.

For a couple of years, Pam and Steve tried to conceive on their own, but it was futile. Concerned, Pam went to a doctor and learned she had endometriosis. "The ironic thing is," laughed Pam, "my family felt Steve was too old when we got married and probably wouldn't be able to have children. And it turned out to be me who had the problem!"

Determined, Pam wanted to go to a reproductive endocrinologist. Steve went along with the idea. However, he was skeptical. In the back of his mind he felt that, perhaps, this doctor was going to take advantage of an unhappy, gullible couple who were desperate to have a baby.

Pam's gynecologist referred them to Dr. Paul Tippet, who was associated with Allegheny General Hospital in Pittsburgh. Dr. Tippet was very cautious and took them one step at a time. "My intuition," Pam said, "told me he was going to help us if he could." However, over the next three years, Pam and Steve were emotionally and physically challenged.

At first, Pam had a laparoscopy to remove scarring and tissue. After she healed, she took her basal temperature every morning to determine when she was ovulating. Talk about sex under pressure! "But Steve hung in there," said Pam.

When that wasn't successful, Dr. Tippet prescribed Clomid, an oral medication to be used for four months. However, Pam felt Clomid caused a great deal of emotional side effects and sadly, wasn't their answer. By now, Pam and Steve were focused solely on becoming pregnant. Basically, their life was consumed with doctors, pregnancy tests, four-hour rides back and forth to Pittsburgh, and disappointment. Pam and Steve decided to take some time off, no doctors, no tests, no drugs.

When they returned to Dr. Tippet, he suggested Pergonal injections as the next phase of treatment, although there was concern over the risk of multiple births and ruptured ovaries. For the next four months, Steve injected Pam with the Pergonal ten days each month. The morning after each injection, Pam went to a nearby hospital for a blood test. The blood was sent by courier to Pittsburgh so that Dr. Tippet could tell them how to modify the Pergonal the next evening.

"The rub was," said Steve, "that the blood wasn't getting to Pittsburgh fast enough." Adding a further burden, the Mileses had to find another hospital about an hour away from their home, closer to Pittsburgh, that was equipped to perform the test.

After five months, Pam and Steve were exhausted and defeated. "I would cry every time Steve gave me the shot," remembered Pam. "It was pitiful...so upsetting."

Depleted, the Mileses abandoned the idea of having a child. Nevertheless after six months, they recovered enough from the emotional and physical drain to try one last time. "I desperately wanted a baby who would be part of Steve and myself," said Pam.

The first month passed with no results, but Pam and Steve trudged on for three more disappointing months. "We then decided to continue for one more month," sighed Pam. "And that would be the end of it." She thought, "How much is enough!"

However this time, Dr. Tippet introduced artificial insemination along with the shots. "Steve just loved that!" laughed Pam. "Yeah," sniggered Steve. "That was one of the most humiliating things I ever went through in my life!" Halfheartedly, they waited.

"It was so strange when it happened," exclaimed Pam. "We didn't believe it. Steve went out and bought three different pregnancy tests just to triple check. When they were positive, it was incredible! We went out and bought some more. For days, we kept testing and testing. Steve and I couldn't believe it!"

Pam's pregnancy was perfect! She didn't even experience morning sickness. Steve was in the delivery room when Stephanie was born. Together, they felt the joy of being new parents. A little bit afraid to look back, Steve now says, "I'm so glad Pam pushed me. If anyone ever videotaped my cooing and gurgling with Stephanie, I know I would be embarrassed. It's so fortunate that we stuck it out."

Dan Cary* was married briefly many years ago, but he didn't have any children. When he met his wife Ellen*, fourteen years his junior, he couldn't wait to have children. Two years later, they had a baby boy. Dan, who is fifty-four years-old, "can't wait to get home at the end of the day and hear about Timothy's* adventures." Dan coaches Timothy's soccer league and serves on the PTA. "I would love to have another child, but Ellen has two children from her previous marriage, and her career is just taking off. I don't think it's in the cards."

A few years ago, *Maturity News Service* conducted a survey of over-fifty fathers. The great majority of those interviewed said that they were better fathers with their second families, more concerned, had more quality time, and found the entire experience delightful. Talking to many W.O.O.M. first, second—third—time around dads, I have learned that even those who fought hard to remain "just the two of us" found that after their babies were born, they enjoyed the attention, the love and youthfulness a young child gives to them.

Sam's fun and adventure of enjoying a third childhood through Sean and Ashley is living proof. He's even convinced himself that having them was *his* idea! While Ashley is glued to *I Love Lucy*, he's tuned into *Full House*. He boasts that he's on his fourth Red Flyer wagon and complains, in jest, about how much it has gone up in price since 1965. Accustomed to clutter, Sam has tripped over his share of decapitated dolls' heads and rollerblade gear. Yet, I know for a fact—because he told me so— he wouldn't trade the experience for all the tea in China!

❦ *Dad's Old Enough to Be My Grandpa* ❦

When torch singer, Andrea Marcovicci was born, her father, a physician, was sixty-three years old; her mother, forties pop singer, Helen Stuart, was twenty-nine. In a *New York Times* interview, Ms. Marcovicci said, "I don't remember a day in my whole life that I wasn't worried about my father dying."

Ms. Marcovicci's dad died when she was only twenty years old, but she remembers with pride, "How gorgeously romantic they looked when they went out." She said her parents gave her the love of music; her father, the classics—Chopin, Debussy, Mozart; her mother, the torch songs. She said, "I grew up with my feet in different decades, but I have always had a special nostalgia for the glamour of the thirties." Ms. Marcovicci always wears black velvet so that people will look at her and be reminded of the past.

Many children of older fathers have the distinct advantage of being raised by men who have both feet on the ground. Having seen a good bit of life, these dads are pretty secure with whom they are. And they convey that security to their children.

In many cases, older dads have more money than their younger, often struggling, counterparts. With finances under control, they are usually better providers. Sometimes, too good—older dads can't say *no!* They can't wait to spoil their latest charges and vicariously, themselves. On many occasions, I have had to step in and remind Sam he can't indulge Sean and Ashley like a grandparent!

Like their moms, these kids have the privilege of living and learning about history through the eyes of their dads. Imagine being the children of Russian author Aleksandr Solzhenitsyn! His oldest son, Yermolai, with younger second wife, Natalia, was born when Solzhenitsyn was fifty-two years old. He fathered two more sons, Ignat and Stephan, after that.

And wouldn't we all like to come back as King Hussein's four youngest children? Although their mother, the practical American-born Queen Noor, nineteen years younger than the king, boasts, "We *don't* have a pool," their playrooms have to remind you of Richard Pryor's *The Toy!*

With homes in London, the English countryside, and the palace in Amman, there is plenty of room for them to be doted on by their eight, much-older brothers and sisters from Hussein's previous marriages.

Realistically though, there are children all over the world from every social strata who benefit from the seasoning, wisdom, and judgment only a less-compulsive older father can provide.

Whatever their older dads lack in the athletic department, these guys more than make up for by providing their children with travel opportunities and projects that use the mind more than brawn. Once they get over the initial shock of being a parent, or a parent again, many older dads are so enchanted with their kids, they make the greatest coaches and confidantes.

Actor Cary Grant was sixty-one years old when he married actress, Dyan Cannon, thirty-five years his junior. Shortly after, his only child from five marriages, daughter Jennifer, was born. He boasted, "Jennifer is the most captivating girl I know—and I have known quite a few."

Before he had a stroke and died at age eighty-two, Grant would take Jennifer boating and horseback riding. "I always knew that his death couldn't be too far away," Jennifer remembers. But he left her a letter of musings that urged her to "Be thankful for ears that can listen to Beethoven and a bird singing on a telegraph wire."

Larry L. Meyer, a professor in his fifties who married a coed in her midtwenties, was so enamored with being a second-time-around dad that he wrote a charming book about staying home one summer and taking care of their new baby. I found it so special that he could let down his masculine guard.

My Summer with Molly is *must* reading for any soon-to-be, over-fifty, second-time-around dad. Like Mr. Meyer, many fathers are so thankful to have gotten a second chance to do it right, they are eager to spend lots of time with their little ones. Sometimes though, that can be irritating to the first family, and dad has to remind himself to play fair.

Dr. Elaine A. Blechman, a professor of psychology at the University of Colorado at Boulder, told Lawrence Kutner, writer of the "Parent and Child" column for *The New York Times*, "Older parents tend to have more respect for the differences between children and adults. They may be more patient and better able to focus on the children's needs."

These kids do, however, get very annoyed when their dads are referred to as their grandpas and defensive when their friends say, "Your Dad's so old!"—placing lengthy emphasis on the "o." In general though, children do not see their dads are older. Jonathon Reiser, a tennis friend of mine, said, "I saw my dad's white hair, but it never registered to me that he was any older than my friends' parents. He was my dad."

Dad gets the benefit of having to stay so-o-o young. He has to dress "right" and gets to play with toys he would, normally, be ashamed to admit he misses. Staying in tune with the latest kid craze is the most fun—he might even buy himself his own Game Boy! He can hardly afford to retire and has a reason to focus on everything youthful. Rather than dwelling on an ache or pain, he concentrates on raising his kids. His fountain of youth was right there in the delivery room!

Having kids can have a positive influence on partying older men who have been single for years. They clean up their act! When Warren Beatty and his wife, Annette Bening, twenty-one years his junior, were expecting, a friend of Beatty's told *People* magazine, "Jack [Nicholson] was very inspirational. Having a baby, stopping philandering, and really loving his little girl must have rubbed off on Warren."

Actors Dennis Hopper, Beau Bridges, and Al Pacino are also over-fifty fathers. Clint Eastwood fathered a child when he was sixty-three! And you know what happens when stars "do it," everybody wants to get in on the fun!

On the downside, a child's time with dad may be short. But that means they can't take each other for granted. "As a little girl, I used to run home from school just to be with my dad," exclaimed twenty-five-year-old Christine English*, whose dad was sixty years old when she was born. "I was very lucky to have had him all to myself. When I was very little, he was a successful executive vice-president with a major corporation. Mom and dad would travel to the Orient for weeks on end. If I had been born when he was younger, I never would have seen him. We would have had a very remote relationship."

When Christine's dad retired, her parents sold their big house and let all the servants go. The Englishes moved to a smaller home, and Mr. English spent most of his time with Christine and her older brother. Christine said, "He was hard on my brother because he wanted to set an example before it was too late." However, her brother burned out from all of the pressure. Disappointed, but taking it in stride, Mr. English channeled all of those dreams and goals to Christine. She chuckled, "No longer was it, 'You'll go to a good girl's school and then you'll get married,' it was, 'When you get a job and are real successful, you'll have limousines picking you up' and so forth."

"It was amazing," said Christine. "While my dad was old in years and traditional, he was definitely not behind the times. In no way was he an old person. He knew what was going on in the world and was very up on things. Dad made me appreciate older people and the experiences they have lived through. It was interesting to watch how he melded his generation with what was currently going on in the world."

Christine said she learned a great deal from her dad. "I was like a sponge, I wanted to absorb so much from him. It's funny, dad lived through the Depression; he told me so much about it. When all of my friends were spending extravagantly in the heyday of the eighties, I gave that a second thought. A lot of people used to tell me when I was growing up that I was very mature for my age. So much of that comes from dad. What he had to say was just good common sense."

Christine lived Mr. English's life through his stories and by following his example. She said her dad was strict but had a really fun side to him because he grew up in the Golden Age of New York. Mr. English was the son of a wealthy Manhattan family and lived a very privileged life.

"I used to poke fun at him," smiled Christine, "when he would lower his voice and proclaim, 'Civilized people don't dine before eight o'clock,' or 'Gentlemen only wear boxer shorts.' Silly quirks like that and old-fashioned politeness were ingrained in me."

Moreover, Mr. English taught Christine and her brother how to love and respect a spouse. His first wife was an invalid, but his old-fashioned values compelled him to stay with her until she died, twenty-five years later. They had no children. When Mr. English met Christine's mother, she was twenty-eight years old; he was fifty-six.

"My mom was a Paris model," boasted Christine. "And she and my dad lived a very charmed life for many years. However, when dad's health failed, I lived through the change in their marriage." Her parents went from lovers to friends. "Even though my mother was very lucky to have married a wealthy man when she was very young," sympathized Christine, "I watched how upsetting it was for her to deal with a husband who was very elderly and quite ill." However, their respect and concern for each other got them through it.

"They were both at a very difficult point in both of their lives," remembered Christine, "but dad insisted she go out with her friends and make a life for herself. If they went to parties, he encouraged her to dance with younger men. He cared, very much, about her happiness and respected that she was young and very beautiful and that his aging and poor health were holding her down. His last year was very difficult for her." Christine realizes you pay in life. She learned there are no easy roads in marriage, and you have to deal with that no matter how much it hurts.

"All my *firsts* were with dad," Christine said. "When I was about twelve, he took me to Laura Ashley in New York and bought me an entire outfit. We were always at his favorite restaurant, Gino's, in Manhattan. On my sixteenth birthday, he took me to 21 to have lunch—just the two of us! I knew he was proud of me and proud of himself when the waiters and maitre'd remembered him and put us in the power dining room."

"When dad was eighty-four, he went into the hospital the second time," Christine said with her first glimmer of sadness. "I got scared. I knew he was dying from cancer." She said it was devastating for her to watch him go down. Christine said her dad was frustrated also because he was as sharp as a tack, but his body had failed him.

"I realized our days together were numbered, but he hung in there, and as sick as he was, no one could believe he walked me down the aisle on my wedding day. My brother was all set to do it, but at the last minute, dad showed more strength and energy than any of us had seen in years. He whipped down that aisle so fast; he made the trip perfectly."

Christine said her dad always had life expectancy goals. First it was to see her graduate from high school, then college. "We never dreamed he would be there for my wedding. When he danced the first dance with me, that was the moment we had all been hoping for. I knew, forever in my heart, I would always be daddy's little girl."

"My dad was eighty-five when he died. I was there to hold his hand and see him take his last breath. I knew I would miss my dad, but I wasn't sad. I knew he was miserable being trapped in that old body."

To this day, Christine says she talks and thinks about him as if he were alive. During all of her business decisions and dealings with everyday life, Christine finds herself weighing every new idea with good old-fashioned common sense. "Living with dad, through his illness and now remembering only the good times," says Christine, "has made me a much stronger person. I don't feel deprived, I feel very lucky."

❦ Securing Your Future... The Emotional Side of Money, Insurance, Legacies ❦

*P*ractically speaking, younger wives have to face the bleak assumption that they could outlive their husbands by, at least, the number of years in the couple's age difference. Over the years, I have tried to encourage wives of older men to become more interested in personal finances. But on the whole, it is an exercise in futility—their participation in securing their future financially is negligible. Yet, at the same time, many worry and complain to me that they are uncertain how well they have been provided for if their husbands predecease or divorce them. Many, including those who are highly educated, don't even know how to balance a checkbook—because they have never had or wanted to do it.

Natalie Dworkin*, an executive's airplane pilot, is a case in point. "I went from my parent's home into a quick first marriage at nineteen, a quicker divorce and married my twenty-six-year-older husband right after that. It wasn't until he left me, when I was well into my forties, that I wrote my first check! I didn't even have a credit card in my name—I couldn't buy gas—boy, was I stupid!" On the whole, it seems home economics are generally *done* for younger wives. But eventually, it could *do* them in.

When I suggest that these younger wives appreciate that a Q-Tip (a specific trust) is not just for cleaning out one's ears, many balk at the discussion. "He's always taken care of that." But what about when *he's* not there anymore, dies unexpectedly without a will, the estate is tied up in litigation, and *she* doesn't have enough cab fare to get to her mother's? Younger wives often respond, "That could never happen to me!" Sure.

Generally, the older husband makes more money than his younger wife; but often, his expenses (alimony, support, legal, mortgage, etc.) are greater. However, in every case—even if he says he doesn't have a nickel to spare, which is usually not the situation—younger wives should insist upon some type of protection. But that raises a complicated and emotional set of circumstances (the gold-digger issue, for one). As distasteful as it is, you're going to have to bring it up. If you know what you're talking about, it will have a lot more impact.

Here are some of the common types of survivor-benefit terms and plans with which you may want to become familiar. It is a brief overview and barely scratches the surface of financial planning. Once you understand these terms, you can visit a financial planner or have a discussion with your husband and not feel like a bimbo. If I have tweaked your interest, your local library has oodles of books and financial periodicals for you to study.

ASSETS—Economically, the important difference between age-disparate marriages and similar-in-age marriages is that our husbands have lived longer. They have had more time to earn more money than their younger wives. In 90 percent of the cases, an older husband will have more real estate, personal possessions, and cash (assets) than his wife.

There are gross assets and net assets. It is important to know the difference. You may think your husband makes two hundred thousand dollars per year, but is that before taxes and expenses are taken out (gross)? Or, after-tax take-home pay (net)? You would be entitled to a percentage of the *net* in case of divorce, and that's the amount you should be aware of when preparing a prenuptial agreement.

Some men, especially those who have been burned by previous divorces, are less cooperative when it comes to estate planning than those who are marrying for the first time or had a financially painless divorce years ago. They will be far more dedicated to drafting a prenuptial agreement that puts the emphasis on protecting them. Obviously, in every monetary bracket. there will be those husbands who will divide their assets more generously than others.

WILLS—Most troublesome to me is how many husbands, married to W.O.O.M.ies, don't have current wills or binding agreements, if at all. A will is a traditional way of making sure that assets are passed on to those the deceased intended to leave his estate. It defines who receives what and is handled under the supervision of the court, using probate laws to validate the decision.

Armond Budish, an estate-planning attorney in Cleveland, Ohio, told *Home* magazine he has seen the fallout when financial arrangements haven't been in order. He has experienced "Long delays in settling; disputes over who gets what; huge payments to Uncle Sam instead of money for heirs; and families—sometimes young children—left with almost nothing."

Martha Mlinarich, a thirty-six year-old W.O.O.M. subscriber, knows just what Mr. Budish is talking about! "I'm by no means an expert, but if one person can learn from my experience, it will be worth it. I'm fortunate that I have always worked and had access to retirement plans, and my husband Jim always stressed putting money aside for the future. However, the one thing we did not do, and should have, is put wills together. Jim and I had talked about it for years, especially since he had four children from a previous marriage. He didn't want any trouble if anything should happen to him. Sadly and unexpectedly, Jim recently passed away—he was sixty-one years-old—we were married for ten years but never followed through with the wills.

"In Texas, without a will, everything becomes community property, and his children are now the owners of half of everything we owned. At one time, I was considered by his children a nice person who made their father happy but not anymore. I'm the wicked witch from hell now. I have a fight on my hands, which could have been avoided if I just would have pushed the issue of putting a will together. It is painless and very inexpensive, considering what it will cost to get the estate cleaned up. To anyone out there who hasn't gotten a will put together, do it. Don't do as I did and put it off—there may not be a tomorrow."

Lydia Tomkins*, a fifty-eight-year-old secretary married for six years to a seventy-three-year-old Secret Service man, said, "I don't think older husbands worry about their second wives as much as the first wife because a lot of them don't have children with them."

There is no excuse for anyone to not prepare a will. When a couple purchases their wedding bands, they should make an appointment with an attorney to prepare their wills. If you have a simple estate, you can write your own will and have it notarized. Computer software programs are available that guide you through a series of questions and forms that explain and produce legally binding wills and living trusts.

Considering that financially structuring an age-gap couple's estate is more complex than that of a couple close in age because of preexisting families that require future protection, premarital cash assets, and established businesses, one can understand, but not excuse, not facing up to the responsibility.

There is another underlying reason, a selfish one. Sheila Kaplan author of an article, "Your Money or Your Wife" that appeared in *Dossier* magazine wrote, "Many analysts say there is a resignation on the part of the older spouse that the younger one will most likely remarry after his death. This is not a thought that tends to bring out one's generous impulses."

Greg Sullivan, president of Sullivan Financial Consultants, told Kaplan, "If a spouse is older, they'll assume the surviving one will remarry, and they don't feel they'll have to take care of her for life." When Sullivan asks some older men how they want to take care of their wife, they'll say, "Oh no. She's so pretty, she'll remarry in a week." Not so.

The majority of W.O.O.M. members who are middle-aged wives of older men disagree with their husbands. Edith Weig from Glen Head, New York, told New York's *Newsday*, "The older man/younger woman marriage worked out for us until my husband had a stroke at sixty-two and I was forty-nine years old.

Our children were twenty and eighteen. For twelve years, I was my husband's caregiver. He died at age seventy-three. My life will go on as usual, nurturing the grandchildren, enjoying my job and my friends. After thirty-three years of marriage, I don't think another marriage is in my future. I kind of like my independence at this time in my life."

Many younger wives suggest that entering the dating scene in their middle age doesn't appeal to them. That's for divorcées, not young widows. Joan Greene, a forty-four-year-old beauty who married Jack Greene, twenty years her senior, from Suffern, New York, says, "I want to be able to be comfortable enough where I don't have to feel pressured to date or remarry." What a lot of guys forget is that this marriage is very special. *They* are a hard act to follow.

There are some experts who feel wills, as we know them, are outmoded. The probate process is slow, and probate costs and attorney fees can be expensive. Couples with more sophisticated estates and considerable assets might decide to set up living trusts.

TRUSTS—In cases where older husbands have children from a previous marriage and they want to set aside part of their estate to protect their children's futures in a way that cannot be contested, they can set up a living trust. These documents allow for the transfer of property—real estate, stocks, bonds, mortgages, insurance policies, bank accounts, and other assets—to beneficiaries within days of the death of the benefactor without going through a lawyer or probate. A trustee—a friend, relative, or business associate—is appointed to administer the trust.

"The biggest advantage of a living trust," says Alan Nadolna, a financial planner with Associates in Financial Planning in Chicago and husband of financial planner Suzanne Averill, twenty-three years his junior, "is twofold. *One*: A husband's assets avoid probate. You save the administrative costs and delays inherent in the probate process. *Two*: In the event of the incapacity of the trustee (the older husband, in our case), his wishes can be set out so you don't get the fights between the kids and the spouse when the older husband is, for example, on life support unable to speak for himself."

Furthermore, Mr. Nadolna said, "The living trust lays out distribution of assets and appoints a power of attorney." In other words, who is going to act on my behalf and take care of my financial matters when I am gone. "It is ideal," says Mr. Nadolna, "perfect for the older husband/younger wife situation. It does everything the husband was doing before he was incapacitated and before his executor takes over when he dies—which is critically important." Judging by the lukewarm relationships between most W.O.O.M.ies and their stepchildren, this is the answer to a father's prayer.

There is a revocable living trust and an irrevocable living trust. The revocable trust allows an individual to sell, spend, or give away assets while still alive. The person can change the conditions at any time prior to death. It is also practical. If an older father has young children when he dies, he can specifically state that he wants apportioned assets to stay in the family. For instance, if a father leaves his assets to a daughter and she dies, he can stipulate the money will go to his grandchildren or another family member. If she were the beneficiary of a will and she dies or divorces, those assets might go to her spouse. Not exactly what dad had in mind.

Another benefit of the living trust that can eliminate hassles comes into play when someone owns a home in one state and a vacation home in another. When the houses are put into a living trust, the will only has to be probated in the designated state. This eliminates paying expensive probate and attorney fees in two states and a lot of headaches.

Less popular because once it is established it is impossible to revise, the irrevocable living trust allows a person to make a "gift" and forfeit all control of the property, while still alive, in order to receive a tax exemption from federal estate taxes.

Edmund Iannaccone, a financial planner for American Express' IDS Financial Services, says, "Irrevocable living trusts save you a substantial amount of money in estate taxes. This trust is advantageous to an older father who has very young children. Rather than giving his kids all the money at once, which he would have to do if he had a will, he can 'gift' it into an irrevocable living trust, build the money up in the trust, and then, after his death, the trust can distribute the money according to his wishes."

Mr. Iannaccone gave a very clear example. "Suppose a father has a half-a-million-dollar estate he wants to leave his kids. He may not want his teenagers to get a half a million dollars to blow upon his death. So he puts this money in an irrevocable living trust. After his death, the trust will distribute the money according to the father's wishes. They could get half when they are thirty-five and the other half when they are forty-five." This is a beneficial way to handle distribution of assets when a fifty-five-year-old father is planning for his two-year-old child's future.

Mr. Iannaccone pointed out still another benefit to having a living trust. It can protect a younger wife if she remarries after her older husband's death. He said, "To safeguard his wife—particularly, if she didn't have a prenuptial agreement [with her next husband]—a husband can stipulate how he wants his money distributed. She could get half of the money at the outset and half ten years later. Or, he could specify that she get a certain amount each year." Good thinking! If she divorces that husband, some Joe he never met isn't living off the fruit of his labor. A husband could select from many living trusts to enact these wishes.

According to *Dossier* magazine a Q-Tip trust (qualified terminable interest property) is another useful strategy to consider when an older man remarries a much younger woman. Author Kaplan reports, "In this type of bypass trust, the investor names the beneficiary, usually a spouse, who upon his death collects the interest from the trust. Upon his spouse's death, the entire trust reverts to a third party, usually a child or several children. This does not give the woman full control—something new brides find disconcerting. Then she might say to him, 'I don't want to be answering to a trustee. Don't you trust me? I'll do what you say.'"

An AB trust is yet another type of bypass trust that allows a wife to live off the interest. She can take up to 5 percent of the principal just by asking the trustee, plus at any time the trustee sees fit, he can give her more if he/she feels it's for her health, welfare, and maintenance. However, prior to setting up a trust, you need to have your lawyer confirm your assets. For example, if you own a million-dollar home in a community property state, don't forget that you are only entitled to include half of that in the trust—your spouse owns the other half!

An irrevocable life insurance trust can be established to carry life insurance on the husband. This trust is totally free of estate taxes. The insurance can be purchased with funds provided either by the husband or the wife. A properly funded trust can provide income for the surviving spouse and, again, have the benefit of avoiding conflicts with other family members.

It is important to note that some of the features of the specific trusts I have mentioned may be applied to other trusts as well. Additionally, when assets are under sixty thousand dollars or so, advisors say a will is simpler and less expensive to prepare and very effective. Trusts are far more complicated and very expensive to arrange.

INSURANCE—Women are sensitive about money matters. Concerned their intentions will be misunderstood, many hesitate to bring up the subject of their future. In the heat of passion, "It's tough to ask a guy to beef up his life insurance policy because he'll probably check out before the college bills arrive," says Sheila Anne Feeney, a writer for the New York *Daily News*. Yet, after these men are dead and gone, the horror stories I hear are distressing. It makes you wonder just how much some of these men loved their wives.

There are two types of life insurance that should interest you. Whole life insurance is very expensive but only has to be purchased once. The advantage to this type of policy is that you may borrow against what you have paid in or cash it in and take out the accrued money at any time while the insured is alive. It sounds good on the surface, but it takes years to build up any equity. Most insurance agents write very few whole life policies.

Term insurance is more practical. As of January 1995, a person may purchase term insurance for a period of fifteen years with a consistent premium. You cannot borrow against what you have paid in or cash it in, but the annual fees are five times *less* than whole life insurance. At the end of fifteen years, the insured has to reapply for another policy or convert it to a whole life policy at much greater expense. There are several term insurance policies that can be purchased, in select situations, which provide coverage for a longer period, but the premium will vary. Every life insurance situation is different. It is important to let your agent help you define your needs and then suggest an appropriate policy.

However, if a husband does not want to pay for insurance, a wife could take out insurance on her husband's life and pay the premium herself. Murray Guth, owner of the Murray Guth Insurance Agency in Fair Haven, New Jersey, warns, "The kicker is she can arrange for the policy, but she still has to ask her husband's permission, and he has to sign the waiver line that makes her the owner of the policy. But once he does that, she can do whatever she wants with it."

If the husband owns the policy and makes his wife the beneficiary, he then controls the policy and could, without telling his wife, change the beneficiary at anytime. "It could be his girl friend," says Mr. Guth.

If a forty-year-old man is healthy and doesn't smoke, a $100,000 term insurance policy, good for fifteen years, will cost under $250 per year. As men age, the premium increases.

The question of how much insurance to buy depends upon how much money the person(s) being protected will need at the time of the death of the individual who has been supporting the family. All of us would like to be the beneficiaries of a million-dollar policy; but it is highly impractical for most of us. The premiums are expensive and unrealistic for many couples. Besides, wouldn't your husband be a bit suspicious if you insisted upon an astronomical amount?

If a woman is twenty-six years old, and she and her fifty-year-old husband have a baby, their needs will be significantly greater than those of a fifty-one-year-old career woman who marries a sixty-six-year-old gentleman whose children are off the payroll. Making it easier all the way around is if this middle-aged younger wife has older children from a previous marriage who are being supported by their father.

However, one never knows how reliable a father's support payments will be. What if he loses his job? Or, *he* dies without a will? A number of wives of older men take out an insurance policy on their life naming the children from a first marriage as the beneficiaries. It's a great idea, but I have seen crazy repercussions when she uses her older husband's money to pay the premium.

A few years ago, I held a W.O.O.M. investments program at Saint Peter's Church in New York City. It was far from reverent! Ed Iannaccone offered to speak to our group about setting up a financial program to protect younger wives. Whether the older husbands intimidated their wives into not participating—"Why do you need to hear about that, haven't I taken good care of you?"—or, the younger wife wasn't interested, the turnout was worse than I expected. Only one couple attended. But that was just the beginning! Within minutes, this couple began to argue heatedly. I thought for sure this guy was going to haul off and belt his wife!

It all started when she mentioned that she had taken out an insurance policy on her life naming her two children from her previous marriage as the beneficiaries. Well, this was *news* to her older husband who came along "for the ride"—with a royal chip on his shoulder. Rather heavy, he turned bright red in the face and bellowed, "You used my money to do *what!*"

She explained her insurance plan project and whispered defensively, "I took it out of my allowance you give me." "What!" he yelled. "You have a nerve! You mean to tell me that if you die, your kids are going to benefit from money I provided *you!*" I'm sure he was silently thinking, *I hate those goddamn kids.* By the way, he ranted on, "How *much* do they get?"

By now cowering in the corner, I wondered, what difference does it make what she spent her allowance on. So she gave up a once-a-week manicure for the sake of her kids—big deal! But this guy went on and on humiliating his younger wife. Feeling responsible, I was really upset. Ed and a tax attorney he brought along were shocked, too. They offered to drive this lady, who was visibly shaken, home. I ran from Saint Peter's to the nearest bar. Ed's reward for his efforts? His car was towed away! *That* was and will be W.O.O.M.'s last financial seminar.

THE IDIOSYNCRASIES OF AGE-GAP FINANCIAL PLANNING—Financial considerations for the age-disparate marriage are complex at best. They are further complicated because the age start-point for each couple differs. If a woman is twenty-two years old, in graduate school, and marries a divorced forty-one-year-old man with two children, she'll have to consider that his lack of cash flow due to alimony and child support may put a damper on their life-style. She may have to go to school at night and work during the day. Often, I find younger wives resent support payments because, as it turns out, many are less well off than the first wife.

When a younger, second wife is pregnant, everyone finds out, real fast, that marrying a younger woman can be a very expensive venture, as well as a big responsibility. The marital scenario changes. And it's far more complicated than the addition of baby bottles, cribs, and strollers.

The couple is a family now; an aura of assets equality surrounds them. The prenup as it stands goes out the window. The wife's status has elevated—this is his new baby's mother! Wills have to be revised, trusts set up, insurance policies purchased, and college investment plans established—all separate from the older husband's first family. Enter the investment banker or stockbroker—money needs to be put aside for stocks and bonds! Smith Barney Shearson broker Al Natale, Jr., says, "They might want to think about annuities." Our new family is going to need a home; the young wife's name appears on the deed. Terms like community property take on a new meaning. Financial obligations can become overwhelming; bills pile up. One positive for her: the younger wife now has more control.

After a few years, the younger wife may want to resume her career. However, in a situation where the husband doesn't want his wife to go back to work (so she will be free to travel around with him—common in the age-disparate marriage), he's going to have to think about compensating her for lost career opportunities. If they have a prenuptial agreement, it could cost!

As the older husband ages, the age difference poses more complicated needs, wants, and future protection. As he reaches sixty-plus, the oldster worries about retirement costs, sickness expenses, and perhaps, money needed for a senior citizen's home for him. His young wife is thinking about acquiring, adding onto the house, and redecorating. At some point very soon, she is going to have to adjust her expectations. Her friends, who have married men their age, may be refinancing their homes and doing great things with the money. But she can't even think about it! Her husband is at a point where he has to reduce debt to protect her future and his young family when he retires, is disabled, or deceased.

FINANCIAL PLANNER—A certified financial planner can help a couple get on target. Some are attorneys or accountants. In many cases, they act as a marital mediator when a couple cannot agree on fiscal priorities. A financial planner will help you understand where you stand now to determine your current requirements, as well as what you will need to meet your future goals. I would highly recommend, a *couple* seek professional advice when setting

up wills, trusts, and all types of estate planning. Usually, these people charge an hourly fee, similar to what an attorney would
charge in a specific geographic area.

Paul Yurachek, a financial planner from Washington, D.C.,
told *Dossier*, "With a fifty-year-old husband and a thirty-year-old
wife, she wants the good life, and he may have already led the
good life and wants to slow down. She wants to spend a bunch
of money for insurance in case he drops dead, on the other hand,
he doesn't want to spend the money on insurance because he'll
be gone. You have to really grab them and shake them and make
them define an objective."

At all times, a couple should preplan well enough to avoid a
court battle if their marriage dissolves. The lawyers will get it all.
If the couple is happy, the older husband should prepare his estate
tightly enough to ensure that after he is gone, his children and
other heirs can't contest his will, take money or investments away
that he intended to leave to his younger wife and different families. The financial planner gets rid of the guesswork.

SOCIAL SECURITY—Many age-disparate couples will rely heavily on the husband's social-security checks to survive financially.
However, advisors suggest that the more affluent older husband
consider social-security benefits as a bonus when planning one's
estate. Those individuals should not regard it as an important
source of income. Supplementary investments, yielding interest,
will be far more critical when relying on day-to-day income for
wealthier couples.

However, many other services fall under the heading social
security and play an important role in every family member's well
being. Under the heading social security, you will find the following divisions and services: old-age, survivors', and disability insurance; medicare, including hospital insurance and supplementary
medical insurance covering other medical costs; supplementary
income; unemployment compensation; aid to families with depen-

dent children; medicaid; social services for adults and children; and maternal and child health and crippled children's services. You can call your local social-security office for more information.

As you can see, there is no set financial formula an age-gap couple should follow. And what may hold true today, will not work tomorrow. Laws change. The important thing is that you act now and don't postpone protecting you and your family to the best of your ability. But first and foremost, don't get so wrapped up in whose money is whose that you lose sight of the love affair that brought you together in the first place. You might not be able to afford to live separately. Nevertheless, money is emotional.

❧ *The Final Hours* ❦

I have talked about the myriad of circumstances surrounding the age-disparate marriage that deal with the inner workings of the relationship. Yet because many younger wives are preoccupied with their husband's death—sometimes from the very moment they fall in love—a heartbreaking, and often frustrating, dimension is added to the mix. Tonie Papaleo said, "Joe is so much a part of my existence that I have silently lived, for many years, in exaggerated fear of his death."

I attribute this premature obsessing to the fact that we often perceive our husbands as old, even when they are merely approaching middle age, because we are so much younger.

Think about the twenty-five-year-old woman who marries the fifty-year-old man. Comparatively, she can't possibly see him as young, yet he certainly is not old. She may spend the next twenty or thirty years plagued by his eventual death. Jill Turndorf said on the former television show *Pittsburgh Today*, "I feel ripped off. I fell in love with a man who is twenty-eight years too old; I am twenty-eight years too young." Jill was teary as she expressed her anger over how little time she and her husband, Gary, a late fiftyish attorney, would have together.

It is almost certain the majority of the age-disparate couples will never celebrate a golden—perhaps not even a silver—anniversary. Younger wives must contemplate whether quality time versus quantity time can measure up to the expected grief and fear of being alone they will endure as premature widows. Often they are left with young children and the responsibility of raising them as single parents.

Every younger woman who falls in love with an older man will be affected by this traumatic but anticipated outcome to varying degrees. However, a greater age difference will heighten the underlying vulnerability for both the husband and wife and influence the security of their relationship. He may resent her youth as a reminder of his aging; at the same time, she worries whether she can make it on her own.

Consequently, a twentysomething married to a forty-year-old man will be less impacted than if she were married to someone sixty. "This, of course, is the downside," author Sally Quinn told *Vanity Fair*. "Marrying the fifty-seven-year-old boss when you're thirty-seven. He gets to the end of the road quicker than you do."

Younger women will find it necessary to weigh the alternative of not marrying an older man and losing what could be years of supreme happiness versus the years of struggling emotionally and perhaps physically on her own after his death. Obviously, the younger the male friend is makes it easier to rule in favor of marriage. However, it is often a personal, lonely decision one has to make. Sadly, there will be few friends and family members who will offer their blessing.

The more difficult decision will be for the younger woman who is fifty or more years old. She will need to seriously examine the ramifications of getting involved with a gentleman fifteen or twenty years her senior. The issues at hand will be his level of boredom after retirement, health and longevity, infirmity, her responsibility in caring for him, and his imminent death. Old age will appear as if it lasts forever as the middle-aged younger wife slows down her life—mimicking an elderly woman—to accommodate him. Aside from worrying about his well being, she will have to deal with her guilt and feelings of selfishness if she wants to continue on with her age-appropriate life-style and career when her husband declines and needs more attention.

Additionally, she will be torn, perhaps resentful, as she watches her middle-aged friends' social lives, lesser familial responsibilities, and general bonhomie bypass her. And most probably, as a young widow, she will feel even more like a third wheel when she socializes with them.

In contrast, there's the flip side to the age-disparate story. Dan Palmer, of the *Kendall News*, wrote an article about W.O.O.M. based on interviews with some of my subscribers. At the very end of the story, he said, "Charlie, my late wife, was fourteen years younger than me. If she were alive today, I know she would be joining W.O.O.M. She'd probably be right there with Jean, Mari, and Jackie, and I'm sure whoever else would be there. Oh the stories and fun they'd have to laugh and help each other."

Sherrie is fifty years old. Her husband of twenty-one years is seventy-six. Sherrie has suffered with bilateral benign paroxysmal positional vertigo for the past eight years, which she says, "has ruined our lives." Add to that her double cataract surgery, breast cancer, and unsuccessful reconstructive surgery that left her mutilated, and you can appreciate her concerns. "I am absolutely terrified every time Herm sneezes."

Sherrie laments, "I often feel if he goes than so do I. I hardly drive anymore, and we do everything together. Fortunately, Herm is a writer and spends the bulk of his time at home with me working on the computer. Even though I am disfigured and ill much of the time, he never lets his love waver. To him, I am the most gorgeous gal on earth. I adore him, and even though I am a mess, he adores me, too."

One can easily recognize how important it is to make the most of each day with our older husbands. Sound advice that may take women married to men similar in age a long time to appreciate. Mary Louise Smythe*, a subscriber in her fifties, regards her marriage to her seventy-seven-year-old husband as a gift. "No one will ever love me more. Each moment we have together is precious. We both interact from that point of view...count our blessings and thank God for the wonderful days we have shared together."

Would You Do It Again?

Yeah, I know! I didn't talk about O.J. Simpson's obsessive control over and battering of his slain, seventeen-year-younger wife, Nicole and whatever outcome that may bring. However, I find it interesting to mention—whether he is guilty or not of murdering her—that as I watched the opening statements of his trial, it dawned on me that of the more than two thousand women who have contacted me over the past seven years, not *one* has complained of physical abuse.

You may be thinking, "Many women who are physically abused are too frightened to talk about it." I agree. But on the other hand, there are another few hundred with whom I have spoken on the telephone who have never told me their names—and I didn't ask. Additionally, I receive lengthy cathartic letters—written as anonymous, emotional releases—from younger wives who sign them with initials and do not use a return address. And yes, they complained about control, feelings of being smothered by their husbands' imposing attitudes, his selfishness in denying them babies, how much they *hate* his kids, how much they hate their husbands, maybe verbal abuse—but never physical abuse.

And what about Heidi Fleiss? I didn't elaborate on the Beverly Hills madam and her clientele and their indiscretions because I think she was given a bad rap. She gets arrested and the guys who bought and paid for her services—who were just as guilty—run back to their wives. These people are in the minority, anyway, the indelicate few who get the gossips working overtime and provide fodder for television talk shows.

Personally, I rather spend my time talking about the majority of decent folks who simply fell in love with someone from a different decade. Oh yes, we may have had our weak moments where each of us lowered our personal standard. But in this day and age, when presidents and national celebrities are forgiven their dalliances, who's to judge?

Most of us are ordinary people who have worked at and enjoyed an exceptional marriage.

And yes, there are going to be times when we will resent or regret our decision to marry an older man. I remember moments sitting in Sam and Joan's court trials and hearings wondering, *What the hell have I gotten myself into?* You have to go into an age-disparate relationship or marriage with wide-open eyes. It isn't for the faint of heart.

Your relationship will be unlike those of your friends married to similar-in-age men. Life in general, decisions, actions, and reactions almost always center around your husband's agenda. Because you are younger and less experienced, you'll find yourself running like mad to outdo him at something! There are greater moments of highs and lows—dissension but seldom boredom. I have a book, *The Gentle Art of Verbal Self-Defense* by Suzette Haden Elgin. The pages are tattered from overuse.

But your husband's support of your endeavors and pride in you will make it all worth putting up with—even if that means you must find the audacity to laugh at and even walk away from his power plays.

Over the years of our marriages, each of us will have the opportunity to venture through two lives at the same time—his and hers—and that's special! We will cherish the good...and the bad? It isn't so bad after all, is it? And even though it's said age-disparate marriages have a very low divorce rate, some of these marriages don't make it. And that's okay, too; it's not for every-one.

When I was almost finished writing this book, a good friend asked me if I would do it again? I said I'm not sure. It took a lot out of me. I opened myself up, told the truth as I have seen it and lived it. There will be some who disagree with me and may even attack me. I don't care. If I had to do it again, I would take the same positions and say the same things, though I'm not sure I could handle the interviews. Often, I was so emotionally involved, I found myself crying.

My friend said, "No silly, I wasn't talking about the book! I was talking about marrying Sam!"

Oh, God...*yes*! In a heartbeat. I can't wait for the next twenty-four years! As Sinatra says, "I Did It My Way." I love you, Sam!

Acknowledgments

Sean and Ashley—Mommie's back! Thank you for coping with my schedule for the past eleven months. I appreciate your encouragement and the push you gave me to finish. Believe me, I don't take your pride in me for granted. I know you are sick of peanut butter and pizza and answering the phone and telling everybody I'm in the shower. Just think—you know how to do your own laundry! You are the best children a mom could ever wish for! Now, run and get out my roller blades. Let's Party!

To my readers—I know I have asked you to take me on my terms. Thank you and good luck!